D1287143

"Where's Larry Gross? You'll find his charisma on every page. You will also find an overview of some major issues in media research."
—Elihu Katz, Professor (emeritus), Annenberg School for Communication at the University of Pennsylvania and Hebrew University of Jerusalem

"Paul Messaris and David W. Park, along with other former students, have composed a volume that could profitably be read for its notable entries on a rich variety of important subjects. But its value goes way beyond the sum of its chapters. All festschrifts celebrate intellectual legacies; this one offers, in the example of Larry Gross, an inspiring vision of the possibilities of scholarship. Read it for a reflection of what it means to do grounded, courageous, humane, and silo-defying intellectual work."
—Tina Huey, Adjunct Faculty, Department of English, University of Connecticut

"What matters? From digital imaging ethics to the role of feeling in politics to the ongoing classed dimensions of queer representation, the authors in this broad-reaching anthology situate their work in a context of social and political commitments. This connective tissue of meaningful intellectual work reflects the extraordinary legacy of Larry Gross. His broad intellectual reach still energizes his former students' research, and his mentorship has produced some of the pioneers of our field. The collection sparkles with inspiration and rigor, glows with love and thanks."
—Katherine Sender, Professor, Communication Studies, University of Michigan

The Inclusive Vision

A CRITICAL INTRODUCTION TO MEDIA AND COMMUNICATION THEORY

David W. Park
Series Editor

Vol. 12

The Critical Introduction to Media and Communication Theory series
is part of the Peter Lang Media and Communication list.
Every volume is peer reviewed and meets
the highest quality standards for content and production.

PETER LANG
New York • Bern • Berlin
Brussels • Vienna • Oxford • Warsaw

The Inclusive Vision

Essays in Honor of Larry Gross

Edited by Paul Messaris
and David W. Park

PETER LANG
New York • Bern • Berlin
Brussels • Vienna • Oxford • Warsaw

Library of Congress Cataloging-in-Publication Data

Names: Messaris, Paul editor. | Park, David W., editor.
Gross, Larry P., honoree.
Title: The inclusive vision: essays in honor of Larry Gross /
edited by Paul Messaris and David W. Park.
Description: New York: Peter Lang, 2018.
Series: A critical introduction to media and
communication theory; vol. 12 | ISSN 1947-6264
Includes bibliographical references.
Identifiers: LCCN 2017059264 | ISBN 978-1-4331-4663-3 (hardback: alk. paper)
ISBN 978-1-4331-4664-0 (paperback: alk. paper) | ISBN 978-1-4331-4665-7 (ebook pdf)
ISBN 978-1-4331-4666-4 (epub) | ISBN 978-1-4331-4667-1 (mobi)
Subjects: LCSH: Visual communication. | Mass media and culture.
Classification: LCC P93.5 I478 2018 | DDC 302.23—dc23
LC record available at https://lccn.loc.gov/2017059264
DOI 10.3726/b13474

Bibliographic information published by **Die Deutsche Nationalbibliothek**.
Die Deutsche Nationalbibliothek lists this publication in the "Deutsche
Nationalbibliografie"; detailed bibliographic data are available
on the Internet at http://dnb.d-nb.de/.

The paper in this book meets the guidelines for permanence and durability
of the Committee on Production Guidelines for Book Longevity
of the Council of Library Resources.

Printed in the United States of America

Contents

Illustrations

Acknowledgments

We would like to express our gratitude to Kathryn Harrison, Acquisitions Editor at Peter Lang, for her support of this project and her valuable guidance. We also thank Michael Doub, Editorial Assistant, and Luke McCord, Production Editor, for their help in getting the manuscript ready for publication. Paul Messaris thanks Michael Delli Carpini, Dean of the Annenberg School at Penn, for providing resources that greatly facilitated Messaris's work on this book. As well, Messaris is grateful to Deborah E. Porter, Senior Building Administrator at Annenberg, for her many contributions to the successful completion of this project. Dave Park is grateful to Lake Forest College for support during the production of this volume. Both editors greatly appreciate the advice and assistance that they received from Scott Tucker.

Introduction

PAUL MESSARIS

Few people have had as much impact on the field of communication studies as Larry Gross has had. Over the course of his long and distinguished academic career, Gross has played a central role in three major scholarly movements. He was a prominent member of the generation that founded visual studies as a graduate research discipline within the field of communication. He was a principal investigator in the Cultural Indicators Project, which, in its time, was perhaps the most influential investigation of the cultural ramifications of the mass media. He was, and remains, one of the most eloquent, illuminating, and productive commentators on the media's portrayal of sexual and other minorities.

The influence of Gross's work as a scholar has been amplified by his extraordinary contributions to the field as a mentor of graduate students and by his tireless participation in editorial activities and administrative service. At the Annenberg School for Communication of the University of Pennsylvania, where he taught from 1968 to 2003, he was the primary advisor on more than 180 masters theses and doctoral dissertations—a record that is not likely to be surpassed. At the University of Southern California, he was the Director of the Annenberg School of Communication from 2003 to 2014. He has served multi-year terms at the helm of two journals, *Studies in Visual Communication* and the *International Journal of Communication*, and he remains the principal editor of the latter. In recognition of the value of his scholarship, teaching, and administrative contributions, he has been the recipient of a Guggenheim Fellowship (1998–1999) and the International Communication Association's B. Aubrey Fisher Mentorship Award (2001). He is an ICA Fellow (elected in 2006) and past-President (2011–2012).

This volume is an exploration of Larry Gross's enduring influence on the field of communication. In three sections that roughly correspond to the three research areas in which he made his most significant contributions, Gross's former students present their own current scholarship. In some of the chapters, the authors comment explicitly about connections to Gross's teaching. In other chapters the ties to Gross are more implicit. Regardless, it is hoped that this book will serve as a bridge between the lines of inquiry that were initiated by Gross and the concerns that are likely to animate the work of future scholars.

The title of the book's first section, "On the Margins of the Art Worlds," is taken directly from one of Gross's publications. Broadly speaking, the essays in this section seek to question cultural distinctions between artistic activities that qualify as elite or approved art and those activities that are rejected as inferior or derided as trash. The book's next section, on "Culture and Power," contains essays that extend the lines of inquiry initiated by Larry Gross, George Gerbner, and their collaborators in the Cultural Indicators Project. That project's aim had been to analyze the ways in which the mass media's portrayal of society serves to reinforce power relationships and social subjugation in real life. The essays in this section discuss the project's impact on later scholarship, and they extend its framework to investigations of present-day social issues. Finally, in the third section, "Towards Inclusion," the book turns to the question that has animated much of Gross's and his students' work since the publication of *Up From Invisibility* (2001), his landmark study of media portrayals of sexual minorities: Who speaks for those who have been less fortunate in the social distribution of power? As a prelude to this collection of essays by Gross's students, the following pages will provide an overview, in roughly chronological order, of those aspects of Gross's work that are most directly related to the themes of each of the book's three sections.

On the Margins of the Art Worlds

Larry Gross's career as a professor began in the Fall of 1968, when he joined the faculty of the Annenberg School of Communications (later renamed the Annenberg School for Communication) at the University of Pennsylvania. Gross had recently received his Ph.D. in social psychology from Columbia, and his training in the logic of hypothesis testing may have been one source of the conceptual rigor and clarity that are such distinctive features of his work. He moved from social psychology to communication because he wanted to study art, and he believed that a communications program would provide a more congenial environment for such a pursuit than a department of psychology would. Looking back on this decision some fifteen years later, he wrote the following: "The field of communications, at least as it was represented at the Annenberg School, appeared to offer a framework in which the varieties of symbolic behavior (especially the kinds that we call art) could be studied with a sensitivity to the role of psychological, social, and cultural determinants" (Gross, 1981, 23).

Gross included that reminiscence in his introduction to a memorial edition of the writings of Sol Worth, who had taught at Annenberg for two decades and had provided the initial impetus for the school's early adoption of visual studies as a field of graduate-level research. Gross has said that his decision to join the Annenberg faculty was motivated to a large extent by Worth's presence. The two of them became close collaborators in their own scholarly work as well as the mentorship of graduate student research. Their collaboration became the nucleus of an expanding group of students interested in visual communication, and it strengthened the intellectual foundations of visual studies at Annenberg.

Some of the most fruitful discussions between Gross and Worth occurred in the presence of their students, in an informal research seminar that met from time to time in Gross's apartment. Disagreement was encouraged at those meetings, and the most vehement—but always polite—disagreement invariably occurred between Gross and Worth. For former students who witnessed them, those clashes about ideas between two close friends have served as enduringly inspiring demonstrations of the value of productive argument. Gross has described his discussions with Worth as major influences on his early work. At the time of their first meeting, Worth had completed the fieldwork for a study of films produced by young Navajos who had had minimal previous exposure to Hollywood movies or television (Worth & Adair, 1972). This attention to cultural difference and to non-professional artistic production is present in Gross's work of that period as well, and it may be one aspect of Worth's influence. However, what is most noteworthy about Gross's work at the very beginning of his professional career is its striking originality.

Gross chose to work in the field of communication because he wanted to do research on art. The most significant results of that research are summarized in a pair of articles that he produced in the early 1970s. His first goal in those articles was to craft a basic theory of art (Gross, 1973a). At that time, art theory had still not completely recovered from the antics of such artistic provocateurs as Marcel Duchamp (for example, his well-known submission of a mass-produced urinal to an artistic exhibition) or John Cage (for example, his musical composition *4'33"*, featuring musicians *not* playing their instruments for 4 minutes and 33 seconds). Instead of appreciating such actions for what they were—amusing gags that would not have been out of place in a *New Yorker* cartoon or a Buster Keaton movie—art critics and theorists had been torturing themselves to produce a theory of art that would encompass both Duchamp and da Vinci, both Cage and Bach in a single definition. Mercifully for his readers, Gross's approach to art was mostly unaffected by such issues. He had little interest in establishing the dividing line between art and non-art, but great interest in the interconnections between art and the rest of life. The central focus of his approach was on the following questions: What is our motivation for experiencing art, and what is the source of that motivation?

In addressing these questions, Gross drew upon his background in psychology, but also on a wide range of material from other fields. On the basis of this prior literature, he argued that what the arts (visual, verbal, musical) have in common is their audiences' attention (explicit or tacit) to performative competence—the fluent handling of the conventions of a particular medium and genre. In other words, what viewers or listeners or readers get out of the arts as a whole is the appreciation of skill. Gross argued further that this type of appreciation is not limited to experiences that are conventionally thought of as artistic. Rather, it is a fundamental human response to any activity whose effective performance is dependent on practice and/or talent. Our appreciation of a well-drawn sketch or a well-played tune has much in common with our admiration for a well-designed piece of furniture, a well-executed football pass, or, for that matter, a well-solved mathematical problem. In that sense, our interest in the arts may be said to derive from a psychological tendency that serves an obvious utilitarian function in our broader lives.

In certain respects, what Gross was proposing was quite similar to the theories of art that have been popularized in recent years by evolutionary psychologists—in other words, theories that seek to explain art in terms of its potential contributions to evolutionary fitness (Chatterjee, 2014; Dutton, 2008; Voland & Grammer, 2003). However, Gross was writing long before such theories had gained the prominence that they enjoy today and, in fact, long before the emergence of evolutionary psychology as a distinct area of research. In that sense, his approach was remarkably original. It was also highly original in one other, very important way.

Gross's main focus of interest, throughout his career, has been on visual media. However, in his theoretical work on aesthetics he took a broader view, encompassing the arts as a whole, regardless of their medium of communication. Aesthetic theory has a long tradition of attempts to define the distinctive characteristics of the various arts, and Gross was certainly aware of this tradition. For example, at the time when he was writing about aesthetics, the reading list of one of his courses included G. E. Lessing's *Laocoön* (1962)— originally published in 1766—one of the most prominent analyses of the differences between visual depiction and verbal description. Nevertheless, as has been noted, Gross has typically been interested in similarities more than in differences. In his work on aesthetics, it was that interest in commonalities and connections that led him to his most creative theoretical formulation.

Writing in publications dealing with social policy and with education, Gross put forth an argument (Gross, 1973b) that was essentially an extrapolation from his conception of skillful communication as the central characteristic of artistic activity and aesthetic experience. He began by noting that the skills that are prized in the use of verbal media are commonly thought of as core constituents of intelligence. Traditionally, the measurement of intelligence has focused primarily on verbal skills and on mathematical skills. However, Gross argued, if skills and competence have value regardless of the medium in which they are deployed, then it makes sense to think of intelligence itself as extending beyond words and numbers. At a minimum, he suggested, we should think of five types of intelligence instead of just one or two: lexical, mathematical, musical, iconic, and social-gestural.

Anyone familiar with the psychology of intelligence will immediately realize that what Gross was proposing was very similar to what is now known as the "theory of multiple intelligences." Today, that theory is a staple of academic discourse about intelligence, and it is also a ubiquitous assumption in educational circles. Much of the credit for the theory's popularity goes to Howard Gardner, whose 1983 book about the theory has justly been called a "classic." But Gross's article on the five types of communicational competence was published half a century ago, and twenty years before Gardner's book. Why has Gross's pioneering contribution to this topic seemingly left no mark on the thinking of contemporary scholars?

The person who can best answer that question is Gross himself. For whatever reason, he never followed up on the ground-breaking ideas about aesthetics, skill, and communicational competence that he had articulated in his early theoretical writings. Those writings make it clear that, if he had wanted to, Gross could have become one of the pre-eminent theorists of artistic communication of his generation. He was a highly original thinker, he had a powerful integrative mind, and his erudition was formidable. But, by the end of his first decade as a professor, he had become involved in research whose political implications were more pressing concerns than its theoretical underpinnings. To be sure, he did produce one more major publication related to his early interests in art and communication. After a heart attack took the life of his colleague and good friend Sol Worth, Gross put together a meticulously curated collection of Worth's articles and papers (Gross, 1981). Thereafter, Gross's work can fairly be described as being increasingly focused on the relationships among media, culture, and social issues.

Culture and Power

From the mid-1970s until the late 1980s, the primary focus of Gross's research was on a series of studies of the content and effects of television fiction. Much of this work was part of the cultural indicators project, a large-scale, feder-ally-funded undertaking that had been initiated by George Gerbner, at that time the Dean of the Annenberg School, and eventually came to include Larry Gross, Michael Morgan, Nancy Signorielli, and James Shanahan as principal investigators. Michael Morgan's chapter in this volume is an authoritative account of the project's aims and methods. As Morgan points out, the proj-ect's research approach—which was labeled "cultivation analysis," because of its focus on the process by which audiences absorb mainstream cultural values from mass media—eventually found its way into some 800 studies published in academic journals, and the project's theoretical framework has become one of the most-cited theories in the history of mass communication scholarship. What follows here is an attempt to assess the project's implications for present-day researchers, in light of the changes that the mass media have gone through during the past quarter century.

The cultural indicators project began as a content analysis of violence on television, with funding that George Gerbner received as part of the US Gov-ernment's response to the social turmoil of the late 1960s. After Gross became involved in the project and the two researchers began to publish together, the project's first major report was an article that appeared in the *Journal of Communication* (Gerbner & Gross, 1976). The article was subtitled "The Violence Profile"—a reference to the fact that it contained an abundance of data about television violence. However, any reader who came to the arti-cle expecting a customary treatment of that topic—i.e., an assessment of the relationship between TV violence and real-world violence—would have been disappointed and perhaps even bewildered by the article's actual approach.

The standard criticism of media violence studies is directed toward meth-odology. Laboratory experiments are typically accused of failing to replicate reality, and surveys are typically accused of failing to establish the direction of causality. Sometimes the criticism is justified, and sometimes—perhaps all too often—it is not, but, in either case, its focus on methodology is almost a given. What Gerbner and Gross's article did was to raise an entirely different challenge to previous research. Instead of questioning its methods, they questioned its theory—specifically, its choice of dependent variable. It may seem self-evident that a study of the effects of media violence should be concerned with violence in real life. But that was not what Gerbner and Gross were looking for. Instead, they argued that television's portrayals of violence are part of a broader set of narratives whose function is to preserve existing social arrangements—to stabilize rather than to disrupt.

This claim was based on the following statement: "We begin with the assertion that television is the central cultural arm of American society. It is an agency of the established order. ... Its chief cultural function is to spread and stabilize social patterns, to cultivate not change but resistance to change" (Gerbner & Gross, 1976, 175). How do we get from this blunt proclamation —which the authors did not label a hypothesis—to the notion that TV violence cultivates resistance to change? Over the years, the cultural indicators project developed a number of different ways of parsing the data from its content analyses of television violence. Two of those approaches to the violence data are particularly relevant to Gerbner and Gross's claim about television as a stabilizer of social patterns: first, demographic analysis of the perpetrators and victims of violence; second, comparison between fictional crime on television and real-world crime statistics.

In its demographic analysis of the fictional characters featured in violent scenes on television, the project was concerned primarily with characters' gender, age, and race. The premise of this analysis was that fictional violence is a symbol of social power. The violent scenarios of television's fictional worlds are implicit lessons about the distribution of social power in the real world. Viewers learn their place in the real world by witnessing the fate of their demographic counterparts on TV.

A graphic illustration of this theory was contained in a large poster that stood on an easel in George Gerbner's office during the project's heyday. The poster, which was loosely based on the mythical story of Perseus and Andromeda, showed a terror-stricken young woman chained to a rock; a horrific monster preparing to pounce on her; and a heroic young man arriving at the last minute to kill the monster and save the woman. Once, when a visitor to Gerbner's office went up to the poster for a closer look, Gerbner offered the following comment: "That says it all." What he meant, presumably, was that the poster, and the ancient myth, contained the same cultural message that was now being transmitted by television—men have power, women don't—and conveyed that message through the same symbolic means, namely, violence.

The idea that people's cultural expectations are influenced by fictional portrayals of demographically similar characters was not controversial, or even new. What was unusual—and, for some readers, startling—about Gerbner and Gross's article was the view of violence as symbolic power. Do audiences really interpret action scenes as metaphors for economic or social stratification? For example, do movies or TV shows about Wonder Woman affect a girl's career aspirations as much as, or perhaps even more, than the presence of real-life women in the top leadership positions of the largest automobile manufacturer in the United States, the wealthiest country in Europe, and the most powerful financial institution in the world? This is not a rhetorical question. It cannot be answered on the basis of intuition, and, unfortunately, it wasn't tackled directly in the cultural indicators project, although related research by Gross and Suzanne Jeffries-Fox (1978) did examine the more general influence of TV on occupational expectations.

In retrospect, then, Gerbner and Gross's theory of symbolic violence can be seen as a tantalizing invitation for further research. For theoretical as well as pragmatic reasons, such research would be a valuable addition to our understanding of the cultural consequences of visual fiction. When the first report of the cultural indicators project was published, Wonder Women had already made her appearance on television. In the forty or so years that have gone by since that time, calls for "empowering" images of women and under-represented minorities have only increased in frequency. Yet it seems true that communication scholars do not yet have an entirely clear sense of what symbolic empowerment consists of and how exactly it works.

In addition to the demographic analysis of perpetrators and victims, the cultural indicators project used its TV violence data to assess the differences between the fictional world of television violence and real-world statistics on crime and law enforcement. This part of the project also examined TV viewers' responses to violence on the screen. The central finding of this examination was that heavy viewers tend to have an exaggerated sense of the amount of violence, crime, and wrong-doing in the real world—a set of beliefs that the researchers labelled "the mean world syndrome." Within the project's broader framework, this finding was interpreted as an indication that television violence serves to reinforce the public's support for stability and authority—for strict policing, tough laws, and strong political leaders.

Of all aspects of cultivation analysis, this one in particular seems most in need of further exploration in the present-day cultural context. In a retrospective assessment of the cultural indicators project that he published in 2009, Gross talked about the importance of revisiting past research findings and methods in light of new developments in the technologies of communication: "changing technologies make a difference in how human beings engage with each other and with the worlds they inhabit. Thus, media studies, far from being stuck in the transmission of conventional wisdom accumulated decades ago, has the opportunity and the necessity of re-asking basic questions and reassessing the methods that are appropriate for finding answers" (Gross, 2009, 68).

The violent imagery that Gerbner and Gross were writing about in the mid-1970s has been affected significantly by the advent of digital media. Fictional violence has become more spectacular thanks to the development of digital special effects, and the increasing technical sophistication of video games has made their violent worlds more immersive. However, from the perspective of cultivation analysis, the changes that have mattered most may be those that have to do with images of real-world violence. The ubiquity of small, mobile digital cameras has led to a substantial increase in the availability of such images, not only from surveillance video and body cams but also—surprisingly or not—from recordings made by the actual perpetrators of violence and their accomplices. Some of those images are acquired by the professional news media, where they become absorbed into established cultural narratives about the nature of good and evil (Mortensen, 2017). However, thanks to the fact that some internet sites are—for the moment—less stringently curated than traditional news outlets, much of the violent imagery captured by amateur sources ends up creating a picture of the world that doesn't fit very neatly into the familiar patterns established by mass-produced fiction and reportage. This contradiction is particularly relevant to cultivation analysis when it involves images of malfeasance by law enforcement officers.

These transformations raise a set of intertwined questions: Does the intensity of special-effects violence (including videogame violence) magnify the "mean-world syndrome," or does the underlying artificiality of computer-generated imagery undermine that effect? Does the increasing availability of real-world examples of violence complement the impact of fictional violence, or is that impact diminished by the proliferation of real-world images that don't fit the moral assumptions of conventional mass-produced fiction—for example, a surveillance clip of an axe-wielding homeless man attacking a charitable stranger who had offered him money (Paul, 2017), or body-cam video of a nurse being forcibly arrested for refusing a warrant-less order to draw an unconscious patient's blood (Wang & Hawkins, 2017).

Some aspects of these questions have been addressed in existing research (e.g., Funk, Baldacci, Pasold, & Baumgardner, 2004; Sumiala & Tikka, 2011; Weaver, Zelenkauskaite, & Samson, 2012). For the most part, however, the digital transformation of media violence remains relatively unexplored, at least as far as the original cultivation researchers are concerned. With the notable exception of a book by Signorielli (2005), the researchers who were most directly involved in the cultural indicators project have tended to broaden their focus beyond symbolic violence in their more recent publications (e.g., Morgan, Shanahan, & Signorielli, 2012). As for Gross, he co-published with the other members of the cultural indicators team as late as 2002 (Gerbner et al., 2002), but by then his primary interest lay elsewhere. The work that he and the others did on cultural indicators and cultivation studies has left us with an abundance of intriguing findings—but also with unanswered questions that may be even more intriguing.

Towards Inclusion

In a speech that he gave as President of the International Communication Association and that was subsequently published as a journal article, Gross talked about the need to cultivate "engaged scholars and scholarship" dedicated to addressing "the most important and pressing real-world issues" (Gross, 2012, 926). No one in the field of communication studies has exemplified that ideal better than Gross himself. In the 1980s and 1990s, at a time when he was serving as Co-Chair of the Philadelphia Lesbian and Gay Task Force (a position that he held for two decades), Gross co-authored a series of large-scale studies of the conditions encountered by members of sexual minorities living in Philadelphia and in the Commonwealth of Pennsylvania. Violence was a major concern of those studies—but now Gross was investigating real acts of violence, not the fictional TV portrayals that he had been analyzing as a participant in the cultural indicators project. The studies' findings were appalling. For example, in a study conducted in 1986–1987, it was found that the annual criminal violence victimization rate in the Commonwealth was twelve times higher for gay men and nine times higher for lesbian women than the respective rates for the adult US adult population (Gross, Aurand, & Addessa, 1988, 4).

The report in which this particular set of findings was presented concluded with four pages of detailed policy recommendations, including proposals for new legislation, training programs, and educational efforts. Thirty years have gone by since that report was issued. It would be an overstatement to claim that all of its recommendations have found a receptive audience, and it would be willful denial of reality to think that violence toward members of sexual minorities is no longer a pressing real-world issue. And yet, as Gross wrote in an article comparing the world of the 1980s with that of the early 21st century, the lives of gay, lesbian, bisexual, and trans people have gone through "profound changes" in that span of time (Gross, 2005, 508). Moreover, as his article went on to demonstrate with an overview of history going back to the 1950s, those profound changes were largely self-authored. They were the cumulative results of the efforts of all those individuals who did the hard work of organizing a community, giving it a voice, and putting that voice to effective use. With characteristic modesty, Gross refrained from any mention of his own outsized role in that arduous, and often dangerous, adventure.

Another characteristic that has contributed to Gross's effectiveness as an "engaged scholar" is the remarkably dispassionate tone of his scholarly writing, even when he is presenting deeply distressing data or describing highly outrageous behavior. Almost always in such circumstances, Gross's text sticks to the facts, leaving it up to the reader to experience the implicit emotions. A rare exception to this pattern occurred in an analysis of journalistic misrepresentations of the lives of gay people (Gross, 1988). In the course of this analysis, Gross examined a 1980 documentary called "Gay Power, Gay Politics," presented by CBS. As anyone who studies visual media should know, when documentaries misrepresent reality, they almost never do so by resorting to any kind of complex technological shenanigans, such as (in today's world) the digital manipulation of images. Instead, using raw, unmanipulated video, they concoct a deceptive fabrication through the use two simple tools: tendentious choice of shots; tendentious sequencing of shots. Gross found glaring instances of these techniques in the CBS documentary, and his dissection of their use was an important contribution to the study of visual ethics, which was the overall topic of the book in which his analysis was published. Elsewhere in his article, Gross made a point of the intentional terseness of his presentation (109). However, when he got to the CBS documentary, he departed from that principle. In addition to calling it "selective and biased and willfully ignorant and manipulative" as well as "an outstanding example of the unethical use of media power," he also confessed: "Although it has been years since the program aired, I am still enraged at its manifest dishonesty" (198–199). That single eruption of emotion says a lot, and its rarity also says a lot.

Of course, there is much to deplore in the conduct of the "news" media, whose avaricious proclivity for the exploitation of moral panics often seems to be exceeded only by their utter disregard for the people whose lives they may be wrecking. Gross gave another example of this kind of conduct in a detailed study of the journalistic practice of publicizing arrests (and, incidentally, providing free publicity for the arresting authorities) without any concern regarding the actual guilt or innocence of those arrested. As part of this study, Gross examined the practices of local TV stations that were "sneaking cameras into public toilets in the hope of catching men engaged in sex." As he noted (without further comment), "For gay men the media do not require an arrest as a pretext for panoptical exposure" (Gross, 2003a, 107). And yet, despite the visceral impact of this phase of his writing career, Gross's most effective work as a scholar is not his dissection of the media's sins of commission but, rather, his explication of their sins of omission. This part of his work is prefigured by one of the aspects of cultivation analysis.

One of the central points of early publications about cultivation theory was the overwhelming importance of media as a source of people's views of reality. The point was stressed in the cultural indicators project's research reports, and it had also been the main topic of one of Gross's first journal articles outside the area of art (Gross, 1974). A vivid illustration of this point is contained in a study that adopted the cultivation analysis approach although it was not a formal part of the cultural indicators project. In this study, a sample of mothers of school-age children were asked to describe the kinds of discussions that they had with their children about the content of television programs. Without more specific prompting, more than a third of these mothers described a recurring anxiety: Their children assumed that the middle-class lives they were seeing on fictional TV represented the norm, and they felt inadequate about their own less privileged circumstances. In one mother's words, "The children seem to feel that that's reality and what they're living in is somehow a mistake" (Messaris, 1986, 524). It is worth pausing for a moment to ponder how much emotional pain is contained in that simple statement.

One measure of humanity's cruelty is the eagerness with which people inflict that kind of pain—the sense of not having a place in society, of being abnormal—on others. That eagerness is also a sign of how terrified most people are of experiencing that pain themselves. Gross touched upon these matters, although with a somewhat different terminology, in an important theoretical piece that he wrote with James Woods, a brilliant scholar who was robbed of life by HIV disease at the age of thirty-two (Gross and Woods, 1999, 4–6). Gross and Woods' text, which was written as an introduction to a book of readings that they had co-edited, could serve equally well as a prelude to Gross's most important work, his book *Up from Invisibility: Lesbians, Gay Men, and the Media in America* (Gross, 2001).

The book is a history of the evolution in the relationship between LGBT people and US mass media over the course of the second half of the 20th century. As the main title suggests, the book tells the story of a monumental series of events that brought about great changes in American culture. The story begins at a time of exclusion and symbolic invisibility, when Hollywood movies had a code explicitly prohibiting any reference to homosexuality, which was designated as a mental disorder by psychiatric authorities. The story culminates (for the moment) in a media environment in which queer youth might encounter images that they are actually able to embrace as their own. Gross tells this story with tremendous verve. At the time when he was writing this book, he was entering his fourth decade as a professor, and he had fully honed a skill that is pathetically rare in the academic world: the ability to write prose that everyday people—not just fellow professors and graduate students—might read with interest and, indeed, with enjoyment. Even on purely stylistic grounds, *Up from Invisibility* is Gross's best work. But what really distinguishes the book as a contribution to scholarship is its point of view.

Most academic analyses of media portrayals are written with the implicit or explicit goal of assessing those portrayals' impact on "mainstream" viewers. In *Up from Invisibility*, however, Gross's biggest concern is for the viewer who approaches the media from a minority position—especially a young person, an adolescent experiencing unexpected and unexplained developmental changes, who has nowhere to turn for an explanation except the mass media. In his analysis of such a viewer's relationship with the media, Gross blends penetrating theoretical observations with carefully chosen illustrations. The nub of that analysis may be gleaned from the contrast between the following two vignettes (presented here in reverse order from that in which they appear in the book).

> Vignette number one: In 1995, a 17-year-old adolescent posted the following question on AOL: "Does anyone else feel like you're the only gay guy on the planet, or at least in Arlington, Texas?" (quoted in Gross, 2001, 227–228)

> Vignette number two: In 1992, when Ryan Philippe, a straight actor, portrayed a gay teenager in the daytime TV serial *One Life to Live*, he received hundreds of letters from young gay men expressing gratitude for his "sensitive portrayal of an experience much like their own, being isolated and vulnerable in a society that would prefer not to know they existed." (Gross, 2001, 218)

As Gross points out, in a world in which no one else seems to share one's identity—the world of the young man in the first vignette—even a fictional portrayal, by an actor known to be straight, acquires profound significance. The media power that Gross had written about many years earlier, when TV was the dominant window on reality, was still very much in evidence at the dawn of the digital age, but now that power was finally beginning to acknowledge the lives of people whom it had once neglected and then maligned.

Gross's chronicle of that hard-won transformation begins in the summer of 1947, when a 26-year-old secretary walked into a lesbian bar in Los Angeles and began to distribute a fifteen-page, type-written magazine that she called, for symbolic reasons that are obvious enough even in retrospect, *Vice Versa*—an event that "signaled the first stirring of the modern gay rights movement in the United States" (Gross, 2001, xiii). Gross ends his story at the cusp of the present millennium, in the world that that brave woman and her successor cohorts have bequeathed to the young people of today. But on the last page of his book he looks even further into the future, envisioning a time when the children of that future age will scarcely be able to comprehend the past's criminalization of love.

With few exceptions, that optimism has been typical of Gross's work, and so too has been his focus on the prospects of the young rather than the misfortunes of the old. *Up from Invisibility* has a coda. A few years after the book's publication, Gross wrote a short article, "Gideon Who Will Be 25 in the Year 2012" (Gross, 2007). Aficionados of European cinema history will recognize the allusion to Alain Tanner's *Jonah Who Will by 25 in the Year 2000*, a 1976 Swiss film about a group of twenty-to thirty-year-olds who have lived through the social upheavals of the 1960s and are wondering if the future will bring a realization of the ideals that they envisioned back then. The film speculates that Jonah, the new-born son of one of the protagonists, may grow up to give form to those ideals.

Larry Gross was a graduate student at Columbia in the late 1960s, and he clearly sees some parallels between his own experiences and those of the characters in Tanner's movie. But, unlike them, Gross is now old enough to have seen the future that the 1960s generation was speculating about. And yet, instead of dwelling on the impact that that future has had on people of his generation, including himself—most notably the fact that he has finally been able to marry the man with whom he shared almost his entire adult life, his spouse now, Scott Tucker—Gross very significantly cast his eyes beyond the present and the recent past, to the life of Gideon—a real young man who had recently come out to his mother in the course of asking her to subscribe to cable so that he could watch *Queer as Folk*. That orientation toward the future permeates Gross's publications (1996, 2003b, 2012), and it is a major reason for the dynamism, the prodigious originality, and the effective engagement with real-world challenges that have always been hallmarks of his work.

This book is lovingly dedicated to Larry Gross by his former students. Some of us have known him almost from the beginning of his professional career. The youngest among us is still (at the time of writing) working with him. All of us have benefited from his extraordinary generosity as a mentor, from his high scholarly standards—demonstrated most prominently in his own work—and from his exemplary career as a socially committed researcher, writer, and teacher. We hope the book is an adequate expression of the depth of our gratitude to Larry. We hope, too, that it will serve to acquaint younger media scholars with his many contributions to our field.

References

Chatterjee, A. (2014). *The aesthetic brain: How we evolved to desire beauty and enjoy art.* New York: Oxford University Press.

Dutton, D. (2008). *The art instinct: Beauty, pleasure, and human evolution.* New York: Bloomsbury Press.

Funk, J. B., Baldacci, H. B., Pasold, T., & Baumgardner, J. (2004). Violence exposure in real-life, video games, television, movies, and the internet: Is there desensitization? *Journal of Adolescence, 27*(1), 23–39.

Gerbner, G., & Gross, L. (1976). Living with television: The violence profile. *Journal of Communication, 26*(2), 172–194.

Gerbner, G., Gross, L., Morgan, M., Signorielli, N., & Shanahan, J. (2002). Growing up with television: Cultivation processes. In J. Bryant & D. Zillmann (Eds.), *Media effects: Advances in theory and research* (2nd ed., pp. 43–67). Hillsdale, NJ: Erlbaum.

Gross, L. (1973a). Art as the communication of competence. *Social Science Information, 12*(5), 115–141.

Gross, L. (1973b). Modes of communication and the acquisition of symbolic competence. In G. Gerbner, L. Gross, & W. Melody (Eds.), *Communication technology and social policy: Understanding the new "cultural revolution"* (pp. 189–208). New York: John Wiley. Also in D. R. Olson (Ed.), *Media and symbols: The forms of expression, communication, and education* (pp. 56–80). Chicago: University of Chicago Press.

Gross, L. (1974). The real world of television. *Today's Education, 63*(1), 86–92.

Gross, L. (1981). Introduction: Sol Worth and the study of visual communication. In L. Gross (Ed.), *Studying visual communication* (pp. 1–35). Philadelphia, PA: University of Pennsylvania Press.

Gross, L. (1988). The ethics of (mis)representation. In L. Gross, J. S. Katz, & J. Ruby (Eds.), *Image ethics: The moral rights of subjects in photographs, film, and television* (pp. 188–202). New York: Oxford University Press.

Gross, L. (Ed.). (1995). *On the margins of art worlds.* Boulder, CO: Westview Press.

Gross, L. (1996). You're the first person I've ever told: Letters to a fictional gay teen. In M. Bronski (Ed.), *Taking liberties: Gay men's essays on politics, culture, and sex* (pp. 369–386). New York: Masquerade Books.

Gross, L. (2001). *Up from invisibility: Lesbians, gay men, and the media in America.* New York: Columbia University Press.

Gross, L. (2003a). Privacy and spectacle: The reversible panopticon and media-saturated society. In L. Gross, J. S. Katz, & J. Ruby (Eds.), *Image ethics in the digital age* (pp. 95–114). Minneapolis: University of Minnesota Press.

Gross, L. (2003b). The gay global village in cyberspace. In N. Couldry & J. Curran (Eds.), *Contesting media power: Alternative media in a networked world* (pp. 259–272). New York: Rowman & Littlefield.

Gross, L. (2005). The past and the future of gay, lesbian, bisexual, and transgender studies. *Journal of Communication, 55*(3), 508–528.

Gross, L. (2007). Gideon who will be 25 in the year 2012: Growing up gay today. *International Journal of Communication, 1*(1), 121–138.

Gross, L. (2009). My media studies: cultivation to participation. *Television & New Media, 10*(1), 66–68.

Gross, L. (2012). Fastening our seatbelts: Turning crisis into opportunity. *Journal of Communication, 62*(6), 919–931.

Gross, L., Aurand, S. K., & Addessa, R. (1988). *Violence and discrimination against lesbian and gay people in Philadelphia and the Commonwealth of Pennsylvania.* Philadelphia, PA: Philadelphia Lesbian and Gay Task Force.

Gross, L., & Jeffries-Fox, S. (1978). What do you want to be when you grow up, little girl? In G. Tuchman, A. K. Daniels, & J. Benet (Eds.), *Hearth and home: Images of women in the mass media* (pp. 240–265). New York: Oxford University Press.

Gross, L., & Woods, J. D. (Eds.). (1999). *The Columbia reader on lesbians and gay men in media, society, and politics.* New York: Columbia University Press.

Lessing, G. E. (1962/1766). *Laocoön: An essay on the limits of painting and poetry.* (E. A. McCormick, Trans.). Indianapolis: Bobbs-Merrill Company.

Messaris, P. (1986). Parents, children, and television. In G. Gumpert & R. Cathcart (Eds.), *Inter/Media: Interpersonal communication in a media world* (pp. 519–536). New York: Oxford University Press.

Morgan, M., Shanahan, J., & Signorielli, N. (Eds.). (2012). *Living with television now: Advances in cultivation theory and research.* New York: Peter Lang.

Mortensen, M. (2017). Eyewitness images in the news. In P. Messaris & L. Humphreys (Eds.), *Digital media: Transformations in human communication* (2nd ed., pp. 24–30). New York: Peter Lang.

Paul, Pritha. (2017, September 8). WATCH: Homeless man attacks good Samaritan outside LA shop with axe. *International Business Times.* Retrieved on 9/10/17 from: http://www.ibtimes.com/watch-homeless-man-attacks-good-samaritan-outside-la-shop-axe-2587628

Signorielli, N. (2005). *Violence in the media: A reference handbook.* Santa Barbara, CA: ABC-CLIO.

Sumiala, J., & Tikka, M. (2011). Imagining globalised fears: School shooting videos and circulation of violence on YouTube. *Social Anthropology, 19*(3), 254–267.

Voland, E., & Grammer, K. (Eds.). (2003). *Evolutionary aesthetics.* Berlin: Springer-Verlag.

Wang, A. B., & Hawkins, D. (2017, September 3). A Utah nurse's violent arrest puts patient-consent law—and police conduct—in the spotlight. *The Washington Post*. Retrieved on 9/10/17 from: https://www.washingtonpost.com/news/morning-mix/wp/2017/09/03/a-utah-nurses-violent-arrest-puts-patient-consent-law-and-police-conduct-in-the-spotlight/?utm_term=.575e754c1e9d

Weaver, A. J., Zelenkauskaite, A., & Samson, L. (2012). The (non)violent world of YouTube: Content trends in web video. *Journal of Communication*, 62(6), 1065–1083.

Worth, S., & Adair, J. (1972). *Through Navajo eyes: An exploration in film communication and anthropology*. Bloomington: Indiana University Press.

Part One

On the Margins of the Art Worlds

1. Toward Art for All: Art Museum Education and the Reinvigoration of American Art Museums

LOIS H. SILVERMAN

Larry Gross' writings about art have yielded profound contributions to art-related scholarship, practice, and education. Gross deepened the understanding of art as a communication process. He showed that the acquisition of artistic competence is a social phenomenon, involving many communication systems and institutions, from American schools to public art movements. He modeled innovation in "art worlds" critique (Becker, 1982) to reveal how communication codes and modes impede or promote the inclusive and democratic practice of art. Collectively, Gross' work demonstrated that while art *is* communication, it is communication *about* art that creates and sustains art's collective meaning. In *On the Margins of Art Worlds*, an edited volume that evinced the broad applicability of his ideas to many art contexts, Gross (1995) made a provocative observation about that collective meaning: "modern Western societies have come to view the arts as a preserve for elites from which most citizens are estranged" (p. viii). As remedy, Gross called for nothing less than "radical changes in the ways our culture conceives of both art and education" achieved through a "restructuring of our educational priorities and methods" (p. 14). Ultimately, Gross linked the future of art to education, offering blueprints for practical change.

Historically speaking, perhaps no institution in the United States has embodied the idea of "the arts as a preserve for elites from which most citizens are estranged" more literally than the art museum. Yet over the past thirty-five years no other art institution has tried harder to remake itself as an essential connective agent between art and American citizens, enacted in large part through the work of art museum educators and their communication about art. Informed by radical change in the ways our culture conceives of *communication*, art museums have actually undertaken their own "restructuring of ... educational priorities and methods" in an effort to redress their exclusionary past. In short, the key themes of Gross' art scholarship prove remarkably prescient and analytically invaluable for understanding the recent movement of art museums toward greater inclusion. In tribute to Larry, this essay will apply both a communication lens and an historical perspective to examine the "paradigm shift" in recent American art museum history, and two communicative strategies by which art museum professionals and educators in particular have enacted greater public orientation and social responsibility: (1) employing audience studies to understand and valorize visitor meaning-making; and (2) promoting new methods, programs, and discourses to engage people with art. How, if at all, have these strategies made any difference for art museums or for art? For context, we begin by defining some key terms, followed by a brief look at the origins of art museums and art museum education in the United States.

The Art Museum Profession and Museum Studies Literature

Despite pervasive stereotypes in popular media of the monolithic, white-columned building, there is, in fact, no singular art museum in the United States. From The Crystal Bridges Museum of Art in Bentonville, Arkansas to the Studio Museum in Harlem, New York, American art museums and their collections are varied and geographically dispersed. What in fact links many institutions is the formally recognized collective of people who work in or for them and/or contribute to the development of their underlying theory and practice: namely, the art museum profession. This includes paid staff members, volunteers, scholars, critics, and employees of professional support organizations, like the American Alliance of Museums and the Association of Art Museum Directors. Along with their counterparts in other types of museums, art museum professionals have forged an interdisciplinary and eclectic body of written knowledge known as museum studies. In this essay, key museum studies writings about art museum theory and practice provide a window on the art museum profession.

A Rose Among Thorns: Early American Art Museums and the Docent as Communicator

Due in large part to post-Civil War affluence and the expansion of philanthropy, the first American art museums were founded in the 1870's: The Museum of Fine Arts in Boston, The Metropolitan Museum of Art in

New York, The Corcoran Gallery of Art in Washington, DC, The Philadelphia Museum of Art, and The Art Institute of Chicago. They all began in urban centers, where inequality thrived. Their wealthy founders professed to gather, preserve, and display great art for public enjoyment, which they did. By many accounts, however, they also looked to art itself, and communication about art in the museum setting, as tools for social reform (e.g., Bennett, 1995; Wallach, 2015). As Roberts (1997) explained:

> Business leaders in the 1870's were faced with tremendous social and economic problems. Labor riots, racial strife, and immigration all threatened to upset the social fabric. Art held the promise of spiritual uplift and social refinement without altering the economic structure that had served business leaders so well. Their sentiments were quite genuine; but … they promoted the values and manners of their class by supporting only those forms of art and culture that they believed would strengthen people's … nature. (p. 29)

In short, early art museums were patriarchal and exclusionary. Indeed, Roberts and others implied that perhaps their most effective communicative function was to maintain the aristocratic image of their founders and leaders and class distinction. As Wallach (2015) stated, "… in practice, as Bourdieu has insisted, the museum helped to constitute a hierarchy in which those who possessed the capacity to comprehend and enjoy works of art were superior to those who did not" (p. 29). Informed by the ideas of the Aesthetic Movement, many early museum leaders felt this capacity to appreciate art required only that visitors quietly contemplate great works from their collections, and by virtue of the art itself, would experience aesthetic pleasure and uplift. Thus, museums needed only to collect, preserve, and display art.

Yet unlike art museums in Europe, American art museums were originally chartered as educational institutions, not only as collecting institutions (Rawlins, 1978). In the United States, a few early museum leaders of more populist bent believed that in fact, visitors needed "trained instruction" and "expert guidance" to be able to engage with art (Kai-Kee, 2011); soon, former art professors and others were recruited to serve as *docents,* or gallery educators, tasked with "giving visitors in the galleries information about any or all of the collections" (p. 20). Visitors indeed availed themselves of these interactions, and before long, most American art museums offered several modes of interpersonal contact with docents, including tours, lectures, and eventually, visits for school children (Kai-Kee, 2011; Roberts, 1997). Thus docents were the early public faces of museums, the communicators-in-chief who attempted to draw visitors closer to art with their "expert" information, thereby shaping their experiences.

The founding of American art museums elevated two competing concepts or meanings of art, namely, art as aesthetic appreciation versus art as educational engagement. Yet proponents of these opposing views found common ground in a key idea: "that the artist's intentions were discoverable in the work of art itself" (Kai-Kee, 2011, p. 24). From the more aesthetically oriented Museum of Fine Arts of Boston to the populist Metropolitan Museum of Art in New York, many early art museums promised to "help us divine what. … [the artists] meant to say" and "translate the message of the artist into terms intelligible to the visitor" (as quoted in Kai-Kee, 2011, p. 24). Thus the concept of art as communication (e.g. Gross, 1973) has also been foundational to American art museum discourse since its inception. Even from this perspective, docents mediated visitors' engagement with art, helping to "divine" and "translate" artists' intentions for others. Early art museum educators did much to shape museum visitors' art encounters.

In sum, American art museum founders implied a desire to serve their surrounding urban communities. In reality, theirs were predominantly patriarchal relationships, aimed at social control and promoting conceptions of art and art appreciation reflective of their elite status. At the same time, these founders essentially empowered docents, early art museum educators, to be institutional communicators-in-chief and mediators of visitors' art engagement. Using highly didactic methods, their efforts were arguably patriarchal as well. Yet, as docent services became popular, seeds were sown for the continued growth of the institutional role of the art museum educator.

From Practices to Profession: Museum Education Matures

The next fifty years saw slow-moving but important developments in American art museums and art museum education. Principles of progressive education fueled the design and success of art museum education programs for adults, children, teachers, and other audiences, and the use of trained volunteer docents as a communications workforce (Kai-Kee, 2011). By the 1960's, art museums offered studio classes programs for children and teens as educators espoused the power of hands-on learning. Increasingly, museum educators looked to other fields like art history, art education, and aesthetic education for theoretical underpinnings to their practices (Ebitz, 2005).

Many writers found communication theory especially applicable to the work of museums, with its concern for successful information transfer from a sender, the museum educator, to a receiver, the visitor, through the "medium" of an exhibit, lecture, tour, or other educational program (e.g.,

Cameron, 1968; McLuhan, 1968). Thus, "Did the visitor get our message?" became a mantra. By the 1980's, museum education was changing from a set of practices to a profession (Ebitz, 2005; Roberts, 1997) as educators from museums of all kinds created theories, research agendas, journals, conferences, standards statements, training programs, and other hallmarks of a profession. Art museum educators across the country were critical to this process.

The Paradigm Shifts: Toward Inclusive Public Engagement

The late 1980's began a significant period of transformation for museums in general and art museums in particular (e.g., Ebitz, 2005; Hein, 2000). Fueled by social, economic, and political changes and increased demand for accountability from their funders and publics, art museums witnessed "a paradigm shift" (e.g., Anderson, 2004; Ebitz, 2005; Silverman, 1995): many turned from an inward to an outward focus, marked by a prevailing aim to engage and serve the nation's diverse public (e.g., American Association of Museums, 1992; Sandell, 2002; Silverman, 2010; Weil, 1997). Not all museum leaders embraced this shift (Cuno, 1997; Moore, 1997). With mandates from professional organizations to change their relationships to their communities, more art museum directors paid heed.

These changes were not unique to museums. Rather, they reflected the influence of the broad cultural sea change in academia and politics known as postmodernism—characterized by the rejection of universalism and the view that "knowledge" and "truth" are socially constructed products of interpretation. Postmodern thought pervaded many disciplines relevant to the art museum profession, including art history, literary studies, and education, and new perspectives in many of these arenas, like constructivism, contributed significantly to art museum education theory and practice (e.g., Hein, 1998; Hein & Alexander, 1998).

Broad in scope, perhaps no discipline carried greater implications for art museums and museum education practice than communication studies. First, it recast the very definition of communication from a one-way linear process of information transmission, to an active negotiation of meaning resulting in multiple interpretations. Second, it highlighted the social nature of communication and its reliance on interaction between and among people, a point quite applicable to the mostly group-based modes of museum education, like tours and studio classes. In short, postmodern communication theory helped the art museum profession enact its new paradigm. Notably, it informed two communicative practices with which art museum educators have arguably moved art museums toward greater inclusivity: (1) employing audience studies to understand visitor meaning-making; and (2) promoting new methods, programs, and discourses to engage people with art. As champions of these practices, art museum educators have evolved to be the primary agents of inclusive public engagement in American art museums.

Art Museum Audience Studies and Visitor Meaning-Making

In order to understand how to engage the diverse public, art museum professionals realized they needed more empirically-based knowledge of peoples' experiences in art museums, as well as reliable channels for soliciting community input into their efforts. They soon found both in the burgeoning practice of art museum audience studies, typically spearheaded by museum educators. While museums have since the 1930's employed some forms of visitor evaluation and market research, this period witnessed a wave of applied research in which professionals acknowledged their insularity and aimed to understand the art museum experiences of people unlike themselves, including first-time visitors (Walsh, 1991), "novices" (visitors without much art background), and "advanced amateurs" (people knowledgeable about art but not career artists) (McDermott-Lewis, 1990).

Among the most-cited findings at the time, first-time visitors in a focus group study across eleven different art museums in the United States said they felt intimidated and disoriented in art museums, and wanted "support in deciding what objects to view and how they could be interpreted" (Walsh, 2011, p. 46). In another key study, "novices" in museums were found to "give no indication they even think about the artist as making deliberate choices in color, composition, etc. to create a work" (McDermott-Lewis, 1990, p. 20) but that they did find value in art that served them as "touchstones for personal associations [or] memories" (p. 17). On one hand, such studies justified the continuing need for professional art museum educators and offered clues about how to better engage people in communicative encounters with art. On the other hand, they also began to suggest that some people found value and meaning differently than art experts.

Before long, some scholars directly applied new communication theory to museum audience studies and recast art museum visitors as active makers of meaning, rather than passive receivers of information (e.g., Hooper-Greenhill, 1992; Perin, 1992; Roberts, 1997; Silverman, 1990). These studies demonstrated that when viewing art in museums, often in the company of others, some visitors may like using or learning "expert" codes of engagement (Gross, 1974; Worth & Gross, 1974), but may *also* or *instead* bring to bear a range of more personal or subjective codes, including past experiences, emotions, memories, social and cultural background, and/or prior knowledge. This period of art museum audience studies made two enduring contributions. It launched the professional practice of applying empirical research to better understand actual and potential art museum visitors and with it, a knowledge base. It also helped document multiple codes and meanings of art, allowing professionals one useful approach to conceptualizing diversity.

New Methods, Programs, and Discourses About Art

By the 2000's, art museums offered a menu of standard educational fare to engage audiences with art, including exhibits, guided tours, community, adult and family programs, classes, specialized tours for school groups, partnerships with other organizations, and online materials and resources (Wetterlund & Sayre, 2009). In addition to their responsibility for creating these modes, art museum educators were increasingly tasked with "audience advocacy," the use of audience research and their own growing sensitivity to address the needs of diverse visitors. Spurred by internal and external pressure to serve more people in more ways, museum educators started working with, rather than against, visitors' varied codes and meanings of art. This transformed the nature of gallery teaching, and inspired a host of program trends in which multiple codes and meanings informed museum goals and ultimately, broadened and diversified museums' discourses about art. Common to these changes was a growing emphasis on the social nature of interpretation and an embrace of group interaction dynamics as a vehicle for meaning-making, inclusion, and education.

Gallery Teaching Transformed

Long the staple of art museum education modes, didactic gallery teaching gave way to new interactive, inquiry-based, and dialogic approaches that made space for visitors' interpretations of artworks. One approach, called Visual Thinking Strategies (VTS) (Yenawine, 2013), used for group art-viewing by many museums, required the museum educator not to provide any information, but to ask only three questions and use only three "facilitation techniques"—paraphrasing, pointing to the work, and linking students' comments' to each other – to guide students to personal meanings of art. Other approaches expressly cast all group participants as equals, including the museum educator. As explained by Burnham (2011):

> The teaching we advocate ... posits that among the most important understandings people have of works of art are those that they arrive at in dialogue with other

visitors, guided but not limited by the teacher's own knowledge ... We realize that we are always as likely to learn from our students as they from us, and we strive to keep our dialogues open to new and unexpected interpretations. (p. 1)

In short, the gallery teacher's "expert meaning" had become the idea that art is multivalent, as the group communication became the teacher.

From Programs to Discourses

The past few decades have witnessed other key developments in art museum educational programming aimed at broader inclusion, from multisensory tours for people with disabilities, to community-curated exhibits. Like gallery teaching, many newer programs have harnessed the social nature of the museum experience, and aimed to "open up" the museum to different people, perspectives, and uses. Art museum initiatives devoted to "access" became more common. While a thorough review of these changes is beyond our scope here, two recent *thematic* trends warrant a closer look: programs about creativity, and programs about social action. As these two cases demonstrate, museum educators' search for ever more inclusive, interactive, and multivalent approaches have in fact given rise to institutional discourses about art that are redefining some American art museums today.

Art as creativity

In the late 2000's, the subject of creativity garnered great attention from government, scholars, and media alike. *Newsweek* magazine deemed creativity a "crisis in America"—as evinced by declining scores on creativity tests in the face of growing demand for creativity in the 21st century workforce (Bronson & Merryman, 2010). Many art museum educators saw an opportunity to join this socially relevant conversation and reframe their work, if not the meaning of art (e.g., Foley, 2014; Munley & Rossiter, 2014). Soon, art museums from The Plains Art Museum in Fargo, North Dakota to the Clark Institute in Williamstown, Massachusetts mounted creativity-themed programs and museum-wide initiatives. Others, like the Dallas Museum of Art and the Columbus Museum of Art in Ohio opened new "Centers for Creativity," and in some cases, even changed their institutional mission (Foley, 2014; Munley & Rossiter, 2013).

Within this art as creativity discourse lie enduring notions of meaning-making and the multivalence of art, and arguably, a multicultural and democratic concept of art. Educators at the Clark Institute, for example, mounted

Clark Remix, placing paintings, sculptures and decorative objects from its collection with a wide array of objects from many different cultures and eras, with the intent of providing a new way to view art and open the possibility of multiple interpretations. Online *uCreate* and *uExplore* features give access to images and information about some 4,000 items in the Clark collection, and invite visitors to create their own "exhibitions" and conduct their own research. (Munley & Rossiter, 2013, p. 4)

Other creativity initiatives, like *Spun: Adventures in Textiles*, have featured the artwork and active participation of contemporary artists from communities that have historically been excluded from most art museum collections and discourses. This institution-wide initiative at The Denver Art Museum highlighted work by Native American artists and community members (Fischer & Munley, 2014). Reflecting on museums' embrace of art as creativity, Munley and Rossiter noted:

> Historically, art museums have … offered people the opportunity to witness the products of exceptionally accomplished artists … [but] art museums are uniquely positioned to do even more. They could augment the opportunities they provide for people to see products produced by others by concentrating attention on engaging people in the creative process itself, thus contributing to the much-needed awareness that creativity is not just the gift of a select few, but it is a basic human capacity that can be developed in everyone. The implications for change in the museum cannot be underestimated. (p. 24)

Indeed, Gross would be encouraged by this positive message about who can be an artist (1983; 1995). Within the discourse of art as creativity, all citizens have the potential to appreciate as well as create art in museums, and the ability to influence each other.

Art as social action

In pursuit of inclusion and social responsibility, many art museums have recently turned for inspiration to the long history of art and activism, and some of its current forms, such as social practice art and protest art (Kennedy, 2013). From the Portland Museum of Art In Oregon to the Queens Museum of Art in New York, museum educators have shaped programs around art that relates to current events and pressing issues that indeed tap visitors' emotional, personal, and cultural codes of engagement. Recognizing the limits of their own training and institutional biases, many educators have reached beyond their walls to a variety of collaborators, including community groups, social service agencies, activists, artists, and others. In so doing, these art museums present art as social action, a highly relevant discourse that, like creativity, holds space for a wide range of people, codes, and meanings.

For example, *It's not just black and white*, a 3-month residency project by Phoenix artist Gregory Sale at the Arizona State University Art Museum in 2011:

used artistic gestures to initiate and host dialogue, aspiring to give voice to the
multiple constituencies of the corrections, incarceration and criminal justice systems … [through] exhibitions, dance and other staged events, discussions and
readings. As the title … implies, the intent of the project is to expose and examine the many often conflicting viewpoints, perspectives and values that are generated from serious considerations of justice and public safety.

Throughout the duration of the project, Sale's art and ideas created interaction among incarcerated people and their families, correctional officers, victims' families, parolees, students, and speakers as different as activist Angela
Davis and former sheriff Joe Arpaio.

In 2017, The Brooklyn Museum partnered with Alabama-based Equal
Justice Initiative (EJI), to organize *The Legacy of Lynching: Confronting
Racial Terror in America*, a group exhibition featuring art from the museum's collection alongside an interactive online presentation of research into
the history of violence against African-Americans, including video interviews
with descendants of lynching victims. The program aimed to prompt "important cultural conversations" (Scher, 2017). Essential to these conversations
were the voices of the artists. As Anne Pasternak, director of The Brooklyn
Museum reflected, "We do believe that art has the power to communicate
truths about an experience, a history, a problem that can't always be effectively done with text … It is urgent we face this history and that's why we are
partnering to make this show a reality" (Scher, 2017).

Like the creativity trend, some art museums have recast their institutional
missions in line with art as social action discourse. For example, The Pulitzer
Arts Foundation in St. Louis, an innovator in social practice art programming,
now states: "Valuing close looking and civic engagement, the Pulitzer is a
place for contemplation and exchange that brings art and people together"
(Pulitzer Arts Foundation, 2017). Building on and beyond the success of its
education programs, the museum has embraced art as social action to rede-
fine its entire institution as multivalent, interactive, and relevant.

Reflections

Little did Larry Gross know that his blueprint for change toward a more communication-based and inclusive art education in America would so perfectly
map the contemporary actions of American art museums, those most historically literal of "preserves for elites from which most citizens are estranged"
(1995, p. viii). Informed by changes in postmodern communication theory, American art museums have, over the past thirty-five years, essentially
enacted their own institutional "restructuring of … educational priorities and

methods" (Gross 1995, p. 14). In service to the highest priority of engaging the diverse American public with art, the "art world" of the American art museum profession has expanded, professionalized, and elevated the essential communicative role and work of art museum education. Its methods have changed in fundamental ways.

Harnessing postmodern ideas about communication, art museum educators have recast the relationship of art museums and the public and used research as a communicative channel to learn about peoples' experiences with art, forging a more empirically-based practice. They have changed gallery teaching approaches to recognize and integrate multiple interpretive codes and meanings, and reshaped programs in a host of museum modes to harness the dynamic nature of group interaction and interpretation. They have embraced collaboration with artists, activists, and people of backgrounds typically underrepresented in art museums, and championed the multivalent nature of art. Museum educators have supported a variety of codes, meanings, and discourses of art as program goals and vehicles of greater inclusion, and ultimately, informed the focus, mission, and reinvigoration of many American art museums today. American art museums may well be contributing to "radical changes in the ways our culture conceives of ... education" (Gross, 1995, p. 14) at least in so far as it now occurs in art museums.

And what about "radical changes in the ways our culture conceives of ... art," the other target of Gross' vision of a more democratic and inclusive art practice in America? Has the restructuring of art museum education priorities and methods wrought change there? It may be a generation or two before we know for sure. But it seems clear that art museum educators have helped broaden the range of discourses and meanings about art that are respected, supported, and promoted in and by American art museums. Many such conceptions of art come from a more genuine understanding of the varied ways in which people relate to and value art. Perhaps most encouraging from Gross' view, the currently popular and engaging discourses like art as creativity and art as social change still promote at their core the essential notion that art is a communication process, and that competence to appreciate and create art can be learned and practiced by all. These current trends in art museum discourse speak directly to a more democratic view of art, as well as how and why art matters to life, which may help motivate people to engage with art.

By many accounts, however, there is still tremendous change required for American art museums to become fully equitable institutions and to reflect the true diversity of this country (Acuff & Evans, 2014). Among recent efforts, professionals are again turning inward, to address and start to rectify the rampant racism, sexism, inequality, and lack of diversity within the art museum profession itself. There is no doubt that a fully inclusive American art museum is very much a work in progress.

When compared to their earliest iterations, however, American art museums have made significant strides toward engaging more people with art in more diverse ways. Through changes in educational priorities, methods, and discourses, many American art museums have become lively centers of community interaction where citizens connect with art, with others both like and unlike themselves, and with pressing issues of relevance to American life today. In these reinvigorated institutions, art museum educators promote learning about the specialized knowledge, skills, products, and language of art while they hold space for disparate people and groups to experience, share, challenge, and co-create its meanings, ever open to the possibility of the unexpected. If that isn't art, then what is?

References

Acuff, J. B., & Evans, L. (Eds.). (2014). *Multiculturalism in art museums today*. Lanham, MD: Rowman and Littlefield.

American Association of Museums. (1992). *Excellence and equity: Education and the public dimension of museums*. Washington, DC: American Association of Museums.

Anderson, G. (Ed.). (2004). *Reinventing the museum: Historical and contemporary perspectives on the paradigm shift*. Walnut Creek, CA: AltaMira Press.

Arizona State University Art Museum. (2011). *It's not just black and white: Gregory Sale – social studies project 6*. Retrieved from: http://asuartmuseum.wordpress-Gregory-sale-social-studies-project-6/

Becker, H. S. (1982). *Art worlds*. Berkeley, CA: University of California Press.

Bennett, T. (1995). *The birth of the museum: History, theory, politics*. London, UK: Routledge.

Bourdieu, P., & Darbel, A. (1991). *The love of art: European art museums and their public*. Cambridge, UK: Polity Press.

Bronson, P., & Merryman, A. (2010). The creativity crisis. *Newsweek*, July 19, 44–50.

Burnham, R. (2011). Introduction. In R. Burnham, & E. Kai-Kee (Eds.). *Teaching in the art museum: Interpretation as experience* (pp. 1–6). Los Angeles, CA: The J. Paul Getty Museum.

Cameron, D. (1968). A viewpoint: The museum as a communications system and implications for museum education. *Curator, 11*(1), 33–40.

Cuno, J. (1997). Whose money? Whose power? Whose art history? *The Art Bulletin, 79*(1), 6–9.

Ebitz, D. (2005). Qualifications and the professional preparation and development of art museum educators. *Studies in Art Education: A Journal of Issues and Research, 46*(2), 150–169.

Fischer, D., & Munley, M. E. (2014). *Tapping into creativity and becoming part of something bigger.* Denver, CO: Denver Art Museum.

Foley, C. M. (2014). Why creativity? Articulating and championing a museum's social mission. *Journal of Museum Education, 39*(2), 139–151.

Gross, L. (1973). Art as the communication of competence. *Social Science Information, 12*(5), 115–141.

Gross, L. (1974). Modes of communication and the acquisition of symbolic competence. In D. Olsen (Ed.), *Media and symbols* (pp. 56–80). Chicago, IL: University of Chicago Press.

Gross, L. (1983). Why Johnny can't draw. *Art Education, 36*(2), 74–77.

Gross, L. (Ed.). (1995). *On the margins of art worlds (Institutional structures of feeling).* Boulder, CO: Westview Press.

Hein, G. E. (1998). *Learning in the museum.* London, UK: Routledge.

Hein, G. E., & Alexander, M. (1998). *Museums: Places of learning.* Washington, DC: American Association of Museums.

Hein, H. S. (2000). *The museum in transition, a philosophical perspective.* Washington, DC: Smithsonian Institution Press.

Hooper-Greenhill, E. (1992). *Museums and the shaping of knowledge.* London, UK: Routledge.

Kai-Kee, E. (2011). A brief history of teaching in the art museum. In R. Burnham & E. Kai-Kee (Eds.), *Teaching in the art museum: Interpretation as experience* (pp. 19–58). Los Angeles, CA: The J. Paul Getty Museum.

Kennedy, R. (2013, March 20). Outside the citadel, social practice art is intended to nurture. *The New York Times.* Retrieved from http://www.nytimes.com

McLuhan, M. (1968). McLuhanism in the museum. *Museum News, 46*(7), 11–18.

McDermott-Lewis, M. (1990). *The Denver Art Museum interpretive project.* Denver, CO: Denver Art Museum.

Moore, K. (1997). Museums and popular culture. London, UK: Cassell.

Munley, M. E., & Rossiter, C. (2013). *An art museum as a creativity platform.* Denver, CO: Denver Art Museum.

Perin, C. (1992). The communicative circle: Museums as communities. In I. Karp, K. Kreamer, & S. Levine (Eds.), *Museums and communities: The politics of public culture* (pp. 182–220). Washington, DC: Smithsonian Institution Press.

Pulitzer Arts Foundation. (2017). Mission. Retrieved from http://www.Pulitzerarts.org

Rawlins, K. (1978). Educational metamorphosis of the American museum. *Studies in Art Education, 19*(3), 4–17.

Roberts, L. C. (1997). *From knowledge to narrative: Educators and the changing museum.* Washington, DC: Smithsonian Institution Press.

Sandell, R. (Ed.). (2002). *Museums, society, inequality.* London, UK: Routledge.

Scher, R. (2017, July 25). Brooklyn Museum partners with Equal Justice Initiative to survey "The Legacy of Lynching." *ARTNEWS.* Retrieved from http://www.artnews.com

Silverman, L. H. (1990). *Of us and other 'things': The content and functions of talk by adult visitor pairs in an art and a history museum*. Unpublished dissertation. University of Pennsylvania.

Silverman, L. H. (1995). Visitor meaning making in museums for a new age. *Curator, 38*(3), 161–170.

Silverman, L. H. (2010). *The social work of museums*. London, UK: Routledge.

Wallach, A. (2015). A very brief history of the art museum in the United States. In K. Murawska-Muthesius & P. Piotrowski (Eds.), *From museum critique to the critical museum* (pp. 15–36). Surrey, UK: Ashgate.

Walsh, A. (Ed.). (1991). *Insights: Museums, visitors, attitudes, expectations: A focus group experiment*. Los Angeles, CA: Getty Center for Education in the Arts.

Weil, S. (1997). The museum and the public. *Museum management and curatorship, 16*(3), 257–271.

Wetterlund, K., & Sayre, S. (2009). *2009 art museum education programs survey*. Retrieved from http://www.museumed.org/research/surveys

Worth, S., & Gross, L. (1974). Symbolic strategies. *Journal of Communication, 24*(4), 27–39.

Yenawine, P. (2013). *Visual thinking strategies: Using art to deepen learning across school disciplines*. Cambridge, MA: Harvard University Press.

2. *Photographic Art in the Age of Digital Image-Making*

Dona Schwartz

Photographic image-making takes place in a wide array of social, cultural, institutional and economic contexts. Among picture making media, photography is arguably the most accessible—more so now than ever before. If I define a "camera" as any device that produces photographs, then I can write with some confidence that most readers of this chapter routinely have a camera close at hand and use it frequently. The marriage of the lens and the smartphone has expanded what we consider to be a camera, and for many photographers it has changed the routines that characterize the practice of photographic image-making. I am using the term "photographer" broadly to refer to anyone making a lens-based still image, no matter what device they may employ. While I use the term to embrace those who engage in a wide range of photographic activities, others may not be so generous, narrowly applying the designation "photographer" to a subset of all camera users—an issue to which I will return later in this chapter. Not only do we keep cameras close at hand, but we also have mobile access to the digital version of a light table we can use to review and select amongst the pictures we've made. Our phone's repository of image files can be called up at will, along with a digital darkroom—the increasingly sophisticated image editing apps that comprise part of a smartphone's default toolkit. More complex editing tasks may require a suite of desktop applications, but these too are widely available, and online training and tutorials makes the acquisition of the necessary skills to use the software accessible to many. Using a cellular network or internet connection, our photographs can be shared with audiences we know and those we don't. Our images circulate in a sea of photographs produced by the millions of photographers making and sharing pictures each day.

For those of us who have championed visual literacy and the development of visual competencies, the widespread activity of photographic image making and the routine practice of communicating by sharing pictures seems to crack open the possibility of learning by doing. By manipulating the technologies, messages and delivery systems that acquaint the picture maker with the vocabulary, grammar, and construction of meanings communicated through photographs, we may become more informed image makers *and* consumers. Framed in this way it is difficult not to applaud the democratization of image-making and the skill set it might engender, although throughout the medium's history there have been those who decried photography's welcoming embrace. Mass participation in photographic image making has been promoted and nurtured by the photography industry. The genius of the Kodak camera was its simplicity, making photography accessible "even" to women and children, as early Kodak ads imply. As the medium of photography has evolved since the mid nineteenth century, industry players—the manufacturers of photographic equipment and materials, as well as service providers of various kinds—have had to morph in order to keep pace with new discoveries, emergent trends, changing and expanding patterns of use. Flux has characterized the history of photography; the medium and its use continue to change.

The earliest photographic practitioners experimented with the hardware and software of their time, contributing to the development of a robust arena of activity that grew and diversified. As the ranks of photographers expanded, categorical distinctions emerged: picture *makers* were soon served by *manufacturers* of equipment and material. Professional designations arose: portrait photographer, landscape and expeditionary photographer, naturalist and scientific photographer, documentary photographer, news photographer, advertising photographer among them. As technology developed allowing photographs to be mass reproduced and published along with print, more specialties emerged. Photographers cultivated audiences and markets for the images they produced. Distinct from these subgroups, other practitioners professed the view that photography was a fine art medium like painting or drawing, giving rise to the construction of an arena devoted to the development of art photography, along with galleries, critics, and connoisseurs. As these professional categories emerged and stabilized they gave rise to their own distinct practices, distribution networks, audiences and aesthetic codes. Before these separate arenas and distinctive practices became recognized and institutionalized, photographers could all be considered amateurs. But there were barriers to participation. The earliest amateurs had access to the financial means, knowledge and skills necessary to be engaged with the medium. Mass production of affordable photographic equipment and material opened the gates to widespread popular activity and an explosion in the ranks of amateurs. Many came together to form camera clubs, groups from which a number of the earliest art photographers emerged. Over time amateur activity could also be partitioned into casual snap-shooters, including family and vacation photographers as well as more avid hobbyists.

In past research, I have examined the construction of a subset of these distinctive arenas of photographic activity, discourse and aesthetics. Three photographic domains particularly attracted my attention, by virtue of circumstance, curiosity and scholarly concern. The worlds of fine art photography, amateur camera club photography, and photojournalism have been the primary subjects of my investigations. My research comparing the worlds of amateur camera club photography and fine art photography in Philadelphia kickstarted my scholarly career and has informed all of my subsequent work, both written and visual. I came to the subject matter as a young photographer—an avid amateur cum aspiring artist. After encountering what seemed to me the vagaries of the art world of photography, I was anxious to try and better understand what made a photograph art, and what made a photographer an artist. Although camera club photographers considered themselves the *true* artists, those outside their world did not bestow the title upon them. I wanted to explore how these social distinctions could be created, recognized, mobilized and sustained. Photography provided me with a model investigative focus—I have been fascinated by the ways in which a single medium can acquire a distinctly different ethos, practice, valuation, aesthetic(s), and status, in accordance with the social arena in which it is employed. Later, my research took a turn down the path of exploring the relationship of photojournalism to other worlds of photographic production, in large part due to the fact that I was a faculty member at the School of Journalism and Mass Communication at the University of Minnesota, where I taught visual communication, the history of photography, and photojournalism. I developed a research agenda simultaneously doing photographic ethnography and studying photojournalism. As I examined the practice of photojournalism, the contradictions between the creed of objectivity and the recognition of exceptional visual artistry among news photographers piqued my interest. If the very best news pictures could be singled out for their visual virtuosity—their display of masterful use of color, light and shadow, composition, and invention—could they still be unbiased reports? If photojournalists keen on earning the highest honors awarded in their field strove to make pictures that stood out from those of their peers, were they straying from their prime directive?

Many of these questions have transitioned to new ones, as the worlds of photojournalism and art have begun to collide. As newspapers and magazines downsized their staffs and photographers could no longer count on finding employment or an outlet for their work as they had in the past, photojournalists began finding new opportunities through museums, galleries and publications outside the realm of journalism. War photographers like Luc Delahaye reinvented themselves as artists (Lennon, 2004). Their aesthetics began to change as the art world incorporated them into the fold—the next new thing to exhibit and market to a robust audience of collectors. Contemporary photojournalism and some art photographs look more alike than ever before. Boundaries have blurred here, and in other arenas as well. The art world of photography, as with other art mediums, hungers for innovation and change.

While professional photographers may be able to jump fences—or help tear them down—and work across formerly strict boundaries, the divide between amateurs and artists remains key to preserving an elite universe of discourse and an art world of photography. The proliferation of digital imaging technology, the ubiquitous presence of cameras, and the routine production of photographic images by camera users of all kinds have made the medium of photography more accessible than ever. How have contemporary art photographers responded to this newest onslaught of photographic image-makers? If there is a perceived need to close ranks, the impulse repeats earlier historical moments, as in the early 20th century, when new technologies invigorated the medium by dramatically expanding the pool of users. In the early 1980s, I outlined a series of principles at work in the construction and maintenance of boundaries separating art from amateur photographic activity (Schwartz, 1986). At that time, there had been no recent change in photographic technology or activity that might have created an urgent need to re-draw and solidify boundaries between these arenas of activity—the principles I gleaned from observations and interviews with camera club and fine art photographers evidenced the results of these photographers traveling divergent paths that had been mapped out in the early 20th century. More recently, the introduction of digital photographic technologies and the consequent explosion of photographic activity has created a more urgent need to mark distinctions between artists and other camera users. A brief review of the principles I outlined in 1986 provides a framework from which to consider and assess distinguishing features currently operating.

Art Photography Is Tied to Other Art Media

In the early 20th century, aligning photography with media like painting and drawing served to make the implicit argument that photography equally occupied the status of *art* medium. This alignment reappeared in statements made by photographers I interviewed. Many eschewed using the term "photographer" when speaking about themselves, identifying first and foremost as artists whose current work happened to be "coming out in photographs."

Art Photography Responds to Its Own History and Traditions

Curators writing about contemporary photography in the 1970s and early 80s noted the revival of early photographic processes. At the time, they wrote that the use of 19th century materials and processes was in vogue. Photographers were then resurrecting labor and skill intensive approaches such as wet plate collodion and hand-colored black and white images. These choices explicitly located photographers' work within the history of the medium both by using past practices and through that use, commenting upon and extending them.

Art Photography Has Its Own Vocabulary

When talking about the process of making photographs and photographic images themselves, a distinctive jargon emerged. Photographers felt complimented when told they had "good eyes" or an image was "well-seen". The act of making photographs involved a process of "discovery". Successful photographs were consistently described as "ambiguous" and "mysterious". Art photographers scorned images with easily discernible meanings, and prized images that required active interpretive engagement and could evoke multiple meanings.

Art Photography Conveys Ideas

Art photographers and the work they produce emphasize ideas and concepts rather than visible content. The photographic artist spends time thinking about what to photograph rather than reacting in response to events and activities—the work engages ideas such as the formal problems of visualization, visual elements like light and shadow, or the nature of the photographic frame.

Art Photography Is Innovative

Like other art media, art photography introduces new ideas, approaches and ways of seeing, expanding existing visual vocabularies. Unlike amateur work which values the successful reproduction of longstanding shared aesthetic codes, artists seek to produce innovative images. Assessments like "I've seen it before" or "It's been done" deliver a devastating blow.

Art Photography Is Personal

Artists use photography as a vehicle for self-expression and the images artists produce are inextricably tied to their histories, values, interests and commitments. They are, in essence, autobiographical. In addition, artists derive personal gratification and pleasure in the act of picture making—intrinsic rewards earned by those who commit themselves to the art-making enterprise.

Art Photography Is a Lifestyle

Artists' identity is tied to their dedication to making images and their commitment to an artist's way of life. Even if that choice were to entail personal sacrifice, alienation from social norms or economic disadvantage, true artists soldier on. To be or not to be is not the question—one's identity as an artist simply is.

Art Photography Participates in the World of Commerce

Despite eschewing art's commodification, artists make objects that circulate within the art market. Success can be measured in terms of the visibility of an artist's work, through exhibitions in for-profit galleries, non-profit art spaces, and museums. Success can also be measured with respect to inclusion in important collections, institutional or private. Most artists happily sell the work they produce to individuals and institutions, and to do so, a market value must be affixed to that work. Despite their focus on living an artist's life and making work, successful photographic artists produce objects that people can buy.

Moving forward, my intention here is not to replicate previous research, but rather to examine the ways in which the findings outlined above might continue to usefully illuminate how contemporary photographic artists define and approach the work they do. I now come to this question from an insider's perspective, and the inferences I offer result from auto-ethnographic participant observation and questionnaire data solicited from practicing contemporary art photographers. Because the trajectory of my own research has shifted, my vantage point on, and access to, the art world of photography has changed. My scholarly interest in the social construction of the art world of photography persists, despite the fact that I consider myself a participant in the arena I previously studied as an interested outsider. Over time, my work has morphed from visual ethnography (Schwartz, 1992) to arts-based social science research (Schwartz, 1998; Schwartz, 2002) to practice-led art research (Schwartz, 2009; Schwartz, 2015). This shift occurred for several reasons.

While engaged in shooting photographs for my first visual ethnography, *Waucoma Twilight*, I became keenly interested in assessing the work the pictures might do, in addition to being used as prompts in photo-elicitation interviewing. Once the material was published I became disenchanted with the secondary role the photographs ultimately played in the overall communication of my research inferences. This had to do, in part, with the poor quality of the image reproduction in my book, but it also stemmed from the role I had ascribed to them—they functioned as supports for the written text. In subsequent research, I labored to give the photographs a more prominent role. Rather than illustrate what the text *already* conveyed, I wanted to give them a different, independent job to do. Still, the problem of audience remained—situated within the context of social science research, my readers gravitated towards what I wrote rather than what I showed. And since scholarly academic publishing optimizes for the reproduction of text, inadequate reproduction quality became a barrier to achieving my goals with respect to the images I was producing. Subsequently, I began showing my research-based photographs to seasoned image-viewers—curators, gallerists, and art photographers. I saw the response to my images change. These viewers looked closely, carefully and intently at what I had painstakingly constructed. They responded to the formal properties of the images and contextualized them within the visual vocabularies with which they were intimately familiar. Their reactions to my photographs enhanced the gratification I felt in making them. It seemed that my attempts to successfully use photographs in visual research might best be accomplished if I crossed into the world I had previously regarded as a site of scholarly inquiry.

Since jumping the fence, I have produced several "bodies of work", exhibited photographs in museums, galleries, and festivals around the world, published in journals devoted to photography as an art, general interest photography magazines, and major publications in the US and abroad. My photographs have been acquired by major museums and I am represented by an internationally respected commercial gallery. I have published two photographic books with essays by important museum curators. I consider the primary reference group for my work the curators, gallerists, editors, publishers, and fine art photographers I have met along the way. I routinely use art world jargon like a native-speaker; it is now a functional part of my lexicon. Rounding out the picture, I am currently a faculty member in a university art department where my research comes out as photographs. Topping it off, I run a photography festival—my duties include exhibition programming, curation, and jurying submissions. My scholarly interest in the functioning of the world I inhabit endures. I simultaneously participate in the art world of photography and assess what I observe and encounter.

From this perspective, I return to the question: in a busy universe of photographic activity, what separates fine art photography and makes it distinct? In what ways might the boundaries have shifted, constricted, or otherwise transformed? The assertions I made in 1986 still hold, although changes have occurred. Innovation and novelty still distinguish artmaking from amateur photography. Novelty may be achieved using new digital technologies and, increasingly, multi-media work has gained attention. Artists who employ photography as a part of their expressive apparatus have proliferated. It is arguably the case that the introduction of digital photography has made the medium more accessible to multi-media artists, and as a result photography is employed as an *aspect* of a larger overall plan of multi-media work. I would venture to suggest that the photographic work appearing in these contexts demonstrates a much more basic level of photographic competence than the work produced by artists who primarily engage with the medium. Multi-media artists do not frame their work within the history of photography—the medium functions as an available resource in a larger media toolkit. Although photography has been appropriated by artists working in other media, the narrower world of art photography continues to thrive.

As evidenced in the late 1970s and early 80s, the history of photography offers a fertile well from which contemporary photographers draw inspiration and make their work distinctive. The aphorism "everything old is new" describes one strategy contemporary photographic artists deploy to separate their work from the mass of image-making. The most recent resurgence of historical processes shows that art photography continues to respond to its own history and traditions. Successful contemporary artists use collodion and cyanotype, among other antiquarian processes. Yossi Milo Gallery in NYC recently introduced Meghann Riepenhoff's work to great fanfare. The work offers a case in point. The gallery press release states:

> Meghann Riepenhoff's experimentations with cameraless photographic processes break down the elements of photography to its basics – paper, light, chemistry and chance. Her *Littoral Drift* series revisits and reconsiders the history of the cyanotype process, linking her to early pioneers in photography and science, as well as to contemporary photography's return to hand-crafted, one-of-a-kind works of art.

Several other photographers represented by the gallery similarly work with historical processes that yield unique, one-of-a-kind images. In general, artists produce a limited "edition" of photographs to protect their monetary value. The fact that artists like Riepenhoff produce single, original works takes this practice to an extreme and further increases the market value of each unique original. Unlike Riepenhoff, Chris McCaw uses cameras to make his images. Again, from Yossi Milo Gallery:

> Chris McCaw builds his own large-format cameras and outfits them with powerful lenses typically used for military surveillance and aerial reconnaissance. Instead of film, McCaw inserts expired fiber-based gelatin silver photo paper directly into the camera. Pointing the lens at the sun, McCaw makes recordings ranging from thirty seconds to as long as 36 hours. The sun, intensified by the lens, scorches its path across the paper while creating a solarized image of the landscape or seascape below—a "direct positive" image made in-camera, without an intervening negative ...

> Chris McCaw's experiments with photography follow in the tradition of the medium's early pioneers, such as Eadweard Muybridge, as well as the history of American landscape photographers, such as Carleton Watkins. While the artist is firmly rooted in photographic history, he confronts the question of what a photograph is and what its elements – time, light, lenses, photo-sensitive paper—can be.

Joni Sternbach also produces unique originals, employing the wet collodion process, to make portraits of surfers from coastal areas around the world. The Rick Wester Gallery press release frames her work in this way:

> The relationship between the surfers and the environment is analogous to Sternbach's own photographic process. Resurrecting the 19th century, the wet-plate collodion process known as tintype, centers on the photographic plates being coated and developed on site, a home cooked method based on experience and control, more art than science. The crux of Sternbach's relationship with her environment is the shared dependency and unpredictability that her subjects have with each rising wave. Developed in an on-site darkroom, each plate is uniquely marked by the conditions of the location. The images are true documentation of each time and place, with no room for manipulation or revision. The raw, umber images are seemingly etched out of the land and sea. Sternbach's one-of-a-kind plates are products of the location in which they are created, just as the surfers' experiences are products of their setting.

These three photographers exemplify a current trend of employing historical processes that yield a single, valuable image. Photographers using these strategies separate themselves from the mass of camera users who employ contemporary technology. Some use photographic materials but not cameras. Others invert photography's reproducibility by choosing approaches that pre-date the introduction of photographic film. They choose novel, infrequently traversed routes to achieve their end products.

Other photographers map out a somewhat less arduous work process, still eschewing the use of digital cameras, but instead choosing to shoot film. The widespread adoption of digital photography is a relatively recent phenomenon that has led to an explosion of new activity by photographers of all ages and skill levels. Pledging their allegiance to film, many art photographers link their work processes and the resulting images to recent photographic traditions that are quickly moving into the category "historical processes". My own recent experience shines a spotlight on the technological shift underway. In 2006, I initiated a photographic project, *On the Nest* for which I chose to use a large format 4 × 5 camera and shoot color negative film. This process involved making test prints before exposing the film, enabling me to check my camera setup, lighting and subject placement. Over the six years I worked on this project, Kodak changed the film stock I had chosen to shoot, and Polaroid ceased manufacture of the instant film I was using to shoot my tests. The price of my film increased. The photo lab I patronized repeatedly decreased the number of days per week they processed 4 × 5 film, and increasingly demonstrated a decline in the level of skill and care their lab technicians brought to the task. I ultimately had to find a new lab to process my film; by the time the elderly employee at my new lab retires there may be no local lab remaining that processes color sheet film. While shooting *On the Nest* I witnessed the gradual dissolution of film photography as an approach to making photographs—photographers choosing to shoot film now confront a range of logistical challenges. Yet many fine art photographers persist.

I asked six accomplished contemporary photographic artists to answer a series of questions about their choice to continue working with film. By insisting on film, at least at the image *capture* stage, these photographers (and many others like them) link their work to an "earlier" era of photographic image-making and to the medium's 20th century history and traditions. I used this line of questioning to provide a way of teasing out attitudes towards making photographic art, ideas regarding the distinctiveness of artistic practices, and views on making photographic art at a time characterized by momentous technological change and widespread participation in photographic image-making activities. The questions I asked follow:

- Why do you choose to shoot film rather than digital?
- As photo technology changes what challenges have you confronted as a result of your choice of film?
- Do you use digital technology anywhere in your practice? If so at what points and why?
- What makes shooting film the right choice for your work?
- Who is the audience for your work?

Audience

Ascertaining the photographers' perceived audience for their work helps to confirm their self-perceived positioning within the art world of photography. When asked about the audience for their work these photographers offered a nearly uniform response that mixed venues for showing their work with those who would see it. Museums and galleries were chief among the audiences listed, and included among the viewing audience were curators, private collectors, artists, and anyone interested in _____, that is, the subject matter of the photographers' work. The consistent focus on this specialized audience clearly marks the photographers as self-identified artists.

Why Do You Choose to Shoot Film Rather Than Digital?

Among the photographers queried, three primary reasons for shooting film were repeatedly cited: the nature of the photographer's personal engagement with the photographic process itself, preference for particular characteristics of "analogue" equipment, and the photographer's own history and facility with the use of film and darkroom based cameras and printing processes. Several of the photographers use large format cameras. This choice accomplishes two primary goals. First, large format negatives allow photographers to capture a degree of detail that supports the production of large-scale photographic prints. Digital printing technologies have contributed to the trend towards increased print size: one of these photographers makes prints sized 55×77 inches, albeit she works with a printer who makes analogue darkroom prints, produced according to her specifications. Large format prints reveal the luscious detail captured on large format film stocks; conversely, they reveal the flaws inherent in consumer and even "prosumer" level digital camera captures and inexpert digital image processing. Few amateur photographers would likely gravitate towards large format cameras, due to their comparative complexity and the greater effort required to use them. Large format film is not the only way to make colossal prints, but few amateurs are likely to have the necessary skill to satisfactorily achieve such print sizes. They are also unlikely to have an appropriate place to handle, store or display large-scale photographs; artists' work is destined for the gallery or museum wall where large scale work is more easily accommodated.

Multiple photographers agreed that shooting film and especially large format "slows down the process," making the act of photographing more contemplative and less reactive. One photographer wrote:

I generally use an 8 × 10″ view camera. The language of that particular camera is difficult to achieve with common digital cameras. Additionally, I enjoy the process of slowing and investing the time and energy to make 1 image. So many technical attributes of photographs are amplified such as framing, focus, depth of field, etc. In addition to the fundamental: 'what is the relationship of the camera to the subject?'.

In addition to the processual and technical attributes of using the 8 × 10 view camera, its use allows this photographer to pursue fundamental ideas with respect to photography. Another wrote about the ways in which shooting film shifts the tempo of image-making:

I love my process better—I like that it slows me down from beginning to end. I am more deliberate in my shooting and I am not distracted looking at the back of the camera. I like that I don't see my work right away and have to wait to get the film back. I like that it forces me to put the camera down when I change film. It gives me the opportunity to talk to my sitters and observe them when the camera goes down—like pressing the reset button.

It makes me feel that I am making art, that I am more invested in the process from beginning to end.

A photographer related her choice of film and large format camera to her work process, and in doing so, invoked the "lifestyle" dimension of art making:

My work process drives my choices in making my work. The work is project based. I spend months at a time driving to a destination that I'm interested in and staying there to engage and make the work, living out of my car, camping when possible to avoid costly motels. I work with a large format 5 × 7 field camera. The camera is simply a box on a tripod, a lens and a piece of glass to view and frame. This particular camera forces me to slow down my process and focus on observing the subject matter. I'm not technical and find myself stumbling through the endless camera settings on a digital camera. The analogue process is superior for me personally in terms of control, color, depth, detail and precision in all aspects of my work. There are no distractions with failed batteries, computers, tethering, downloading and the various bells and whistles that a digital camera involve.

Photographers may also be invested in long-term affinities for idiosyncratic ways of working. One writes:

I have been using large format cameras for over forty years and still use film for several reasons but primarily because I prefer old lenses and the history untold within them. I am interested in the quiet beauty inherent in the impermanence and patina that comes with age and the use of old lenses helps me achieve this. I also like the meditative aspect of working under the dark cloth, and the detail provided with a large negative.

A few of the photographers suggested that digital printing differs from analogue darkroom printing in terms of quality, and therefore choose to print their own darkroom prints or contract with a printer to have their prints printed according to their specifications.

> I like the quality of film/darkroom prints. This may be analogous to what I hear people say about the sound from vinyl records versus digital sound. Film and darkroom prints have depth and subtlety, while digital photographs seem to me like information on the surface of the paper. Added to that—I'm a black and white photographer. Black and white darkroom prints can be quite beautiful. It's very hard to print equivalent quality black and white digital prints.

And:

> I have found that digital output can sometimes appear hyperreal, unnatural color and depth is lost. Things flatten out. I struggle with the differences that I see that others have said I merely need to get used to those differences.

For one photographer, choosing film extends a habitual manner of working, developed over time:

> Not sure I have chosen one form of capture over the other, I grew up using film. I feel more fluid in thought and practice when I use analog photosensitive materials. This I would suspect because of the many hours I have spent exposing and processing film. If I was 18 today not 50 with the choice of which way to invest film or digital the way I work would most likely be different.

As Photo Technology Changes What Challenges Have You Confronted as a Result of Your Choice of Film?

Photographers who choose to shoot film instead of adopting digital imaging technologies face a variety of challenges as previously mentioned. Changes in the industry have led to increases in price, materials and equipment becoming obsolete or difficult to find, and the retirement or unavailability of expert technicians who can provide analogue-based services such as film processing and printing. Despite these difficulties, artists are still wedded to their choice of film over digital technology. Photographers' responses to this question about the challenges they face were uniform and unambiguous.

> 8″ × 10″ film is still readily available, but many of my favorite gelatin silver papers are no longer being produced.

> There is no doubt that the variety of films and available format sizes has diminished since digital has blossomed. Though I have also seen in recent years, as the

interest in hand-made pieces has grown, a resurgence in enthusiasm for film and film production. The fact that fewer folks are processing film has also affected the availability and price of peripheral products such as darkroom chemicals, paper, tools etc.

Film is getting harder to find and more expensive.

Sheet film is expensive and takes huge amount of time to develop. Carrying large numbers of film holders around is difficult when traveling. Darkroom printing is very time consuming and tiring, and also expensive not easily repeatable. You can't "Save" your print, and simply push print another day. Materials are harder to find, and have an uncertain future.

There are far fewer choices available in film. The cost of my film in particular has tripled and needs to be special ordered from Kodak in large batches. There are fewer labs to process film and to make prints. And fewer people in the industry such as retouchers who perfect the final prints.

Do You Use Digital Technology Anywhere in Your Practice? If So at What Points and Why?

Despite the fact that shooting film is integral to their artistic practices, the majority of photographers responding to my questions have developed hybrid workflows that employ digital technology, most commonly when making prints. Darkroom printing—the necessary equipment, materials, chemistry, and expertise—has become more expensive and less accessible, while inkjet printing continually improves, in terms of print quality, archival permanence and ease of use. The hitch in the film shooter's workflow enters in when the photographic negative must be digitized in order to make a digital print. High resolution film scanners themselves are becoming obsolete. Most artists use or contract with a service to use a drum scanner, the best option available to produce high resolution digital files. To my knowledge drum scanners are no longer being manufactured; owners of the machines often buy additional used scanners in order to harvest parts as they fail. Finding an expert to service the equipment would prove difficult and costly. Acquiring the expertise to use the machines involves a fairly steep learning curve. Photographers devoted to shooting film may themselves own drum scanners and contract with fellow photographers to provide their services. In my own workflow, I sought someone in my city with whom I could work; finding a service provider required knowing the right people to ask—other artists with the requisite local knowledge. These and other challenges make it difficult to continue working with film, as one photographer attests:

Expense [is a challenge]. Film processing options are slim, esp. with large format materials. I drum scan all my negatives and digitally edit them so this slows the production, at times, to a crawl. My scanning equipment is from the last century (!) so upkeep and calibration will continue to be more difficult.

Early in the evolution of inkjet printing, questions regarding print permanence and archival standards made curators and gallerists wary of digital prints. As inkjet printing technology has evolved and advanced, digital prints commonly appear in museum and gallery contexts; curators purchase them for their collections without hesitation. Digital printmaking has been widely adopted within art photography as in other arenas of photographic activity, although artists pay special attention to archival ink sets and papers necessary to produce "museum quality" prints.

Even photographers who prefer the slow pace of large format image capture and express their love for historic processes and equipment see the utility in making digital prints.

I don't have a problem blending technologies. I have scanned my negatives to create pigment prints as well as digital silver prints but I still prefer to use my darkroom when possible. I think it is remarkable and great that there are so many options to create work.

Digital technology may make the process of editing and print processing easier than using traditional analogue processes:

I scan my negatives to make contact sheets at first and then when I make my selections, I make high res scans of individual negatives. The final prints are pigment prints from the scanned negative, spotted and adjusted files.

Digital technologies also facilitate making large-scale prints by decreasing the space required to set up and maneuver the prints themselves, a painstaking task requiring care and, depending on size, an extra pair of hands.

I have negatives drum scanned and then make digital prints when I want a print larger than 16 × 20″—typically to make 40 × 50″ prints. It's the best option for large prints.

Darkroom space available for large-scale color printing is rapidly vanishing. While consumer grade inkjet printers are readily available to amateurs, large format printers have a substantial footprint. They are expensive to purchase and keeping them fed with ink and other supplies can be enormously expensive. Producing these prints requires multiple kinds of expertise, and amateurs—especially casual shooters—are likely to be intimidated by the necessary inputs and the space required.

Photographic artists working in black and white are the most likely to continue making analogue darkroom prints. These photographers may choose digital when working in color:

> I do have a digital camera. I use it for most of my color work. I also use both film and flatbed scanners to digitize analog work. Though I don't use my printer much for final works, I do use it for proofing and producing digital negatives.

What Makes Shooting Film the Right Choice for Your Work?

Despite detailing at length the challenges posed by working in film, photographic artists accept those difficulties in order to pursue the work in the manner they feel suits it, and them, best. Returning to a discussion of process, a photographer writes that film is the right choice in the following way:

> Several reasons, notably process. Making photographs becomes an 'event' (or at times a spectacle), specifically in regards to portraiture of any sort. The camera itself demands a certain psychological response from subjects.

Considering the ubiquitous presence of cameras and the routine activity of making photographs, shooting film and, especially, employing an unusual device like a large format camera, complete with the performative aspect of the photographers' disappearance beneath a dark cloth, the artist's camera-related activity stands apart. Subjects may respond differently and, if they recognize the process involved, so too might viewers attribute special status to photographs that result from a laborious, arcane process.

The impression made on photographic subjects as a result of using unfamiliar technologies also appears in this description of the image making process:

> It slows me down. I photograph young women who have grown up in a digital iPhone age. The fact that I am shooting them with film (they don't even know what negative film is!) and that they cannot see the results make them take the photo session more seriously.

Shooting film and employing an unknown process imbues the interaction between photographer and subject with an importance that separates the artist's photographic activity from the activity engaged in by amateurs and casual snapshooters—very likely distinguished from the activities of the subjects themselves.

Love of the equipment itself may be enough of an incentive to tackle the challenges presented by analogue photography. Old lenses may produce unanticipated results and surrendering control to the artistic process itself means that "mistakes" made by amateurs may be reframed as an artifact of the artist's engagement with the mysteries of the medium.

> My decision to shoot film is tied to my love of old lenses. I enjoy experimenting with lenses, from lenses that don't cover my 8″ × 10″ film plane to long lenses that have amazing bokeh, to lenses that are very sharp, depending on what I am photographing. I still get excited when I look at my film after it is developed. Because photography is somewhat of an exacting medium, it can be intriguing to let go of some control by using long exposures and lenses that bend and blur to the edges of the frame.

And for some, the romance of the darkroom eclipses the bright glow of the computer screen:

> I can't sit still and I like using my hands. I never really enjoyed working too long in front of a computer screen. When working digitally I was quickly turned off by the hours of editing, retouching, and printing I was doing while sitting.

Reviewing the rationales provided by art photographers for continuing to produce their work using film, and in several of these cases using large format equipment, sheds some light on ways contemporary art photography remains distinct from amateur activity. The photographers quoted above clearly articulate the challenges of utilizing technologies as they become obsolete; my own experience echoes theirs. In some cases, these photographers linked their choice to the expense of acquiring new digital gear. Others espoused the view that the complexity of digital distracted them from the important fundamentals of photographic image-making. Photographers outlined the advantages of the slower pace of working with film, and some asserted a difference between the image quality of analogue versus digital processes. The choice of film over digital technologies marks the photographer's commitment to the medium—its history and traditions. Making photographs the hard way separates artists from casual snapshooters. Most all of the photographers quoted here willingly utilize digital imaging in their overall workflows, especially when it comes to making photographic prints. They do not rigidly shut out new technologies when they usefully enhance their art practices.

A logical extension of this chapter would explore the work of artists who solely employ digital technology, from image capture to editing process, to printing and display of the work. Examining the ways in which artists' use of digital photography departs from amateurs' use of the technology would help identify additional boundary markers. Markus Brunetti, who, like Riepenhoff and McCaw, is represented by Yossi Milo Gallery in New York, provides an instructive case in point. Brunetti creates colossal hyperreal photographic prints, often measuring 60 × 70″, that represent architectural facades in stunning detail. To achieve his end result, he makes a large number of digital captures of his subject and stitches the images together using digital editing software. Brunetti's prints, according to the gallery press release, extend "the tradition of Bernd and Hilla Becher's serial documentation of German industrialization." The press release does not divulge exactly how Brunetti makes these photographs. The virtuosity and singularity of Brunetti's use of digital imaging technologies sets his photographs apart from what others are able to do with digital tools.

Drawing together my own experience as a participant observer, a review of galleries' positioning of their artists' work in their written press releases, and the questionnaire responses of accomplished art photographers who choose to shoot film in an era of technological change, what might be concluded regarding the distinctions that currently separate fine art photographers from other camera users? Returning to the principles set out earlier in this chapter, it seems appropriate to ask whether these boundary markers persist, and if so in what ways. As discussed previously, contemporary multimedia artists integrate photography into their work, employing the medium as one tool amongst a larger range of artmaking approaches. In this way, photography is explicitly linked to art making through its incorporation into other genres. Many commercial galleries represent both photographers and artists working in other media—art photography no longer solely operates in its own institutional arena. Museums of photography exist, and in addition most major art museums also have photography collections and curators who purchase the work of contemporary photographic artists.

All of the photographers participating in this study consider curators, collectors and artists the audience for their work. Photographers often network with art world gatekeepers and may sell directly to institutions and individuals, or do so through their gallerists—contemporary art photographers produce images that convey ideas, as they simultaneously function as commodities. It might be argued that the strength of the ideas present in contemporary work, whether or not those ideas are accessible to a general viewing public, relates to the monetary value attributed to the work. A track-record of exhibitions, sales and acquisitions certainly does correlate with the prices artists' work fetches. In contemporary photographic art, innovation persists as a value. Innovation may take the form of introducing a never-before-seen approach to making photographs. Digital technology that *is not available* to all sets apart what artists can uniquely do. Resurrecting historical processes and bending them to contemporary uses makes a statement that curators, gallerists and collectors notice. The rapid rise to prominence of photographers like Meghann Riepenhoff and Chris McCaw evidence the thirst for something old made new. Pieces featured in Riepenhoff's recent exhibition of cyanotypes at Yossi Milo that measured up to 42 × 97″ demonstrate the value of old made new, made colossal, conforming to the ongoing trend towards large scale work, suitable for display in only the outsized architectural settings generally found in museums and galleries.

While the principles separating fine art from amateur photography continue to hold, in the digital age key distinctions may rest with ways in which the *technology* related to photographic image making is deployed. Using film. Using large format cameras. Using historical processes. Using camera-less processes. Using proprietary software. Using expensive equipment. Art photographers counter amateurs' easy access to digital cameras and printers, personal computers and online outlets for sharing photographs with their withdrawal from the technologies others routinely use. Art photographers who do embrace digital technology develop alternative approaches to its commonplace use.

I am constantly surprised by my 20-something art students who express a deep affinity for photographic film, citing its je ne sais quoi. I wonder how long these practices will last. To what lengths will artists go in order to keep using film? When the diminishing markets for film compel manufacturers to quit making the supplies photographers now pay dearly to use, what turn will art photographers take? When I researched the boundaries between amateur and fine art photography years ago, the digital revolution that has fundamentally altered the medium was unimaginable. Distinctions between amateurs and artists could be drawn by mapping the milieus in which photographic activity occurred, the audiences conceived for the work, and the ethos surrounding the photographic practices employed. These boundary conditions endure and have been refined and elaborated since they were established in the early 20th century. When the next wave of technological invention hits, what choices will artists make that differentiate their work from what other camera users do? Time and technology will tell.

Note

I would like to thank the photographers who so kindly responded to the list of questions that informs this discussion: Rania Matar, Linda Foard Roberts, Victoria Sambunaris, Brad Temkin, Bob Thall, Brian Ulrich, and Ryan Zoghlin.

References

Lennon, P. (2004). Weekend: THE BIG PICTURE: Luc Delahaye made his name as a photojournalist and war photographer. He is still immersed in the fray, but now the aim of his vast panoramas is capturing history–making art. What is the distinction, Peter Lennon asks him. *The Guardian* (London, England).

Schwartz, D. (1986). Camera clubs and fine art photography: "the social construction of an elite code." *Urban Life, 15*(2), 165.

Schwartz, D. (1992). *Waucoma twilight: Generations of the farm*. Washington: Smithsonian Institution Press.

Schwartz, D. (1998). *Contesting the super bowl*. New York: Routledge.

Schwartz, D. (2002). Pictures at a demonstration. *Visual Studies, 17*(1), 27–36.

Schwartz, D. (2009). *In the kitchen*. Heidelberg: Kehrer Verlag.

Schwartz, D. (2015). *On the nest*. Heidelberg: Kehrer Verlag.

3. *Cultural Competence in the Art World of Video Games*

BILL MIKULAK

Introduction

Video games are a realm of contemporary culture that is hotly contested. Critics bemoan their violence, addictiveness, and negative stereotyping of women and minorities. Their champions consider them artworks, whose cutting-edge technologies immerse gameplayers in vibrant, challenging environments that can communicate emotionally intense narratives and improve mental and physical aptitudes.

I will first describe the popularity of video games, then give examples of cultural institutions that have judged them to be art. Next, I will consider arguments against that designation, and use theories of Larry Gross and Howard S. Becker to shift away from romantic preconceptions of art and artists toward a more sociological and communication-based view of art worlds, into which video games fit well.

I delineate the major genres of video games and then turn to a central aesthetic concern within this art world, playability. Finally, I turn to some members of the video game community who have applied playability to solving real-world problems.

Genesis of This Inquiry

In 1996 under the guidance of Paul Messaris, Larry Gross, and Joseph Turow at the Annenberg School for Communication at the University of Pennsylvania, I wrote a dissertation, *How Cartoons Became Art*, which asserted that animation is an art form within an art world of participants who understood its hybrid origins in the graphic arts and motion pictures as a strength rather than a weakness. Museums began to collect and screen animation; art dealers, galleries, and auction houses began to sell production art from animated films; critics began to seriously consider animated films as art.

During the course of my research, I noticed that an increasing number of students in art schools who majored in animation were taking jobs at video game companies. So, here I am over 20 years later looking a bit more closely at video games. They share a similar marginalized status that has plagued animation, both of which have multiple creators working in teams, eluding easy identification of the true singular artistic vision behind them. There are many genres of video games that vary in complexity, design elements, interactivity, story, characters, and gameplaying platforms. This makes it difficult to discuss them en masse.

The Growth of Video Games

One claim we *can* make for video games as a whole: They are extremely popular. According to the Entertainment Software Association's *2017 Essential Facts About the Computer and Video Game Industry*, "Sixty-five percent of American households are home to someone who plays video games regularly." The ESA's survey also found: "Gamers age 18 or older represent 72 percent of the video game-playing population, and the average gamer is 35 years old"; "Adult women represent a greater portion of the video game-playing population (31 percent) than boys under age 18 (18 percent)"; and "Seventy-one percent of parents feel video games positively impact their child's life." All told, the ESA tallied $30.4 billion spent on the video game industry in 2016, up from $23.5 billion in 2015.

The Pew Research Center's 2015 report "Gaming and Gamers" found that 49% of Americans play video games (50% of men and 48% of women surveyed). Pew reported that game players generally have more favorable views of video games than non-players, agreeing more often with statements that video games promote problem solving and teamwork, while disagreeing more often with statements claiming video games are a waste of time and that they portray minorities and women poorly (Duggan, 2015).

Such surveys indicate that video games are played by a much broader portion of the public than is often assumed, in terms of both age range and gender. As more people are exposed to gaming, they view video games more positively. Parents are no longer so fearful of the games' negative effects on their children. In fact, the ESA reports, "Sixty-seven percent of parents play video games with their children at least once a week" (2017).

The Legitimation of Video Games as Art

A number of museums have exhibited and collected video games, providing institutional evidence that distinguished cultural arbiters have ordained them "art." The Museum of the Moving Image in Astoria, NY, began collecting video games in 1989 for the exhibit "Hot Circuits: A Video Arcade" and has exhibited them multiple times since then. In 2012, the Smithsonian American Art Museum's Renwick Gallery held the exhibit "The Art of Video Games," which included 80 games selected with the help of the public. In 2012, the Museum of Modern Art in New York announced the acquisition of 14 video games to initiate their collection within the medium (Antonelli, 2012).

Another indication that video games have arrived as an art form is the Video Game Art (VGA) Gallery, founded in 2013 in Chicago. In addition to hosting temporary video game art exhibits and educational forums, it sells high-fidelity giclee prints of stills from video games (https://www.videogameartgallery.com). And in 2011 the Supreme Court accorded video games First Amendment protections in *Brown v. Entertainment Merchants Association*, 564 U.S. 786, which struck down a California law prohibiting the sale or rental of "violent video games" to minors.

Contesting the Artistic Status of Video Games

The chorus welcoming video games into the hallowed halls of high culture is far from universal. Many dispute their aesthetic legitimacy, and such gatekeeping vigilance against this medium is an instructive counterpoint to the above approbation.

Roger Ebert is hardly alone in denying video games the honorific of "art," but he was prominent in the debates over the artistic status of video games from the mid-2000s to his death in 2013. This may have to do with his lifelong championing of the film medium, which had its own tortured path to artistic acknowledgement. The newest entrant to high society must watch his back for those coming behind.

Ebert's first argument against video games is: "No one in or out of the field has ever been able to cite a game worthy of comparison with the great poets, filmmakers, novelists and poets" (2010). Perhaps one exemplar might have arrived that compared favorably in his eyes to the unnamed greats of older art forms, but he found none "that will deserve my attention long enough to play it."

Another objection Ebert makes is categorical: "One obvious difference between art and games is that you can win a game. It has rules, points, objectives, and an outcome" (2010). The interactivity and indeterminacy of games leave so much of the experience up to gameplayers, they cannot be in the same category as artworks. He contrasts games with "a story, a novel, a play, a dance, a film. Those are things you cannot win; you can only experience them." The artistic production, in his eyes, cannot be completed by the audience's reception of it; gameplayers cannot be artistic collaborators with game developers.

Finally, Ebert hits upon the essence of what he knows about art, "that it grows better the more it *improves* or *alters* nature through a passage through what we might call the artist's soul, or vision" (2010). Video games are usually the result of an elaborate division of labor at a game developer company. Passage through that many souls necessarily diffracts the artistic vision, if there ever was one.

Defenders of the artistic validity of video games also seek that singular visionary upon which to bestow the title of artist. The Academy of Interactive Arts & Sciences (AIAS) inducts an individual each year into its Hall of Fame, most of whom are co-founders of video game companies, their CEOs, or other high-level executives, with a number of game designers and game directors listed as well.

AIAS's first Hall of Fame honoree in 1998, Shigeru Miyamoto of Nintendo Co., Ltd., is often cited for his work on the *Super Mario*, *Legend of Zelda* and *Donkey Kong* series of games. As Kyle Chayka writes in *The Atlantic*, "Miyamoto's oeuvre, with its postmodern sense of play and worlds-within-worlds-within-worlds, is as defining a body of art as we can hope to have for the twenty-first century" (2010).

Video game critic Tom Bissell (2011) singles out a handful of creative visionaries within complex production organizations, praising the narrative minimalism of *Left 4 Dead*'s designer Michael Booth (Valve Software) and giving extended coverage to Cliff Bleszinski, design director at Epic Games (*Gears of War*); Drew Karpyshyn, head writer of BioWare's *Mass Effect;* and Sir Peter Molyneux, designer of Lionhead's *Fable II.* Of those Bissell focuses on, only Jonathan Blow independently produced his own game, *Braid.*

Some critics have challenged a bias among game reviews favoring "indie" games over those produced by large developers (called "AAA" games). For example, Edward Smith cautions, "I think that by continually deifying indie games regardless of their material, and doing the total opposite to AAA games, we're drawing a line in the sand between what's ok to discuss as art and what isn't. I think we're drowning out a lot of voices" (2013). Certain indie game producers, e.g. Jason Rohrer, developer of *Passage*, are elevated into a realm of "artgames," leaving behind those who create within larger developer companies (Parker, 2013). This is not unlike the selection of a few comics artists, e.g. George Herriman, Art Spiegelman and R. Crumb, for exhibition in museums while denying artistic legitimacy to the medium of comics as a whole (Beaty, 2012).

In fact, video game producers do not always accept their products' status as art. Hideo Kojima, primary creator of the game *Metal Gear* series, exhibited ambivalence about the aesthetic status of his video game, calling it "something of a service. It's not art. But I guess the way of providing service with that videogame is an artistic style, a form of art" (quoted in Gibson, 2006). This ambivalence is reminiscent of the attitudes of certain canonized comics artists, as when critical darling Chris Ware's work "evinces a distrust of, and disdain for, the art world" (Beaty, 2012: 224).

Many Artists for One Video Game

The above discussion calls attention to an ingrained romantic view of artistic production that Larry Gross traces back to the Renaissance and the Protestant Reformation, which focused attention on the individual in place of feudalistic and Catholic emphasis on group affiliations. "In the realm of the arts these shifts are reflected in the increasing focus on the individuality of the artist and of artistic creation. ... Achievement in art comes to be identified with innovation, as the artist's genius is manifested in the originality of style and execution. ... The resulting pattern of constant innovation in the arts undermines their ability to embody the common experiences and meanings of the society, to serve the central communicative functions of socialization and integration" (Gross, 1995: 2–3).

Howard S. Becker offers a corrective to the romantic isolation of the solitary artist in *Art Worlds* (2008, 1982). He identifies conception, production, execution, distribution, exhibition, rehearsal, performance, appreciation, patronage, support services, training, and state authority as aspects of art worlds that yield the works for which each world is known. This collective activity is often overlooked under the romantic rubric of art, but Becker gives the examples of two seemingly solitary artists to show how interdependent they are with other art world members: "Poets depend on printers and publishers, as painters do on distributors, and use shared traditions for the background against which their work makes sense and for the raw materials with which they work" (2008, 1982: 14).

The division of labor in the video game industry fits squarely into this conception of art worlds. According to Ben Saywer of Digitalmill (Flew & Humphries, 2005: 101–114), six layers comprise the video game industry:

1. Capital and publishing layer: involved in paying for development of new titles and seeking returns through licensing of the titles.
2. Product and talent layer: includes developers, designers and artists, who may be working under individual contracts or as part of in-house development teams.
3. Production and tools layer: generates content production tools, game development middleware, customizable game engines, and production management tools.
4. Distribution layer: or the "publishing" industry, involved in generating and marketing catalogs of games for retail and online distribution.
5. Hardware (or Virtual Machine or Software Platform) layer: or the providers of the underlying platform, which may be console-based, accessed through online media, or accessed through mobile devices such as smartphones. This layer now includes network infrastructure and non-hardware platforms such as virtual machines (e.g. Java or Flash), or software platforms such as browsers or even further Facebook, etc.
6. End-users layer: or the users/players of the games.

Looking at just the product and talent layer, the degree of specialization has grown enormously. Josh Jenisch notes that over time, programmers have relinquished more duties to artists: "On larger games, it is not uncommon to see artists outnumber programmers by a ratio of three to one. As before, concept artists get their projects rolling—but now, instead of giving their work to programmers, they turn instead to 3-D modelers, who render their creations in virtual space and ensure that a character's movement will be realistic and practical. Next come the texture artists, who add layers of color, shading, and surface texture over the models for a realistic final appearance" (2008: 14).

While these visual artists are using computers to accomplish much of their work, some are finding a need to return to the fundamentals of figurative drawing and painting developed over centuries of fine art. For example, Chris Solarski realized his background in computer animation inadequately prepared him compared to artists who had a "mastery of classical art principles that placed them in the enviable position of being first to visualize characters and environments in the development process" (2012: 9), so he took two years off to study these principles.

Evan Skolnick warns that at too many game developers, the role of the writer or narrative designer is often overlooked, because as the industry grew, specialization of roles occurred on the visual design side much sooner than on the narrative side of production (2014: 102). Rather than game conception beginning with a writer, as in film production, he notes: "Games don't start with stories any more than movies start with scores. A new game almost always begins with a decision on genre, followed by a concept within that genre. At this formative stage, few if any specific narrative elements are yet determined" (2014: 115).

Video Game Genres

"Genres are categories of games characterized by particular kinds of challenge, regardless of setting or game-world content" (Adams, 2013: 67). They have evolved along with hardware, software and accessories, taking advantage of computing power and responsiveness to player input. As the internet has expanded, so, too have online games, which enable many geographically disparate players to inhabit one game space.

The typography of genres is dizzying (Adams, 2013: 67–80), but a major category is action games, within which are platform (scrolling) games such as *Super Mario Bros.*, shooter games such as *Doom*, fighting games such as *Mortal Kombat*, stealth games such as *Metal Gear*, and survival games. An early category that has declined is adventure games, which allowed slow-paced exploration of a setting, calling upon the gameplayer to solve puzzles. *Myst* was a prominent example of this kind of game.

Today, role-playing games (RPGs) are a growing segment of the industry, as players take on characters that may be variously configured. Western RPG games have developed differently from Japanese RPGs, which are known as JRPGs. The ubiquity and high connection speeds of the Internet have allowed massively multiplayer online role-playing games (MMORPGs) to greatly expand the role of players in determining the course of gameplay. *World of Warcraft* is a popular subscription-based game of this genre. Action-adventure games combine gameplay experiences, the *Grand Theft Auto* series being a "sandbox" version of this, where players can opt for different missions within the fictional world.

Simulation games may simulate operation of various vehicles (aircraft, race cars), control of artificial lives, all the way up to constructing cities, businesses, governments and civilzations. Sports games also have a large following. Strategy games present battles from a bird's eye view, based on their genesis in board games. Among smartphone users, casual games (with simplified and colorful interfaces and quick rewards for short-term play) have grown explosively. These games have greatly expanded the demographics of gameplayers to include older women with titles such as *Candy Crush*.

What developers of these different game genres share is a concern for the player's experience. This is expressed in terms of a game's playability. The aesthetics of the visuals, the narratives, and the themes being explored are subservient to the imperative to create a game that people want to play.

Aesthetics of Game Design and the Gameplaying Experience

José Luis González Sánchez et al. (2012: 1033–54) discuss the following properties of playability: **Satisfaction**, **Learning**, **Efficiency**, **Immersion**, **Motivation**, **Emotion**, and **Socialization**. Game designers go to great lengths to evoke these desired responses from gameplayers.

Jane McGonigal argues that **satisfaction** is derived from a sense of accomplishment: "Games make us happy because they are hard work that we choose for ourselves, and it turns out that almost nothing makes us happier than good, hard work." (2011: 28). As a gamer reported to me, "RPGs, JRPGs, puzzle games and strategy games all require a high level of thinking and problem solving that keeps me engaged and makes completing levels—and the entire game—all the more satisfying and rewarding."

To incorporate **learning** into a game's playability, some games include tutorials to convey the procedures and rules, resources available, the point system, all of which together are called "game mechanics." Tom Bissell laments, "One feels for game designers: It would be hard to imagine a formal convention more inherently bizarre than the video-game tutorial" (2011: 8). The most elegant solution to the problem of getting gameplayers past the tutorial is to avoid one entirely. "It's a truism in the game industry that a well-designed game should be playable immediately, with no instruction whatsoever" (McGonigal, 2011: 26). Sometimes no matter what a gamer does, the way forward is elusive. One gamer acknowledged to me, "I've gone online to sites such as GameFAQs.com to look up how to beat a boss or solve a puzzle, but only after trying every possible solution I can think of."

The quality of **efficiency** can be understood in terms of tight feedback loops in the best designed games: "There seems to be no gap between your actions and the game's responses. You can literally see in the animations and count on the scoreboard your impact on the game world. You can also feel how extraordinarily attentive the game system is to your performance. It only gets harder when you're playing well, creating a perfect balance between hard challenge and achievability" (McGonigal, 2011, 24). A gamer described to me his frustration when a game's feedback was buggy and his progress was not properly recorded by clunky gauges.

Game designers that create narrative-based games seek to **immerse** players in that fictive world as fully as possible, so the players suspend their disbelief and merge with the character they are playing. When successful, "There is no other medium where the audience or person experiencing it empathizes with it so heavily that they use personal pronouns when describing what they experienced" (Deardorff, 2015).

But there are many obstacles to overcome to keep a player from bouncing out of the game world. Evan Skolnick describes two parts of a game's storyline that may clash: (1) the framing story, which is often provided in "cut scenes" that are mini-movies setting the situation; and (2) the gameplay story, which must accommodate the player's actions. "This dissonance may come from the narrative depiction of the main character not being consistent with what that character actually does in gameplay. Or it may result from the player's desires and the player character's desires (or required objectives) being at odds" (2014, 39).

A frequent complaint of critics and gamers is that narrative-based games have hackneyed stories with stilted dialogue, which must be endured to get to the much superior action of gameplay. One senses gratitude in Christopher East's review of *Uncharted 4: A Thief's End* when he reports: "But where *Uncharted 4* stands out even more is in its clever writing and stellar voice-acting. Oh, the pirate-treasure plotline is the usual heightened reality nonsense, but the characters are well defined and superbly performed. The dialogue is well written, with a deft sense of humor" (2017).

Other barriers to immersion are visual in nature. Tom Bissell notes: "By mistaking realism for believability, video games have given us an interesting paradox: the so-called Uncanny Valley Problem, wherein the more lifelike nonliving things appear to be, the more cognitively unsettling they become" (2011, 75). This trend toward greater photorealism continues with virtual reality (VR) headsets like the Oculus Rift, which may not solve the Uncanny Valley Problem, but coordinates visual stimuli with your head's movements to submerge you further into the created visual environment. Another technological advance is augmented reality (AR) games, in which a smartphone's camera view has game elements superimposed over real-life visuals, as in Nintendo's *Pokémon Go* game.

Adam Bargteil (2017) sees arising an interesting alternative to slavish photorealism in video games, whose stylistic progress he compares to painting and traditional animation. He argues that *Bambi* "heralded a new development in animation: a shift away from visual realism, and toward abstractness," especially for its backgrounds. This parallels painting transitioning from seeking ever greater realism toward experimenting with abstraction and stylization. In the video game industry, he says, "The advent of the iPhone in the late 2000s led video games back away from realism. The new devices almost immediately spawned thousands of simple, two-dimensional, abstract and often highly stylized games."

Developers structure games carefully to maintain a player's **motivation** to complete the game. Those that involve competition against other individuals or teams build such motivation the same way sports do. Other genres of games are structured as a series of challenges, and the completion of each leads to the next level of the game. The phrase "leveling up" has escaped the boundaries of gameplay to refer to self-improvement and the gain of status in other contexts. As a gamer reported, single-player RPGs with an emphasis on story can be a massive time commitment to complete the narrative. He singled out the science fiction world of *Mass Effect* for allowing his progress to continue from *Mass Effect 1* to *Mass Effect 2*, rewarding the time he put into the succession of games.

Jane McGonigal notes that the combination of a clear goal and actionable next steps toward achieving that goal are primary motivators (2011, 55), but equally important is the game's design of "fun failure." She writes: "In many cases, that hope of success is more exciting than success itself. Success is pleasurable, but it leaves us at a loss for something interesting to do. If we fail, and if we can try again, then we still have a mission. Winning tends to end the fun. But failure? It keeps the fun going" (2011, 68).

By inserting gameplayers into narratives, video games can elicit surprisingly strong **emotions**. Tom Bissell describes a point in *Mass Effect* in which he has to decide which of two remaining squad members to save, each of whom has a fraught relationship with his character. He describes a "sensation that the game itself is as suddenly, unknowably alive as you are. ... To say that any game that allows such surreally intense feelings of attachment and projection is divorced from questions of human identity, choice, perception, and empathy—what is, and always will be, the proper domain of art—is to miss the point not only of such a game but art itself" (2011, 126–7).

Socialization has grown as an aspect of playability in many ways. Jane McGonigal describes such party games as *Rock Band* and *WarioWare: Smooth Moves*, which are played together in groups, and make use of input devices and optical sensors that allow full body actions to be incorporated into the games, and, more importantly, they make for bonding experiences through "happy embarrassment" (2011, 83–86). Even those multiplayer online games that allow for gamers to play alone still provide benefits of "ambient sociability" when they are exposed to other players in the background (McGonigal, 2011, 89–91). And beyond players teaming up in "co-op" play mode on MMORPGs is the opportunity for mass-scale collaboration, like when *Halo 3* players around the world pitched in to score 10 billion kills of the alien enemy, the Covenant (McGonigal, 2011, 95–96).

Gameplayers contribute to communities that grow around the games they play together. They record and post videos of their own gameplay sequences to YouTube. They create game content for open-source games like Will Wright's *Spore* (McGonigal, 2011, 274–5). They produce online Wikis and discussion groups that provide a knowledge base for other players to use. Much as I found that Warner Bros. animation fans created their own fan fiction and art (Mikulak, 1998), video gameplayers explore similar avenues of self-expression and interaction.

Games for Change

The medium of video games contains multitudes, which has inspired a number of people to conceive of ways to employ games for real-world purposes. Keith Stuart notes: "... intelligent, thoughtful designers such as Navid Khonsari want to make games about serious issues like the 1979 Iranian revolution. ... Ryan Green is making *That Dragon, Cancer*, a game about how he and his wife are coping with the terminal illness of their youngest son" (2014). Heather-Ann Schaeffner recommends *Freshman Year* and *Mainichi*, which give gameplayers experiences as a female student in a bar and as a transgender female, respectively (2017, 29).

Jane McGonigal's superb discussion of the emotional, intellectual and social value of video games (and games in general) paves the way for her to advocate game-like approaches to solve real-world problems, given gameplayers' intense satisfaction from the productive immersion in gameplay. She writes, "The great challenge for us today, and for the remainder of the century, is to integrate games more closely into our everyday lives, and to embrace them as a platform for collaborating on our most important planetary efforts" (2011, 354). Asi Burak and Laura Parker have also taken up this cause, detailing the development of games about Middle East peace (*PeaceMaker*), civics lessons (*iCivics*), feminism in Saudi Arabia (*Saudi Girls Revolution*), and several other topics of note (2017). Burak is the former executive director and current chairman of the nonprofit Games for Change, which promotes social impact games.

One interesting area for the application of games to real-world problems is crowdsourcing research. McGonigal details how *The Guardian* received a large data dump about the expense accounts of Ministers of Parliament that it did not have the resources to sift through. The paper made the data available online and gave instructions for citizens to find unauthorized expenses, which tens of thousands did (2011, 219–24). Burak and Parker discuss how an online puzzle game called *Foldit* crowdsourced the solution to a problem of the configuration of proteins of an AIDS-causing monkey virus. "The problem had eluded scientists and supercomputers for more than 15 years. The gamers had solved it in just ten days" (2017, 152).

Conclusions

Guided by theories and perspectives of Larry Gross and Howard S. Becker, I have argued in this brief survey that video games are an art world. In this world are participants creating, distributing, playing, and critiquing games, much as there exist a similar range of participants in the art worlds of painting, music, theater and film. Over the decades that video games have existed, technology has advanced greatly, and games have gained in sophistication and ambition. Likewise, video game players have adjusted their connoisseurship, demanding ever more challenging experiences. Their active participation in response to a game's playability is crucial to the artistic production of gameplay. Social impact video games employ players' interpretive, problem-solving and team-building skills to address a range of educational, social and political problems we confront.

References

Academy of Interactive Arts & Sciences D.I.C.E. Special Awards. Retrieved on 24 August 2017 from: http://www.interactive.org/special_awards/index.asp

Adams, E. (2013). *Fundamentals of game design* (3rd edition). San Francisco: New Riders.

Antonelli, P. (2012, November 29). Video Games: 14 in the Collection, for Starters. Inside/Out, A MoMA/MoMA [Blog post]. Retrieved on 25 August 2017 from: https://www.moma.org/explore/inside_out/2012/11/29/video-games-14-in-the-collection-for-starters/

Bargteil, A. (2017, August 7). How 'Bambi' paved the way for both 'Fallout 4' and 'Angry Birds.' *The Conversation*. Retrieved on 25 August 2017 from: http://theconversation.com/how-bambi-paved-the-way-for-both-fallout-4-and-angry-birds-81885

Beaty, B. (2012). *Comics versus art*. Toronto: University of Toronto Press.

Becker, H. S. (1982). *Art worlds* (25th Anniversary Edition). Berkeley, CA: University of California Press.

Bissell, T. (2011). *Extra lives: Why video games matter*. New York: Vintage Books.

Brown, Governor of California, et al. v. Entertainment Merchants Association, et al. (Decided 2011, June 27). 564 U.S. 786, Supreme Court of the United States. Retrieved on 24 August 2017 from: https://www.supremecourt.gov/opinions/10pdf/08-1448.pdf

Burak, A., & Laura P. *Power play: How video games can save the world*. New York: St. Martin's Press, 2017.

Chayka, K. (2010, May 5). Why video games are works of art. *The Atlantic*. Retrieved on 24 June 2017 from: https://www.theatlantic.com/entertainment/archive/2010/05/why-video-games-are-works-of-art/56205/

Collection spotlight: Video games at moving image. Museum of the Moving Image. Retrieved on 25 August 2017 from: http://www.movingimage.us/collection/videogames

Deardorff, N. (2015, October 13). An argument that video games are, indeed, high art. *Forbes* Retrieved on 25 August 2017 from: https://www.forbes.com/sites/berlinschoolof-creativeleadership/2015/10/13/an-argument-that-video-games-are-indeed-high-art/#2475f827b3c7

Duggan, M. (2015, December). Gaming and gamers. *Pew Research Center*. Retrieved on 26 March 2017 from: http://www.pewinternet.org/2015/12/15/gaming-and-gamers/

East, C. (2017, March 28). Video game: Uncharted 4: A thief's end [Blog post]. Retrieved on 25 August 2017 from: http://www.christopher-east.com/2017/03/28/video-game-uncharted-4-a-thiefs-end/

Ebert, R. (2010, April 16). Video games can never be art. *Roger Ebert's Journal*. Retrieved on 24 June 2017 from: http://www.rogerebert.com/rogers-journal/video-games-can-never-be-art

Entertainment Software Association. *2017 Essential facts about the computer and video game industry*. Summary retrieved on 23 August 2017 from: http://www.theesa.com/article/2017-essential-facts-computer-video-game-industry/. Full report retrieved on 23 August 2017 from: http://essentialfacts.theesa.com/mobile/

Exhibitions: The art of video games: March 15, 2012–September 29, 2012. Smithsonian American Art Museum Renwick gallery. Retrieved on 25 August 2017 from: http://americanart.si.edu/exhibitions/archive/2012/games/ Flew, T. & Sal, H. (2005). Games: Technology, industry, culture. In T. Flew (Ed.), *New media: an introduction* (2nd ed., pp. 101–114). Oxford: Oxford University Press.

Gibson, E. (2006, January 1). Games aren't art, says Kojima. *eurogamer.net*. Retrieved on 26 August 2017 from: http://www.eurogamer.net/articles/news240106kojimaart

González Sánchez, J. L., Gutiérrez Vela, F. L., Montero Simarro, F., Padilla-Zea, N. (2012) Playability: analysing user experience in video games. *Behaviour & Information Technology, 31*(10), 1033–54.

Gross, L. (Ed.). (1995). *On the margins of art worlds*. Boulder: Westview Press.

Jenisch, J. (2008). *The art of the video game*. Philadelphia: Quirk Books.

McGonigal, J. (2011). *Reality is broken: Why games make us better and how they can change the world*. New York: Penguin Books.

Mikulak, B. (1998). "Fans versus time Warner: Who owns Looney tunes?" In Kevin S. Sandler (Ed.), *Reading the rabbit: Explorations in Warner Bros. animation* (pp. 193–208). New Brunswick: Rutgers University Press.

Mikulak, W. A. (1996). *How cartoons became art: Exhibitions and sales of animation art as communication of aesthetic value* (Dissertation). Annenberg School for Communication, University of Pennsylvania, Philadelphia, Pennsylvania.

Parker, F. (2013). An art world for artgames. *The Journal of the Canadian Game Studies Association, 7*(11), 41–60. Retrieved on 3 September 2017 from: http://journals.sfu.ca/loading/index.php/loading/article/view/119

Schaeffner, H.-A. (2017, Summer). Digital media: A new kind of game. *STAND: American Civil Liberties Union*, ( ) *4*(2), 29.

Skolnick, E. (2014). *Video game storytelling: What every developer needs to know about narrative techniques*. Berkeley: Watson-Guptill.

Smith, E. (2013, January 24). Why games matter blog—Indie games aren't art games. *International Business Times* Retrieved on 3 September 2017 from: http://www.ibtimes.co.uk/why-games-matter-indie-movie-fez-meat-427544

Solarski, C. (2012). *Drawing basics and video game art*. New York: Watson-Guptill.

Stuart, K. (2014, January 8). Video games and art: Why does the media get it so wrong? *The Guardian*. Retrieved on 26 August 2017 from: https://www.theguardian.com/technology/gamesblog/2014/jan/08/video-games-art-and-the-shock-of-the-new

4. On the Digital Margins of Art Worlds: Art and Vernacular Creativity in Online Spaces

Ioana Literat

"On the Internet, nobody knows you're an artist ..."

—Ed Halter

Riffing off of the famous New Yorker cartoon ("on the Internet, nobody knows you're a dog"), critic and curator Ed Halter (2015, p. 236) brings up a crucial issue regarding the status of Internet art within the larger context of contemporary digital culture: given the vastness of creative digital content—from memes to remixes to collaborative fiction—produced and circulated online, the boundaries between art and non-art on the Internet are becoming increasingly blurry. These distinctions are further complicated by the prominence of contemporary artists' engagement with vernacular digital content (i.e. collecting, reframing and/or remixing user-generated content), as in Cory Arcangel's *Working on My Novel*, a compilation of tweets containing the title phrase, or Eric Oglander's *Craigslist Mirrors*, a collection of user-submitted photographs of mirrors posted for sale on Craigslist. Moreover, in many cases, this indistinguishability is a core feature of the work, as in Joel Holmberg's *Legendary Account*, a series of profound philosophical questions posted among the otherwise banal inquiries on Yahoo Answers.

This essay examines the positioning of Internet art vis-a-vis vernacular digital creativity, interrogating the shifting boundaries between art and (what is traditionally considered) non-art in the online environment. If a work of Internet art and, respectively, of vernacular online creativity (such as a meme or a Youtube mashup) live in the same space, use the same tools and often address the same networked audiences, where do the key differences between them still lie? In view of the specific patterns of production and circulation that characterize the online environment, how might today's digital creative culture make us rethink—or reinforce—our notions of "art" and "artists"?

Two contemporary artistic practices that illustrate the complexity of this relationship between Internet art and online vernacular creativity refer to the embrace of user-generated content and, respectively, vernacular aesthetics in online art. These practices, briefly mentioned in the opening paragraph, will be referenced throughout this chapter due to their potential to facilitate a more nuanced understanding of the key questions at the heart of this inquiry, while anchoring this analysis in contemporary online art practice. Thus, they merit further explanation and exemplification.

The first trend refers to artists appropriating and reframing found user-generated content, with the goal of repositioning it and inscribing it with new meaning. In addition to Oglander's *Craigslist Mirrors* and Arcangel's *Working on My Novel*, mentioned previously, examples of this practice are Guthrie Lonergan's *Recent Music Videos*, a collection of found photos compiled into archetypal YouTube videos, or Penelope Umbrico's photographic installations made up of found user-generated content, such as *Suns from Flickr* or *TVs from Craigslist*. In some of these projects, the modification involved in working with the found digital material is substantial, as in Olivier Laric's *50/50*, where the artist painstakingly pieces together hundreds of different performances of 50 Cent's hit song "In Da Club" posted to YouTube, recreating the entire original song. At other times, it consists of collection or compilation, as in *Craigslist Mirrors* or *Working on My Novel*.

The second type of practice that illuminates the increasing interrelation between art and non-art on the Internet is stylistic mimicry, where contemporary Internet artists adopt the "subamateur" vernacular of the web (Halter, 2009). While these artists generally do not integrate found user-generated content in their work, their creations reflect—and thus comment on—the particular aesthetics of vernacular online creativity. This type of work is exemplified by Joel Holmberg's work on Yahoo Answers, Lorna Mills' animated GIFs, Petra Cortright or Alexandra Gorczynski's webcam videos, and Michael Manning's aptly titled Mirroring.net, which is a collection of clickable animations of mundane objects and popular culture characters, reflecting an already outdated Internet aesthetic.

Both of these practices illustrate how the boundary between art and grassroots online creativity becomes further confounded, bringing up important questions regarding our considerations for legitimating a creative product as art. Of course, these dynamics are not entirely new—there is an important

Figure 4.1: User-Generated Content in Oglander's *Craigslist Mirrors* (2016).

Figure 4.2: User-Generated Content in Lonergan's "Kids in Hampers" From the *Recent Music Videos* Series (2012).

Figure 4.3: Animated GIF by Lorna Mills (2015).

Figure 4.4: Still From Petra Cortright's VVEBCAM (2007).

tradition of pro surfer work (Olson, 2008) and embrace of amateur aesthetics in new media art (Greene, 2004; Tribe, Jana, & Grosenick, 2006). However, these practices—and the implications they hold for culture and creativity—are becoming increasingly significant and prevalent in today's digital culture, as the sphere of online media is becoming saturated and the volume of vernacular online creativity keeps growing, with more and more people producing more and more content online. As critics Cornell and Halter (2015) put it,

> in a world in which new forms of software have made the creation of music, images, video and new software easier than ever to master, and the Internet has fostered an unprecedented amount of activity in terms of showing, sharing, and remixing this work, how does the work of artists utilizing the same practices differ in any fundamental respect? (p. xxiii)

The prevalence of Internet art that engages with vernacular content and aesthetics can be explained, at least in part, by the idea of saturation, which many artists and commentators feel has come to represent our contemporary online environment. Guthrie Lonergan, for instance, has stated that his art is, to a certain extent, born out of "the feeling that there's so much stuff out there already that it seems pointless to make something new, from scratch" (Lonergan, quoted in Beard, 2008, n.p.). The vastness of online creativity also makes the field more competitive. As Cory Arcangel muses, "as a conceptual artist, it's tough because chances are that some 14-year-old kid from Brazil has already beat you to your new project" (Arcangel, quoted in Cornell, 2006, n.p.). Artist Brad Troemel memorably called this new approach to art-making "athletic aesthetics": "a by-product of art's new mediated environment, wherein creators must compete for online attention in the midst of an overwhelming amount of information" (Troemel, 2013, n.p.).

Cory Arcangel, one of the pioneers of net art, refers to the proliferation of online grassroots creativity as both a source of inspiration and soul-searching reflection: "All this stuff out there made by all these people is probably better than the stuff I'm making. How do you deal with that? … As an artist, what is my role on the Internet?" (Arcangel, quoted in Arcangel et al., 2015, p. 104). Thus, the questions addressed here are not only of theoretical importance; indeed, they carry significant implications in terms of the ontology of art and the social, cultural and economic positioning of art and the artist in society.

The distinctions between art and non-art on the Internet are also important because questions of artistic legitimacy precede those of aesthetic appreciation: "unless and until they are satisfied that the object/event in question is indeed a work of art, audiences will not be willing to respond to it appropriately" (Gross, 1973, p. 122). The increasingly intertwined and complex relationship between art and vernacular creativity on the Internet also shapes the way we respond to these creative products, both critically and heuristically. For instance, what happens when, as Arcangel suggested above, online user-generated content might be "better" than a professional artist's work? What are the aesthetic hierarchies that are being drawn between works of art and vernacular online creativity, and do we need to take these relationships—both aesthetic and ethical—into account when assessing online creative works? In this sense, these questions speak to the significance of context in tracing the boundary between art and non-art, but also to new practices of circulation, distribution and exhibition within the artistic realm.

Danto (1986) famously declared that, in the latter half of the 20th century, we had reached "the end of art," not meaning, of course, that no more art would be produced, but rather that art as we had known it—a progression of movements evolving out of one another—had come to its natural conclusion in the mid to late 20th century. "The future of *our* art is very dim," he wrote, "but … a new cycle will begin, with its own peaks, and we can no more imagine it than *we* could have been imagined from an earlier cycle. Art will have a future, it is only that *our* art will not" (p. 794). The plurality of art practice has only widened since Danto's writing; the forms and materials of art (including traditional two- and three-dimensional media, new media, performance-based and time-based work, conceptual art, and socially-engaged art, to name a few) have continued to expand, as have the venues through which such works are shared and interpreted. Art of today might not be defined by its materiality (or lack thereof), or any sort of stylistic similarities defining the work of an entire era. Rather, contemporary art can best be conceptualized in terms of the process, practices, and ideas with which artists engage. Some of the key guiding principles characterizing art today are: escaping the confines of museums; collapsing boundaries between high and low; rejecting originality; appropriating; simulating; hybridizing; mixing media; layering; mixing codes; recontextualizing, and irony, parody, and dissonance, among others (Barrett, 2006). Indeed, Internet-based art, while a diverse and heterogeneous field, certainly epitomizes these features and proposes intriguing combinations between them.

But if it has been established that art can take any form (including no physical form at all), how is it agreed that a work of art is a work of art, and what are the implications of these definitions on the boundaries between Internet art and vernacular online creativity? This essay starts from the premise that, in online spaces, it is particularly difficult to imagine "purely formal criteria that would distinguish art from any number of very art-like creations" (Halter, 2015, p. 236). Furthermore, I would add, given the appropriation of form and content that is at the heart of many contemporary works of Internet art, exclusionary criteria (i.e., x is art if it is *not* y or z) become problematic as well, and challenging to apply in practice. So then, by what processes do we differentiate them, and how are these processes complicated by the idiosyncrasies of the Internet as both context, raw material and exhibition/distribution channel?

According to Carroll (1999), "stated precisely, the aesthetic definition of art maintains: x is an artwork if and only if (1) x is produced with the intention that it possess a certain capacity, namely (2) the capacity of affording aesthetic experience" (p. 162). In suggesting a theory of art as experience, Dewey (1934) similarly argued that what makes something a work of art is not any quality inherent in the work itself, but rather, the experience of engaging with it—both in the creation and the viewing or interpretation of it. At the same time, it is important to note that all creative works—and not just those that we would readily consider as art—can trigger an aesthetic experience. Yet, aesthetic theory suggests that artworks "afford a unique kind of experience… They abet a peculiar—that is to say, distinctive—type of contemplative state" (Carroll, 1999, p. 160). Framing found online material as art is, in a sense, about putting the audience in the right frame of mind to look at something anew, in much the same way that the readymade asks us to consider it in a different light (Cortright et al., 2015, p. 285). Sometimes this is done through the subtle manipulation of user-generated material, as in Lonergan's *Recent Music Videos*, a collection of found YouTube videos that the artist set to MIDI music. Often, as exemplified for instance by Oglander's *Craigslist Mirrors*, Arcangel's *Working on My Novel*, or Laric's *50/50*, this reframing of meaning is done via compilation. In such cases, the collective presentation of vernacular online material creates a new narrative by way of association, in the same way that the "Kuleshov Effect" functions in film (Olson, 2008): the whole becomes greater than the sum of its parts.

However, a crucial prerequisite here is the existence of a shared "symbolic code" between artist and audience. As Gross (1973) explains,

> artistic communication is a form of culturally determined symbolic behavior in which an artist creates or arranges object(s) and/or events, purposefully, so as to imply meaning(s) and emotion(s) according to the conventions of a symbolic code… For artistic communication to occur it is not necessary for the artist and the audience to co-exist in either time or space. However, according to this definition, it is necessary that, to a significant extent, they share a common symbolic code. (p. 115)

It is this shared symbolic code that allows these creative works to be read as art—or, as a highly reflexive commentary on what we simultaneously understand as non-art (i.e. vernacular online creativity; user-generated content). Furthermore, as Gross (1973, 1974) aptly observed, the development of competence in a symbolic mode is based on familiarity and repeated encounters with communication in that same mode. Here, this applies to both Internet art and online user-generated content; we need to understand the ethos of each of them in order for the relationship between them to exist in an artistic sense.

However, there is another key element that enables user-generated content to take on new meanings. Namely, it is the prerogative of the artist to reframe non-art as art, and this is also a vital process whereby these differences in interpretation are facilitated. In other words, the fact that a creative work is made by an artist (or not) still matters—for all art, but perhaps even more so for Internet art, which lives side by side with and among huge volumes of vernacular online creativity. The question of authorship is particularly important for works that are camouflaged or that try to mimic and thus comment on vernacular forms of digital creativity. Gene McHugh (2015) argues that, by mimicking vernacular online content, works of Internet art function as readymades, solely because of their authorship by an artist. He writes:

> If you were not acquainted with Cory Arcangel as an artist and you came across his YouTube video of U2's 'With or Without You' mashed up with footage of the Berlin Wall coming down, it would read as a normal YouTube video. It seems like something that is native to YouTube and not to art… However, *Arcangel is an artist and anything creative he does will inevitably function as an artwork* in an art context. (McHugh, 2015, p. 187, emphasis mine)

Starting in the twentieth century, with the turn of modernism, the formal designation of cultural products as art ceases to be a matter of inherent properties, and becomes the prerogative of the artist (Danto, 1986; Dickie, 1969; Gombrich, 2006; Meecham & Sheldon, 2000). As Dickie (1969) defines it, a work of art is an artifact "upon which some society or some sub-group of a society has conferred the status of candidate for appreciation"; Dickie further notes that "the status [of candidate] must be conferrable by a single person's treating an artifact as a candidate for appreciation" and that usually this person is the artist himself (p. 785). In practice, however, this status is most often conferred by elements and institutions within the surrounding art world (Gross, 1973).

In its broadest sense, an "art world" might simply be thought of as a receptive audience willing to consider the work as art, and with the ability to legitimize it as such and amplify the artists' work for a broader audience. Significantly, as Arora and Vermeylen (2013) note, the meaning of art criticism and expertise is changing in the digital age, with the rise of social media and the celebration of crowd wisdom across different spheres of sociocultural activity. However, notwithstanding these important changes, the traditional institutions that make up the formal art world—chiefly, museums, galleries and critics—maintain their central position in terms of contextualizing and legitimating art (Arora & Vermeylen, 2013).

Contemporary curation is often about the meaning inherent in making certain selections as much as it is about the works of art themselves, and museums recognize their role in influencing public opinion about what constitutes a work of art (Haacke, 1986). In the case of Internet-based art, although the physical object has disappeared, museums, galleries and other art world institutions continue to play a role in recognizing and legitimating this work as art, by collecting and exhibiting such work in both traditional and alternative venues. The Whitney, for instance, has a dedicated online exhibition space, ArtPort, which features commissions and new media exhibitions; the New Museum sponsors Rhizome, the "leading art organization dedicated to born-digital art and culture" which plays both an archival, curatorial and educational role. Additionally, museums and galleries also feature works of Internet art—or, sometimes, representations of these works—within their physical spaces (Joel Holmberg at the New Museum, Lorna Mills at Transfer Gallery, Aaron Koblin at the MoMA, Kyle MacDonald at the the Victoria and Albert Museum, and many more). In 2015, the art and culture website Hyperallergic released its first top-ten list of Internet-specific art, highlighting work that had been produced or exhibited that year (Meier, Vartanian, & Voon, 2015). Although the contenders could presumably have come from anywhere, the list included projects affiliated with MoMA, the Victoria and Albert Museum, The Whitney, the Museum of the Moving Image, and a project directly inspired by Obrist, curator for the Serpentine gallery.

But while the contemporary art world still plays a crucial role in amplifying Internet-based work and lending an aesthetic validity to such work, it is also important to note that a work of Internet art can be encountered in different contexts: institutional (that is, institutionally endorsed or contextualized) *and* "at large" on the Internet. How does this multiplicity—and, most often, synchronicity—of being alter its meaning, interpretation and status? At first, traditional art institutions and mass culture (including the Internet) were mutually exclusive as distribution networks; Rachel Greene noted this tension between Internet art's institutionalization and its underground existence in her influential early history of net art (Greene, 2000). But later, the multi-platform approach to the distribution of Internet art become more widely embraced and a key feature of its aesthetic prerogative (Cornell & Halter, 2015). So can the same work then lead multiple lives, and have multiple statuses as art and non-art depending on context? Or, if a work of Internet art lives or circulates on vernacular online platforms (Youtube, Facebook, Tumblr, Yahoo Answers, etc.) and is, at least on the surface, indistinguishable from the user-generated content that surrounds it, does it "stop being art if someone's not thinking about it as art?" (Halter, quoted in Cortright et al., 2015, p. 285). These are the kinds of idiosyncratic questions that online creativity invites—the kinds of questions that ultimately problematize the boundaries between art and vernacular creative activity on the Internet.

* * *

As this essay has aimed to illustrate, the contemporary proliferation of creative activity in online spaces—in terms of both sheer amount and diversity—represents an important opportunity to consider the relationship between art and vernacular creativity online. To a large extent, Internet art challenges the notions of fine art developed in the West during the Renaissance and Enlightenment—especially in terms of the idea of the romantic artist, the relegation of art to "the fringe of society" (a "reservation" outside of quotidian life) and the emphasis on individuality, originality and uniqueness (Gross, 1995). In particular, Internet artists' commentary on both the form and content of user-generated creativity, reveal a complex and complicated relationship between art and vernacular creativity online. While remix and reappropriation are not new concepts specific to the digital age (Lessig, 2005), there is a need to pay attention to the ways in which the Internet is making these processes more prevalent both within and beyond the art world.

Furthermore, it is important to consider how authorship is evolving in the digital age, as it is becoming more distributed, modular and, often, more difficult to ascertain (Literat, 2012). Facilitated by digital technologies and online participatory practices, contemporary remix and appropriation practices are challenging conventional notions of authorship; we must ask, "how is authorship conceptualized in an environment where individuals can easily appropriate, share, and remix?" (Diakopolous et al., 2007). These developments have a crucial impact on the art world, yet are insufficiently acknowledged and interrogated. As critic and curator Karen Archey (2015) notes, "one of the great failures of post-Internet [art] is its dogmatism towards conventional modes of authorship (the objective, intellectual auteur) and the aesthetics paired with it"; furthermore, Archey is right in suggesting that such an approach "seems cognitively dissonant with the Internet's cultural democratization that it seeks to address" (p. 451).

In addition to the theoretical considerations that this evolution of authorship entails, there are ethical and practical consequences that also need to be considered, especially as they relate to the practice of Internet artists incor-porating vernacular online content. This content is most often incorporated without any kind of attribution of credit, and imbued with new meanings that are out of the original creators' control. While crafting these new mean-ings and recontextualizing existing material is the prerogative of the artist, and while content in online spaces is quintessentially dynamic, it is none-theless important to pay attention to the relationships that are produced as part of these works. This is especially significant when factors like gender, race and class are salient aspects of the appropriation dynamics. For instance, Barron (2014) argues that the class dynamics which are at the basis of Arcan-gel's *Working on My Novel* are rather problematic. Similarly, Richard Prince's controversial series *New Portraits*—where he appropriates Instagram posts (belonging overwhelmingly to young attractive women) for gallery exhi-bition, often adding his own lewd remarks as Instagram comments on the images—has attracted significant criticism along gender lines. Furthermore, when there is a commercial element to projects that rely on the appropriation of user-generated content, the ethical (and, sometimes, legal) implications are all the more crucial to consider. Both Arcangel and Prince, for example, profited from these projects: Arcangel released a book compiling the tweets, while Prince sold each Instagram print-out for $90,000 (Parkinson, 2015).

Ultimately, I come back to the question that started this inquiry: namely, has there ever been a time—since the "invention" of art, or Art with a capital A (see Kristeller, 1951, 1952; Shiner, 2001)—that art and non-art have lived so close together, used the same tools, shared the same space, breathed the same air? How are the conventional distinctions between art and vernacular creativity evolving in the Internet age, as the scope and diversity of online creative participation continues to grow? As Weitz (1956) argued, the criteria of evaluation as to what is or is not art are fundamentally fluid, and the value of aesthetic theory is that it makes us examine and re-articulate these criteria. He writes:

> The problem with which we must begin is not "What is art?," but "What sort of concept is 'art'?" ... If I may paraphrase Wittgenstein, we must not ask, What is the nature of any philosophical x?, or even, according to the semanticist, What does "x" mean? ... but rather, What is the use or employment of "x"? What does "x" do in the language? (Weitz, 1956, p. 30)

Thus, Weitz emphasizes the need to refocus our attention on "the rela-tion between the employment of certain kinds of concepts and the conditions under which they can be correctly applied" (p. 30). Such a view is valuable when it comes to interrogating the changing meanings of "art" and "artists" in the Internet age; as several scholars have argued (e.g. Bruns, 2008; Jenkins, 2006; Sinnreich, 2010), what we are currently witnessing is not simply the enhancement or evolution of pre-existing practices of production and consumption, but rather their dethronement by a new cultural paradigm that both combines and confounds them. Acknowledging this paradigm shift—and its momentous implications for art and culture—is a necessary first step towards reassessing the field of contemporary creativity and better understanding the opportunities and challenges brought about by the Internet as both a locus and a medium for widespread creative engagement.

References

Arcangel, C., Bell-Smith, M., Connor, M., Jones, C., Olson, M., & Staehle, W. (2015). Net aesthetics 2.0 conversation, New York City, 2006: Part 1 of 3. In L. Cornell & E. Halter (Eds.), *Mass effect: Art and the Internet in the twenty-first century* (pp. 99–106). New York, NY: MIT Press.

Archey, K. (2015). Bodies in space: Identity, sexuality and the abstraction of the digital and physical. In L. Cornell & E. Halter (Eds.), *Mass effect: Art and the Internet in the twenty-first century* (pp. 451–468). New York, NY: MIT Press.

Arora, P., & Vermeylen, F. (2013). The end of the art connoisseur? Experts and knowledge production in the visual arts in the digital age. *Information, Communication & Society, 16*(2), 194–214.

Barrett, T. (2006). Approaches to postmodern art-making. *FATE in Review 28*, 2–14.

Barron, J. (2014, November 13). Working on my novel. *Bookforum*. Retrieved from http://www.bookforum.com/review/13895

Beard, T. (2008, March 26). Interview with Guthrie Lonergan. *Rhizome*. Retrieved from: https://rhizome.org/editorial/2008/mar/26/interview-with-guthrie-lonergan/

Bruns, A. (2008). *Blogs, Wikipedia, Second Life and beyond: From production to produsage*. London: Peter Lang.

Carroll, N. (1999). Art and aesthetic experience. In *Philosophy of art: A contemporary introduction* (pp. 155–204). London: Routledge.

Cornell, L. (2006, February 9). Net results: Closing the gap between art and life online. *Time Out New York*. Retrieved from: https://www.timeout.com/newyork/art/net-results

Cornell, L., & Halter, E. (2015). Hard reboot: An introduction to Mass Effect. In L. Cornell & E. Halter (Eds.), *Mass effect: Art and the Internet in the twenty-first century* (pp. xv–xxxiv). New York, NY: MIT Press.

Cortright, P., McCoy, J., McCoy, K., & Moody, T. (2015). Net aesthetics 2.0 conversation. In L. Cornell & E. Halter (Eds.), *Mass effect: Art and the Internet in the twenty-first century* (pp. 285–288). New York, NY: MIT Press.

Danto, A. (2003). The end of art. In S. M. Cahn (Ed.) *Philosophy for the 21th Century: A comprehensive reader* (pp. 788–798). New York, NY: Oxford University Press.

Dewey, J. (1934). *Art as experience*. New York, NY: Pedigree Press.

Diakopoulos, N., Luther, K., Medynskiy, Y., & Essa, I. (2007). The evolution of author-ship in a remix society. Proceedings of The Eighteenth Conference on Hypertext and Hypermedia, (pp. 133–136), New York, USA.

Dickie, G. (1969). Defining art. *American Philosophical Quarterly, 6*(3), 253–256.

Gombrich, E. H. (2006). *The story of art*. New York, NY: Phaidon.

Greene, R. (2000). Web work: A history of Internet art. *Artforum International 38*(9), 162.

Greene, R. (2004). *Internet art*. London: Thames & Hudson.

Gross, L. (1973). Art as the communication of competence. *Social Science Information, 12*(6), 115–141.

Gross, L. (1974). Modes of communication and the acquisition of symbolic compe-tence. In D. O. Olson (ed), *Media and symbols: The forms of expression, communi-cation, and education* (pp. 56–80). Chicago, IL: National Society for the Study of Education.

Gross, L. (1995). Art and artists on the margins. In L. Gross (ed.), *On the margins of art worlds*. Boulder, CO: Westview Press.

Haacke, H. (2012). Museums: Managers of consciousness. In K. Stiles & P. Selz (Eds.). *Theories and documents of contemporary art: A sourcebook of artists' writings*. Oakland, CA: University of California Press.

Halter, E. (2009, April 29). After the amateur: Notes. Retrieved from: http://rhizome.org/editorial/2009/apr/29/after-the-amateur-notes/

Halter, E. (2015). The centaur and the hummingbird. In L. Cornell & E. Halter (Eds.), *Mass effect: Art and the Internet in the twenty-first century* (pp. 231–242). New York, NY: MIT Press.

Jenkins, H. (2006). *Convergence culture: Where old and new media collide*. New York, NY: New York University Press.

Kristeller, P. O. (1951). The modern system of the arts: A study in the history of aesthetics, Part I. *Journal of the History of Ideas 12*(4), 496–527.

Kristeller, P. O. (1952). The modern system of the arts: A study in the history of aesthetics, Part II. *Journal of the History of Ideas 13*(1), 17–46.

Lessig, L. (2005, October). Re:MixMe. Plenary address to the annual Network for IT-Research and Competence in Education (ITU) conference, Oslo, Norway.

Literat, I. 2012. The work of art in the age of mediated participation: Crowdsourced art and collective creativity. *International Journal of Communication, 6*, 2962–2984.

Lonergan, G. (2015). "We did it ourselves!" aka "my favorites." In L. Cornell & E. Halter (Eds.), *Mass effect: Art and the Internet in the twenty-first century* (pp. 167–184). New York, NY: MIT Press.

McHugh, G. (2015). Excerpts from post Internet. In L. Cornell & E. Halter (Eds.), *Mass effect: Art and the Internet in the twenty-first century* (pp. 185–198). New York, NY: MIT Press.

Meecham, P., & Sheldon, J. (2000). *Modern art: A critical introduction*. New York, NY: Routledge.

Meier, A., Vartanian, H., & Voon, C. (2015, December 29). Best of 2015: Our top 10 works of internet art. *Hyperallergic*. Retrieved from: http://hyperallergic.com/263538/best-of-2015-our-top-10-works-of-internet-art/

Olson, M. (2010). Lost not found: The circulation of images in digital visual culture. In C. Cotton & A. Klein (Eds.). *Words without pictures*. New York, NY: Aperture Foundation. Retrieved from: http://language.cont3xt.net/wp-content/uploads/2011/01/olson-lostnotfound.pdf.

Parkinson, H. J. (2015, July 18). Instagram, an artist and the $100,000 selfies—appropriation in the digital age. *The Guardian*. Retrieved from: https://www.theguardian.com/technology/2015/jul/18/instagram-artist-richard-prince-selfies

Shiner, L. (2001). *The invention of art: A cultural history*. Chicago, IL: University of Chicago Press.

Sinnreich, A. (2010). *Mashed up: Music, technology, and the rise of configurable culture*. Amherst, MA: University of Massachusetts Press.

Tribe, M., Jana, R., & Grosenick, U. (2006). *New media art*. London and Cologne: Taschen.

Troemel, B. (2013, May 10). Athletic aesthetics. *The New Inquiry*. Retrieved from: http://thenewinquiry.com/essays/athletic-aesthetics/

Weitz, M. (1956). The role of theory in aesthetics. *The Journal of Aesthetics and Art Criticism 15*(1), 27–35.

2016, 200). It also kept it well suited to curricular change, particularly as widespread dissatisfaction with the status quo—driving intellectual developments like poststructuralism, postmodernism and postconolonialism—and increasing access to information technologies played into the notion's fluid, interactive and hyper-textual attributes. Performance promised, in one view, to "be to the 20th and 21st centuries what discipline was to the 18th and 19th, that is, an onto-historical formation of power and knowledge" (McKenzie, 2001, 176).

However, as its study spread across the curriculum, little about its essence remained lucid, constant or reliable. For some, the term came to comprise a set of related terms rather than one sole idea, with its invocation "so baggy [and having] mopped up so many possible meanings and applications, that discourse about performance is becoming damaged ... oratorically grandiose and intellectually vacuous" (Shepherd, 2016, viii-x). In semiotics, Peirce (1998, 265) was so bothered by the phenomenon of conceptual deviation that he called for an "ethics of terminology," envisioning thought police to offset the "shameful offense against the inventor of the symbol and against science, [where] it becomes the duty of others to treat the act with contempt and indignation." Few, however, acted on his lament.

Instead, performance's study emblematizes a strong pattern of concept creep, where energetic horizontal expansion is accompanied by similarly vigorous vertical growth. Four main instances of creep have been instrumental in its semantic enlargement: performance as a staged production, an interpersonal strategy, social structure and culture. Interchangeably used and artificially separated here only as an analytical construct, they represent various kinds of activity, issues and situations that no longer necessarily share core attributes. This raises the possibility that performance may be approaching the exhaustion of its invocation, and that it may no longer be able to adequately address the phenomena it is tasked with describing. Though deviating from a term's original meaning is necessary for intellectual growth and unloading aspects of a concept is necessary when adding new ones, the imprecision that surrounds performance today suggests that the concept's growth may have outpaced its capacity to lend clarity. As Raymond Williams (1976, 87) once said about the word "culture":

> Culture is one of the two or three most complicated words in the English language ... mainly because it has now come to be used for important concepts in several distinct intellectual disciplines and in several distinct and incompatible systems of thought.

So too may be the case with performance, whose uneven appropriation stands out on closer examination of its concept creep.

Performance as Staged Production

The idea of performance at its most fundamental level positions it as a staged production, a "unique coming together of a special occasion, performers, a tradition involving past experiences ... and an audience capable of observing and judging by aesthetic criteria" (Abrahams, 1979, 70). This view articulates concrete attributes that one might associate with a theater or concert hall: an actual spatial setting, a predictable and regularized time span of activity, an identified set of performers, an intentional audience, some type of performative modality and clear criteria for evaluation. Relevant here is the notion of competence, which goes straight to the heart of a performance's definition: Bauman (1975, 293), for instance, defined performance as a "communicative phenomenon [with] responsibility to an audience for a display of communicative competence."

This view of performance caught on quickly in the late 1960s and 70s, where it was soon being widely used to address music (Blacking, 1973), verbal displays (Gossen, 1974), dance (Hanna, 1979), oral narrative (Scheub, 1977) and oral poetry (Finnegan, 1977) as well as the performative liveness—described as "twice behaved behavior" (Schechner, 1985, 36)—that unfolds as part of theatrical staging (Burns, 1972). In each case, scholars laid out performance's technical and formalized accouterments—written or oral, visual or acoustic.

In keeping with the mood of the time, competence generated skepticisim among those who felt it amounted to no more than formalized rules of grammar, and they attempted to minimize its hold on performance. Gross (1973, 1974), for instance, saw competence as a complex interplay of creation and appreciation, while Hymes (1972, 283) attempted to dislodge the two more fully: Noting that "performance, as an event, may have properties not reducible to terms of individual or standardized competence," he envisioned a range of performances for every degree of competence, freeing performance to become "culture in action" that emphasized "speech over code; function over structure; context over message; the ethnographically appropriate over the ethnologically arbitrary" (Hymes, 1964, 6,11). Over time, this facilitated performance's invocation in discussions of the formal aspects of productions as widespread as shouting matches on the US-Mexican border (Abrahams, 1981), shamanistic ceremonies of ritualistic healing (Laderman & Roseman, 1996), refugee theater (Jeffers, 2011) and flash mobs (Molnar, 2014).

Not surprisingly, performance's relationship with competence opened the door to the term's metaphorical appropriation, with concrete performances increasingly put in step with a different kind of competence suggested by broader notions of display. Across Debord's (1967) "society as spectacle," Foucault's (1970) "theatrum philosophicum" or Baudrillard's (1981, 69) "stage of the body," notions of performance moved easily from concrete to ephemeral, imagined and symbolic. Using performance to address wide-ranging activity with varying degrees of consonance to the term's original contours has thus enhanced the term's "catch-all" quality, facilitating claims that performance is "what you say it is. And what you say it is depends on who you are and where you are speaking" (Shepherd, 2016, 183).

Despite its relatively lucid and concrete moorings, then, work on performance as a staged production exhibits signs that its framing cannot contain what it is tasked with clarifying. Even in its most contained invocation, one fixated on articulating the precise contours of an actual staged production, the notion of performance threatens to bust the seams of its prescribed use. This has remained the case as concept creep continues to broaden.

Performance as Interpersonal Strategy

Performance's intellectual promise compels scholars seeking to explain inter-personal encounters as performative activity. Though this connection was suggested early on in Cooley's (1902) seminal essay "The Looking Glass Self," the idea that a person's self-image depends on social interaction took flight with the work of Goffman (1959, 1963, 1981). His sociological regard for "the arrangement which transforms an individual into a stage performer" (Goffman, 1974, 124) relied on performance to describe the interpersonal strategies that unfold as part of social relations. His creative melding of existing scholarly work on dramaturgy (Burke, 1952), symbolic interaction-ism (Blumer, 1969) and Bateson's (1972) notion of frame fostered a prism through which to productively consider the acts of everyday life as performa-tive activity. By showing that individuals order experience so as to sustain social equilibrium, Goffman's investment in performance as interpersonal strategy—which straddled multiple works over a 25-year time span—generated a social gaming approach to action that gave the idea of performance depth: front, back and off stage spaces; public/private dimensions; practices con-nected to role distance, scripts and border crossing.

Goffman's elaboration of the presentation of self fostered scholarship that extended from focused dyadic or small group interactions to large scale, public settings. Included here has been work by ethnomethodologists, con-versation analysts and ethnographers of communication, who traced the performative patterning of everyday talk (Katriel, 1985; Sacks, Schegloff & Jefferson, 1974); scholarship on the framing activity of social movements and political discourse (Gitlin, 1980; Gamson, 1992); and dramaturgical analyses that address "the metaphor, perspective and reality of life as theater" (Edgley, 2013, 1), such as self-presentation strategies in online dating (Ellis, Heino & Gibbs, 2006) or the dramaturgical elements of airport security checkpoints (Altheide, 2013).

While invoking performance as interpersonal strategy broadens the term from contained and regularized productions to the settings of everyday life, it continues to blur multiple aspects of the term's core meaning: differences between stage and social roles, the intentional presence of audience and performers, a setting occurring in spatial and temporal boundaries, a clear performative modality and evaluative criteria. The metaphoricity introduced here leaves scholars to ponder what exists beyond the performative frame. From standing in elevators to entering a cocktail party, the situations analyzed by Goffman and others turn all everyday activity into performance, suggesting that concept creep fosters the notion's horizontal growth, even as it transforms and continues to loses sight of some of the idea's most constitutive vertical features.

Performance as Social Structure

Invoking performance as a prism on social structure further broadens the term, offering a platform on which to consider details relevant to the maintenance or diminution of socio-structural arrangements, mostly concerning power's uneven distribution. From Bateson's (1972) anthropological theory of play, fantasy and metacommunication to Turner's notions of liminality (1969) and social drama (1974, 1982), performance here is constitutive of periods of heightened activity during which a social group or society's presuppositions are most exposed. In discussing the regularized form of social dramas that disturbances take, for instance, Turner (1974, 32) delineated the stages of breach, crisis, redress and reintegration (or schism) that they necessarily accommodate, with Ndembu ritual performances offering one case, among many, in which "a cultural form (theater) is the model for a social science concept."

Performance's potential to concretize uneven power flows has easily fostered the analysis of settings addressing social structural issues but without explicit attention to their ever-widening temporal and spatial frames, diminished intentionality of audiences and performers and/or increasingly muddied evaluative dimensions. Thus, though all address social structure as performance, there is an uneven commonality linking the analyses of ideological participation in US rodeos (Stoeltje, 1981) or South African women's role-taking in Truth and Reconciliation Commissions (Oboe, 2007) with discussions of retributive silence in Apache culture (Basso, 1970) or virtual dissidence during the Arab Spring (Allam, 2014). Relevant here is the consideration of large scale public events invested in putting social inequities on display—demonstrations, sit-ins and mass protests. In his discussion of social movements as performance, for instance, Eyerman (2007, 49) noted the broad social impact of such movements, themselves reliant on "corporality and presence, acting and acting out, the role of drama and the symbolic":

> If social movements articulate frames of understanding, the performance of protest actualizes them ... Performance focuses on corporality and presence; performance is what makes a movement move and helps it move others.

Drawing from an understanding that performance can be fundamentally political—demonstrating what Taylor (2016, 147) recently called "the continuation of politics by other means"—performance becomes in this view an integral dramaturgical feature of protest and it enhances its ability to challenge social order: pro-Nazi rallies in 1930s Germany (Baxandall, 1969), student protests in Beijing's Tianenman Square (Kershaw, 1997), ACT-UP demonstrations across the US (Foster, 2003).

Concept creep's horizontal spread, then, is accompanied by vertical expansion that further fosters the concept's depletion. Blurred further are performance's constitutive features—activity taking place in a concrete setting, with identifiable actors, audience, modality and evaluation. As with those studying performance as interpersonal strategy, scholars are not easily able to extricate performance from its surrounding social structure, raising questions about its analytical use-value.

Performance as Culture

Finally, the appropriation of performance to explain culture writ large invites a focus on large-scale cultural patterns and impulses, where, as metaphoricity continues to grow, notions of culture and performance are increasingly treated as substitutional frames for each other. Consonant with the scholarship of anthropologist Clifford Geertz (1972, 1973), the embedded dimensions of cultural systems like common sense or religion depend on being performed without reflection or hesitation. As Geertz (1983, 168) noted,

> The instruments of reasoning are changing and society is less and less represented as an elaborate machine or a quasi-organism than as a serious game, a sidewalk drama or a behavioral text ... The analogies are coming more and more from the contrivances of cultural performance.

Operating on the premise that all culture is public and capable of being appropriated through performance, this work situates performance and culture as necessarily in service to each other. In Turner and Bruner's (1986, 81) words, culture and performance make sense as ways of explaining each other because "man is a self-performing animal—his performances are, in a way, reflexive, in performing he reveals himself to himself."

Many scholars employ performance as a direct stand-in for culture: Discussions of carnival in Trinidad (Stewart, 1986) and Brazil (Da Matta, 1984) or analyses of the Olympic Games (D'Agati, 2011; MacAloon, 1981) track multiple performative levels at play within events as a means to understanding their surrounding cultural formations. Studies of media events, necessarily invested in a break between the experiential and mediated, or the cultural and performed, rest on the argument that the mediated experience is better (Dayan & Katz, 1992). As with other invocations of the term, unclear in these efforts is the point of crossover between performance and culture.

Performance becomes here a "laboratory for studying cultural and social forces" (Fischer-Lichte, 2009, 1), with performative activity figuring in culture's very definition, as in discussions of gay culture (Roman, 1998) or organizational culture (Kotter, 2008). No surprise, then, that the term's accommodating nature easily fits theories insisting on flux and fluidity—Bakhtin's (1975) idea of dialogism or De Certeau's (1984) approach to mobility—where performance is expected to champion "radical critique, breaking of boundaries, process and energy rather than stasis and product, liberation rather than containment" (Shepherd, 2016, 59). Further blunted by these efforts is consonance across terms, as performance readily surfaces in forms that make little sense when closely juxtaposed to each other: Consider, for instance, Butler's (1990) "punitive performatives" alongside Lyotard's (1984 [1979]) idea of "performativity." Bringing performance "out into the public world where ethical judgment can get at it" (Geertz, 1968, 139) does not necessarily foster conceptual cohesion.

For studies of performance, then, as the notion's usage has broadened spatially, its grip on its own core attributes has come loose. Across all four instances of concept creep, a surplus of metaphoricity depletes the term's meaning as its invocations move progressively away from its original grounding—a concrete performance, staged in real time and space with identified actors, intentional audience, performative modality and criteria for evaluation. Instead, current invocations of performance—which now regularly signify interpersonal strategies, social structures and culture writ large—omit key aspects of the root concept, as they are used to describe displays that are imagined or abstract, immaterial or intangible, inanimate or enacted to no one in particular. Lost in these more metaphorical appropriations is the capacity to recognize where and when performance ends. Instead, the concept bleeds into the context it is tasked with explaining, and, in so doing, it loses much of its conceptual clarity.

Exhausting the Tipping Point of Performance

One of the academy's less-articulated but widely-used practices is that of broadly adopting terminology current to the moment. Academics, wrote Sunstein (2001, para. 3, lines 1–6), are subject to "cascade effects," fads and fashions in intellectual thought by which they

> start, join, and accelerate bandwagons, ... are subject to the informational signals sent by the acts and statements of others, ... participate in creating the very signals to which they respond, ... and are susceptible to the reputational pressures imposed by the (perceived) beliefs of others. They respond to these pressures, and by so doing, they help to amplify them.

Resonant with what Gladwell (2002) labelled "tipping points," academic fashions often generate frenzied periods during which certain ideas or points of view are widely adopted. Sometimes, but not always, these periods of intense growth are followed by the same concept being depleted as frenetically as it had been picked up.

Such a scenario may be facing performance. At present, "there is no culturally or historically fixable limit to what is or is not 'performance,'" which remains largely "fragmented rather than unified, decentered rather than centered, virtual as well as actual" (Schechner, 2013, 2, 27). Though now widely embraced across the curriculum, it no longer occupies "a single, 'proper' place in knowledge" (Schechner, 2013, 27). Rather, its "capacious intellectual productivity" (Shepherd, 2016, 198) has encouraged it to stand-in for an array of phenomena associated with performative activity, though not enough attention has been paid to what is being lost or transformed along the way.

Bateson (1972) established long ago that values ripe in an environment erupt in their own meta-language about that environment. It should thus be no surprise that performance has become its own meta-term. While grounded terms of reference respond to the ongoing intellectual desire to explain undecipherable phenomena, this analysis suggests that across both its concrete and metaphorical appropriations, the notion of performance is being stretched out of use, potentially exhausting its tipping point. Though this reflects a concern that sharing terms across disciplines always runs the risk of neutralizing the notion's original value, it points to the need for embracing semantic enlargement with more care. If the notion of performance has become part of an interdisciplinary metalanguage, there is need to be explicit about what gets lost or transformed when the concept disseminates. Otherwise, the value of sharing terms across disciplines comes to naught.

In Shakespeare's *As You Like It*, the notion of *theatrum mundi* prompted one of the play's characters to muse that "all the world's a stage." This discussion of performance suggests that staging the world may not be such an enviable goal, after all.

Note

1. The ideas contained in this chapter germinated while I was a graduate student in the late 1980s at the University of Pennsylvania. Larry Gross was my advisor at the Annenberg School, and he was key in supporting my journeying across the Penn curriculum. Those journeys resulted in a certification in folklore and performance studies, chaired by Roger Abrahams, with one of my folklore courses, taught by Dan Ben-Amos, producing an earlier version of this chapter. The topic of performance remained central as Larry and I wrestled toward a dissertation topic. I share this chapter for three reasons: to pay tribute to the extraordinary interdisciplinary training I received at Penn; to honor the memory of Roger Abrahams, who sadly passed away in the summer of 2017, and to celebrate Larry Gross, whose tough but nurturing hand kept me simultaneously on call while in deep generative thought. For his mentorship, enriched long ago by friendship, I will always be grateful.

References

Abrahams, R. (1979). In and out of performance. *Folklore and Oral Communication* (special issue of *Narodna Umjetnost*, Yugoslavia), 1981, 69–78.

Abrahams, R. (1981). Shouting match at the border: The folklore of display events. In R. Bauman and R. Abrahams (Eds.), *And Other Neighborly Names*. Austin: University of Texas Press.

Allam, N. (2014). Blesses and curses: Virtual dissidence as a contentious performance in the Arab Spring's repertoire of contention. *International Journal of Communication, 8*, 853–870.

Altheide, D. (2013). Media dramas and the social construction of reality. In C. Edgley (Ed.), *The drama of social life* (81–96). New York: Routledge.

Austin, J. L. (1962). *How to do things with words*. Cambridge: Harvard University Press.

Bakhtin, M. (1975). *The dialogic imagination*. Austin: University of Texas Press.

Bascom, W. R. (Ed.). (1977). *Frontiers of folklore*. Washington, DC: AAAS Selected Symposia Series,

Basso, K. (1970, Autumn) To give up on words: Silence in Western Apache culture. *Southwestern Journal of Anthropology, 26*(3), 213–230.

Bateson, G. (1972). *Steps to an ecology of mind*. New York: Ballantine.

Baudrillard, J. (1981). *Simulacra and simulacrum*. Ann Arbor, MI: University of Michigan Press.

Bauman, R. (1975). Verbal art as performance. *American Anthropologist, 77*(2), 290–311.

Baxandall, Lee. (1969). Spectacles and scenarios: A dramaturgy of radical activity. *The Drama Review*, 13(4), 52–71.

Ben-Amos, D. (1971, Jan-March). Toward a definition of folklore in context, *Journal of American Folklore, 84*(331), 3–15.

Blacking, J. (1973). *How musical is man?* Seattle: University of Washington Press.

Blumer, H. (1969). *Symbolic interactionism*. Englewood Cliffs, New Jersey: Prentice Hall.

Burke, K. (1952). *A grammar of motives*. Englewood Cliffs, New Jersey: Prentice Hall.

Burns, Elizabeth. (1972). *Theatricality*. London: Longman.

Butler, Judith. (1990). *Gender trouble*. London: Routledge.

Conquergood, D. (1985). Performing as a moral act. *Literature in Performance, 5*(2), 1–13.

Conquergood, D. (1995). Of caravans and carnivals: Performance studies in motion. *The Drama Review 39*(4), 137–141.

Cooley, C. (1998) The looking glass self. In H. J. Schubert (Ed.), *Self and social organization* (pp. 20–22). Chicago: University of Chicago Press.

D'Agati, P. (2011). *Nationalism on the world stage: Cultural performances at the olympic games*. New York: UPA.

Da Matta, R. (1984). Carnival in multiple planes. In J. MacAloon (Ed.), *Rite, drama, festival, spectacle*. Philadelphia: ISHI Publications.

Dayan, D., & Katz, E. (1992). *Media events*. Cambridge: Harvard University Press.

Debord, G. (1967). *Society of the spectacle*. Detroit: Black and Red.

De Certeau, M. (1980). *The practice of everyday life*. Berkeley: University of California Press.

Edgley, C. (ed.). (2013). *The drama of social life*. New York: Routledge,

Ellis, N., Heino, R., & Gibbs, J. (2006). Managing impressions online: Self-presentation processes in the online dating environment. *Journal of Computer-Mediated Communication, 11*(2), 415–441.

Eyerman, R. (2005). How social movements move. In H. Flam & D. King (Eds.), *Emotions and social movements* (pp. 41–56). London: Routledge.

Finnegan, R. (1977). *Oral poetry*. Cambridge: Cambridge University Press.

Fischer-Lichte, E. (2009). Culture as performance. *Modern Austrian Literature, 42*(3), 1–10.

Foster, S. L. (2003). Choreographies of protest. *Theater Journal, 55*(3), 395–412.

Foucault, M. (1998). Theatrum philosophicum. In J. Faubion (Ed.), *Essential works of foucault, Vol. II*, New York: New Press, 343–368.

Gamson, W. (1992). *Talking politics*. New York: Cambridge University Press.

Geertz, C. (1968, Summer). Thinking as a moral act. *Antioch Review, 28*(2), 139–158.

Geertz, C. (1972). Deep play: Notes on a Balinese cockfight. *Daedalus, 101*(1), 1–37

Geertz, C. (1973). *The interpretation of cultures.* New York: Basic Books.

Geertz, C. (1983). *Local knowledge.* New York: Basic Books.

Gitlin, T. (1980). *The whole world is watching.* Berkeley: University of California Press.

Gladwell, M. (2002). *The tipping point.* New York: Back Bay Books.

Goffman, E. (1959). *The presentation of self in everyday life.* New York: Free Press,

Goffman, E. (1963). *Behavior in public places.* Glencoe, IL: Free Press.

Goffman, E. (1974). *Frame analysis.* Boston: Northeastern University.

Goffman, E. (1981). *Forms of talk.* Philadelphia: University of Pennsylvania Press.

Gossen, G. (1974). To speak with a heated heart: Chamula canons of style and good performance. In R. Bauman & J. Sherzer (Eds.), *Explorations in the ethnography of speaking.* Cambridge: Cambridge University Press.

Gross, L. (1973). Art as the communication of competence. *Social Science Information* 12, 115–141.

Gross, L. (1974). Modes of communication and the acquisition of symbolic competence. In D. R. Olson (Ed.), *Media and symbols.* Chicago: University of Chicago Press.

Hacking, I. (1991, Winter). The making and moulding of child abuse. *Critical Inquiry, 17,* 253–288.

Hanna, J. (1979). *To dance is human.* Austin: University of Texas Press.

Haslam, N. (2016). Concept creep: Psychology's expanding concepts of harm and pathology. *Psychological Inquiry, 27*(1), 1–17.

Hymes, D. (1964). Toward ethnographies of communication. *American Anthropologist, 66*(6.2), 1–34.

Hymes, D. (1972). On communicative competence. In J. B. Pride & J. Holmes (Eds.), *Sociolinguistics.* London: Penguin.

Jakobson, R. (1960). Closing statement: Linguistics and poetics. In T. Sebeok (Ed.), *Style in language.* Cambridge: MIT Press.

Jeffers, A. (2011). *Refugees, theater and crisis: Performing global identities.* London: Palgrave MacMillan.

Katriel, T. (1986). *Talking straight: Dugri speech in Israeli Sabra culture.* Cambridge: Cambridge University Press.

Kershaw, B. (1997). Fighting in the streets: Dramaturgies of popular protest, 1968–1989. *New Theatre Quarterly, 13*(3), 255–276.

Kotter, J. (2008). *Corporate culture and performance.* New York: Simon and Schuster.

Kuhn, T. (1962). *The structure of scientific revolutions.* Chicago: University of Chicago Press.

Laderman, C., & Roseman, M. (Eds.). (1996). *The performance of healing.* New York: Routledge.

Lyotard, J-F. (1979). *The postmodern condition: A report on knowledge.* Manchester, UK: Manchester University Press.

MacAloon, J. (1981). *This great symbol: Pierre de Coubertin and the origins of the modern olympic games.* Chicago: University of Chicago Press.

McKenzie, J. (2001). *Perform or else: From discipline to performance.* London: Routledge.

Molnar, V. (2014). Reframing public space through digital mobilization. *Space and Culture, 17*(1), 43–58.

Oboe, A. (2007). The TRC women's hearings as performance and protest in the New South Africa. *Research in African Literatures, 38*(3), 60–76.

Paredes, A., & Bauman, R. (1972). *Toward new perspectives in folklore*. Austin: University of Texas Press.

Peirce, C. S. (1998). *The essential peirce: Selected philosophical writings, Vol. II*. Blomington, IN: Indiana University Press.

Roman, D. (1998). *Acts of intervention: Performance, gay culture and AIDS*. Bloomington, IN: Indiana University Press.

Sacks, H., Schegloff, E., & Jefferson, G. (1974). A simplest systematics for the organization of turn-taking for conversation. *Language 50*(4), 696–735.

Schechner, R. (1985). *Between theater and anthropology*. Philadelphia: University of Pennsylvania Press.

Schechner, R. (2013). *Performance Studies: An Introduction* (3rd edition). London and New York: Routledge.

Scheub, H. (1977). Performance of oral narrative. In W. R. Bascom (Ed.), *Frontiers of folklore* (pp. 54–78). Washington, DC: AAAS Selected Symposia Series.

Shepherd, S. (2016). *The Cambridge introduction to performance theory*. New York: Cambridge University Press.

Stephens, J. (1998). *Anti-disciplinary protest: Sixties radicalism and postmodernism*. New York: Cambridge University Press.

Stewart, J. (1986). Patronage and control in the Trinidad carnival. In V. Turner, & E. Bruner (Eds.), *The anthropology of experience*. Urbana, IL: University of Illinois Press.

Stoeltje, B. (1981). Cowboys and clowns: Rodeo specialists and the ideology of work and play. In R. Bauman, & R. Abrahams (Eds.), *And other neighborly names*. Austin: University of Texas Press.

Sunstein, C. R. (2001). On academic fads and fashions. 99 *Michigan Law Review* 1251. Retrieved from: http://nrs.harvard.edu/urn-3:HUL.InstRepos:13614522

Taylor, D. (2016). *Performance*. Duke University Press,

Turner, V. (1969). *The ritual process*. Ithaca: Cornell University Press.

Turner, V. (1974). *Revelation and divination in Ndembu ritual*. Ithaca: Cornell University Press.

Turner, V. (1982). *From ritual to theater*. New York: Performing Arts Journal Publishing Collective.

Turner, V., & Bruner, E. (eds.). (1986). *The anthropology of experience*. Urbana, IL: University of Illinois Press.

Williams, R. (1976). *Keywords*. London: Oxford University Press.

Part Two

Culture & Power

6. *Larry Gross and Cultivation Analysis*[1]

Michael Morgan

Larry Gross made essential, profound, and far-reaching contributions to the area of media effects research known as cultivation analysis. This chapter tells the story.

But in order to tell it, a bit of background is required.

The story begins with George Gerbner, who became Dean of the Annenberg School for Communication at the University of Pennsylvania in 1964. After about ten years of conducting a variety of discrete studies of media content and institutions, in the mid-1960s Gerbner began to formulate a more comprehensive theoretical framework for studying mass communication. He sought to draw attention to the historically distinct institutional qualities of mass communication; he argued that the rise of mass media meant that culture was now being mass produced by commercial organizations, and that this transformation had enormous implications for collective consciousness.

By the late 1960s, Gerbner began to refer to his scheme as "Cultural Indicators." *Economic* indicators (e.g., unemployment, inflation) were regularly reported in the news, and a movement was emerging to provide periodic reports of *social* indicators (e.g., health and illness, social mobility). Gerbner hoped to establish *Cultural* Indicators to complement these efforts, providing cumulative and comparative information about the mass-produced cultural climate.

Cultural Indicators was envisioned as a three-pronged approach to examining relationships among "message systems, corporate forms and functions, collective image-formation, and public policy" (1970, p. 71). First, *institutional process analysis* would study the institutions that create the messages, in order to illuminate how the mass production of messages is organized, controlled, and managed. Second, *message system analysis* would systematically document the "facts of life," perspectives, and relationships expressed in media messages, reflecting not what any individual sees but what large and diverse communities absorb over time. And third, *cultivation analysis* would reveal the common assumptions that message *systems* cultivate, over and above single or selected messages or individual and selective responses.

Cultivation analysis represented a different way of thinking about media effects. At the time, most studies looked at whether media messages could modify how you feel about a political candidate, convince you to buy a different brand of toothpaste, lead you to engage in violent behavior, and so on. But Gerbner wanted to know if the patterns and "lessons" found in message systems, in the aggregate, are reflected in audiences' shared assumptions, ways of perceiving, and general world views. He sought to develop cultivation as a theory that would

> define mass communication effects as the relationship between mass-produced and technologically mediated message systems and the broadest common terms of image-cultivation in a culture. It would ask not so much how to *change* ideas and behavior, but what public perspectives, conceptions and actions different types of mass communication systems tend to *cultivate*. (1966, p. 433)

Institutional process analysis and message system analysis both had detailed conceptual frameworks and straightforward methodologies. The former would be based on interviews, observation, and the analysis of records and documents; the latter would use the methodology of content analysis, emphasizing the body of media messages *as a system*, in order to investigate how that relates to other systems (i.e., of institutional processes and public beliefs).

But there was no road map for cultivation analysis. Even as Gerbner refined and expanded his thinking about Cultural Indicators and the social implications of the mass production and consumption of cultural texts, the cultivation component remained relatively undeveloped. In many of his early writings, it almost seems as if "cultivation" was simply asserted, taken for granted, as something that could be inferred through careful analysis of media messages and close scrutiny of their symbolic functions.

Enter Larry Gross, who arrived at The Annenberg School in 1968, fresh out of graduate school. (In an interesting coincidence, one of Gerbner's first pieces that used the term "Cultural Indicators" was published in a special issue of *The Annals of the American Academy of Political and Social Science* [Gerbner, 1970]. The issue, devoted to the topic of "Political Intelligence for America's Future," was edited by Gross's father, Bertram Gross, who played an important role in the Social Indicators movement.)

Gerbner and Gross soon began to have regular discussions about the conceptual and methodological challenges of assessing and documenting the "effects" of television—a medium that was increasingly dominating Americans' time and attention, with most people watching mostly the same programs on the only three networks that existed. As Gross (2009) put it, he was "drawn into conversations" with Gerbner "about the role of the media, television in particular, as the primary vehicle through which culture was transmitted in contemporary American society" (p. 66). These conversations led to a remarkably productive and synergistic collaboration, resulting in a unique and influential body of work that neither of them would have been likely to achieve on their own, one with immense ramifications that continue to echo strongly—and even intensify—today.

With graduate training as a social psychologist, Gross was well acquainted with existing research on the effects of exposure to messages. But conceptually, the idea of cultivation posed daunting methodological challenges for the research techniques commonly used in those studies. For one thing, as noted, existing research was concerned mainly with measuring *change* following exposure to messages, whereas cultivation implied *stability*—the steady nurturing and continual reproduction of shared beliefs, perspectives, and assumptions about the world. How does one apply techniques designed to detect change to study the *absence* of change? And existing research tended to look at individuals' immediate or short-term responses to single messages or campaigns, while cultivation was interested in the long-term contributions of exposure to large bodies of media content among broad and heterogeneous communities.

At the time, Gerbner was heavily involved in (and becoming well-known for) annual studies of the portrayal of violence on prime-time network television, starting in 1967. This effort was supported with funding from various federal agencies, with an annual "Violence Profile" released each year. Gross formally joined him as co-investigator on the Cultural Indicators project in 1972, when they received funding from the National Institute of Mental Health for a two-year pilot project to explore methods for investigating how television might cultivate viewers' images and conceptions—specifically, they sought to establish "the feasibility of indicators of the relationships between pervasive cultural trends represented by network television drama, and popular conceptions of reality in critical areas of health, behavior, and policy" (Gerbner & Gross, 1973a, p. 1).

In that period, Gross sharpened and deepened Gerbner's conceptual framework for cultivation and devised a methodological approach that would provide a way to put the idea of cultivation to empirical test. It is true that "the assumptions we made and the methods we adopted were grounded in a set of circumstances that now seem both quaint and distant" (Gross, 2009, p. 66). Yet, although the approach that emerged would evolve a great deal through many studies (and critiques) over the years, it remains the basic technique of cultivation analysis to this day. It was simple, it was elegant, and it lit a spark.

Gross asked us to imagine a hermit who lives in a room (in some of his writings it was a cave), whose only connection to the outside world is prime-time network television. If everything that hermit knew about the world came from what he saw on television, what sorts of images, assumptions, and beliefs about life and society would he have? This is of course reminiscent of Plato's allegory of the shadows on the wall of the cave, or Jerzy Kosinski's novel *Being There*, about a simple gardener who tends his garden and watches television and knows practically nothing about "real life." (The book was published in 1970; the well-known film came out in 1979.)

We all live in the cave, but some of us get out a little bit more than others. The trick was to compare those two groups: those who live mostly in the cave, and those who enjoy a change of scenery now and then.

> The basic assumption ... is that television drama is in the mainstream—or is *the* mainstream—of the symbolic environment cultivating common conceptions of life, society, and the world. No member of society is unaffected by its dominant cultural trends. However, living deep in the mainstream, being a heavy consumer of its images and messages, means more intensive acculturation and tighter integration of the myths and rituals of the symbolic world into one's view of how the real world works. ... Therefore, while all Americans are influenced by the persistent symbolic structures of the cultural mainstream, more heavy viewers of television than light or non-viewers tend to conceive of reality as they experience it in the symbolic world of television drama. (Gerbner & Gross, 1973a, p. 2)

Coming from a social psychological perspective, Gross was drawn to the use of semi-projective techniques to tease out people's inclinations, assumptions, and world views. The idea was to focus on areas in which the "facts of life" in the world of television (as revealed through the message system data) diverged most sharply from the real world. By comparing (1) public beliefs about the real world with both (2) television images and (3) the actual "facts,"

> we can build a composite picture of the relationships between these three images of the world. In many cases it is possible to trace a line extending between the image of the world via television and that image which presumably reflects the true world of fact and then place our respondents at various points along this dimension. In such cases we may be able to see how close our viewers come to seeing the world as would our hypothetical hermit in solitary confinement with a television set. (Gerbner & Gross, 1973b, p. 15)

In a hand-typed memo dated May 1971, Gross sketched out the contours of a possible three-year longitudinal study of children and television that could serve as a prototype for cultivation analysis. Potential focal areas included violence, sex roles, occupational roles, family life and structure, and images of past and future societies. For each of these, "questions and 'tests' will be developed or adapted to assess the child's knowledge, i.e. what are the facts, his sense of priorities and values, i.e. what is important, what is good, what should be changed." Media consumption measures would include "amount of television viewing, type of television viewed, usage of other mass media (including comic books), and the relation between parents' and children's viewing and media usage."

A broad range of possible topics to be studied included "perceived satis-factions from television—why do they watch?" The question of "why" they watch was to be fleshed out in terms of:

- informational benefits? (reported? exhibited? incidental learning of information? of behavior?)
- how do they feel about TV?
- how do they feel about TV vs. other media?
- how do they feel about TV vs. other sources of info.?, vs. other source of entertainment?

Data were to be collected through "intensive interviews with children and their parents." For "'Cultivation' effects testing" (yes, the word was put in quotations marks), "direct questioning would be combined with indirect and projective methods developed or adapted for these needs." Candidates for methods and measures to be used included:

– DeFleur Occupation Test, used to estimate knowledge of occu-pational roles, and of occupational status. Could be modified and expanded to reflect sex-role knowledge and values;
– Hammond's Error Choice technique, could be used to assess infor-mational and attitudinal biases related to the cultivation effects of TV's world view, e.g., in the area of violence, the relative incidence of various kinds of violence, the role of the police, etc.;
– TAT-type story telling techniques, in which children might be asked to make up or complete a story which resembles a typical television situation. Possibly they might be given some as TV and others as news stories, and asked to generate endings, etc. ...
– Attitude scales, such as the Children's F (Lovibond), as related to viewing patterns and preferences.

Not all of these would be used in cultivation analysis; for example, the question of how people "feel" about TV came to be seen as irrelevant to cultivation. The idea of having children complete a story did find its way into other research on the interpretation of visual narratives (e.g., Messaris & Gross, 1977), but did not become part of the cultivation approach. From all the possibilities laid out in this memo, and with the funding from NIMH, two avenues emerged for pilot testing: semi-projective picture tests with small samples of children and a telephone survey of adults.

Groups of children were shown a large sheet with passport-type photographs of 40 people. Although it was not immediately apparent because they were spread out randomly, 20 of the photos were of males and 20 of females; 20 were white and 20 were black; and they were equally divided between older and younger people. The children were asked to indicate who they thought would be a murderer, and who would be likely to be killed. Or they were asked to pick out which one(s) would be a hero, and which a villain. Or they rated each picture in terms of how likely that person was to commit violence, to be a victim, to be a winner or a loser, and so on.

In the pilot tests, Gerbner and Gross (1973b) found that the children's stereotypes of violence and victimization vis-à-vis gender, race, and age closely paralleled television's dominant portrayals (Gerbner, 1970). Although the samples were very small, they also noticed that the heavier viewers reproduced the TV patterns even more sharply; for example, the children who watched more television were even more likely than the lighter viewers to select males as heroes and females as victims.

This suggested that a more focused look at differences between heavy and light viewers (those who spend more vs. less time in the cave) could be fruitful. The distinctive idea was to ask people not what they thought about *television*, but simply to ask them about what they *thought*—to gauge their beliefs about *society*. In this way it would be possible to investigate television's contributions to viewers' conceptions without directly asking them about television. Then, the question of whether or not amount of television viewing made a difference in conceptions could be explored. This was not a minor methodological departure.

Given Gross's interest in semi-projective measures, they drew on "forced error" questions, which require respondents to select one of two (or more) closed-ended answers to a factual question (Hammond, 1948). All answers are actually incorrect but they reflect either an over- or under-estimate of some phenomenon. One response was tilted more toward the way things are on television—this was called the "TV answer"—and the other was tilted more in the direction of reality (or, at least, farther away from the TV "world").

The idea was not to test whether respondents knew the correct answers, but to see if there was a systematic bias such that heavier viewers would be more likely to give the response that was biased in the direction of the "facts" as presented on television.

In April 1973, Gerbner and Gross commissioned the Starch/Hooper firm to conduct telephone interviews with about 600 adults in four metropolitan areas. Respondents were pre-screened to produce two equal-sized groups of light (less than two hours of television a day) and heavy (4 hours or more) viewers. They were asked a series of these "forced error" questions, such as:

- During any given week, what are your chances of being involved in some type of violence? 50–50 (the TV answer) or 1 in 100?
- What percent of all crimes are violent crimes like murders, rape, robbery and aggravated assault? Is it 8 percent, 18 percent, or 28 percent? (the TV answer was either 18 or 28).

The hypothesis was that if television viewing cultivates assumptions about the facts of life that reflect the medium's most recurrent portrayals, then heavy viewers should be more likely than light viewers to choose the "TV answers," indicating greater perceived chances of being involved in violence and an overestimation of the prevalence of violent crime. The margin of difference between the percentages of heavy and light viewers who give some TV answer was dubbed "the Cultivation Differential" (CD). A positive CD means that heavy viewers are more likely than light viewers to give the TV answer—that is, they are more likely to see the real world as it is portrayed on television. The CD can be compared easily across different questions and within different subgroups.

The first cultivation results were reported in Violence Profile No. 5 (Gerbner & Gross, 1973c). The data that were presented—with great fanfare—consisted of a grand total of two Cultivation Differentials, along with a few sentences. For "What percent of all crimes are violent?" the CD was +8.1%, and for "What are your chances of encountering violence?" it was +12.8%. Heavy viewers were indeed more likely than light viewers to overestimate the percentage of violent crimes as well as their chances of being involved in violence. Both of these were statistically significant. This represented "the first clear evidence of a relationship between television viewing and conceptions of social reality that conform to the world of television but contrast with real life" (Gerbner & Gross, 1973c, p. 4; in Congressional hearings held in April 1974, Gerbner called these results "startling").

Subsequent Violence Profiles expanded on these sorts of questions with other samples, and also examined the CDs within specific subgroups defined by education, sex, age, race, and so on. No more small-sample experiments with pictures and other semi-projective tests such as asking respondents to interpret ambiguous scenes of people in interaction. Since that initial 1973 pilot study, cultivation analysis has been synonymous with the use of survey data to look at the difference that amount of television viewing makes with regard to people's conceptions of social reality.

The recipe is straightforward. First, message system analysis provides clear-cut, reliable evidence of how something is portrayed on television. Next, based on those findings, hypotheses are developed about what heavy viewers would be expected to think about the topic, if they think about it the way it is presented on television. Finally, researchers collect (or use existing) survey data that asks people questions about the topic at hand, and then compare responses according to how much time respondents report spending watching television. Although cultivation analysis has evolved a great deal and has drawn on increasingly sophisticated analytical techniques over the decades, at its core it still compares the responses and beliefs of heavier and lighter viewers, other things held constant.

In 1976, Gerbner and Gross published "Living with Television: The Violence Profile," the first scholarly publication that laid out the full range of conceptual assumptions and methodological procedures of cultivation analysis. This article remains the most comprehensive manifesto of what cultivation theory and research are all about. It was also Violence Profile No. 7, and it presented the world with the first published cultivation data. As noted above, some of the conditions it describes are indeed "quaint and distant," but much of the paper remains remarkably current over 40 years later.

Among many key contributions that Gross made in that article, one was to stress that television drama relies on a particular style of "representational realism" that is the dominant convention in Western narrative in general. This does not mean that programs are "real" in a documentary sense (and of course documentaries are also selective symbolic constructions). It means that no matter what happens in the foreground of the story, no matter how contrived or absurd the plot is on the surface, viewers demand (and expect) things to be "realistic"—that is, to fit conventional criteria for what is *considered* to be "realistic." No matter how aware we are that we are watching a made-up story, television drama

> offers to the unsuspecting viewer a continuous stream of 'facts' and impressions about the way of the world, about the constancies and vagaries of human nature, and about the consequences of actions. The premise of realism is a Trojan horse which carries within it a highly selective, synthetic, and purposeful image of the facts of life. (Gerbner & Gross, 1976, p. 178)

They go on to make the point even clearer:

> How many of us have ever been in an operating room, a criminal courtroom, a police station or jail, a corporate board room, or a movie studio? How much of what we know about such diverse spheres of activity, about how various kinds of people work and what they do—how much of our real world has been learned from fictional worlds? To the extent that viewers see television drama—the foreground of plot or the background of the television world—as naturalistic, they may derive a wealth of incidental 'knowledge.' (Gerbner & Gross, 1976, p. 179)

The next four years saw the publication of Violence Profiles No. 8, 9, 10, and 11, each with increasing quantities of cultivation findings. By then cultivation analysis was receiving a great deal of attention—and not all of it positive. Critics broadly attacked many of cultivation's assumptions (e.g., that viewers watch non-selectively, that their interpretations of television content are irrelevant, and that overall exposure is more important than what specific types of shows people watch, among others) and its methodology (including concerns about sampling, question wording, and especially the techniques used for data analysis, which raised questions about causal order and spuriousness).

The issues raised in these attacks, responses, and rejoinders are too numerous and complex to discuss here (but see Shanahan & Morgan, 1999, for an extensive discussion of the critiques). One important issue, however, revolved around the use of statistical controls. Briefly, the early cultivation studies controlled for one variable (age, sex, education, etc.) at a time, and found that the associations between amount of viewing and "TV answer"-type beliefs mostly held up. Several other researchers, however, found that when those controls were implemented *all at once, at the same time*, the relationships tended to disappear, which suggested they were spurious and cast serious doubt on the validity of cultivation.

It soon emerged, however, that even with multiple controls applied all at once, relationships often held up *within particular subgroups*. These cases tended to reflect a consistent pattern that was called "mainstreaming." The term was based on Gerbner and Gross's argument that television provides "a common symbolic environment that now binds diverse communities" (1976, p. 173) and their frequent explicit references to television as the mainstream of the culture.

Essentially, mainstreaming suggests that television viewing cultivates a kind of homogenization among "otherwise" diverse groups of heavy viewers. Among light viewers, various background and demographic factors play a strong role in shaping people's views and perspectives. But among heavy viewers, that diversity is often reduced, and heavy viewers of all groups tend to converge toward similar views—even under multiple controls (see Gerbner, et al., 1980).

This suggested that heavy viewers might then see *themselves* as "mainstream"—normal, average, moderate, and prone to eschewing what they perceive as extreme or deviant. Gross came up with a powerful way to test this prediction, based on how people locate themselves on the political spectrum. The General Social Survey (GSS), an omnibus opinion survey that has been fielded to representative national samples since 1972, asks respondents where they fit on a seven-point scale of political ideology, ranging from "Extremely Liberal" to "Extremely Conservative," with "Moderate, middle of the road" at the midpoint. If heavy viewers prefer to situate themselves in the safe, comfortable mainstream, Gross reasoned, then they should be more likely to self-identify as "moderate" and less likely to say they are *either* liberal *or* conservative.

This is exactly what the data showed (Gerbner, et al., 1982). Heavy viewers were significantly more likely to say they were "moderate," and less likely to call themselves liberal or conservative, regardless of controls (for sex, age, education, political party, and other factors). This finding was replicated in numerous other datasets (Gerbner, et al., 1984).

Despite the massive institutional and technological changes that television has seen, the "moderate" pattern has held ever since then and continues to be the case today. Figure 6.1 shows the association between amount of viewing and political self-designation in 25 General Social Surveys conducted between 1975 and 2016, divided into eight five-year periods. (There are either three or four surveys in each five-year period; each sub-chart contains data from 3500–5000 respondents.) Over all these years, heavy viewers are still significantly and consistently more likely to claim the "moderate" self-designation (solid line), and less likely to say they are liberal (dotted line) or, especially, conservative (dashed line).

This does not mean that their actual *views* are "moderate," however. In "The cultivation of intolerance: Television, blacks, and gays," Gross (1984) found that heavy viewers' were more likely to hold racist and homophobic beliefs, regardless of political ideology. But there's a twist: liberals expressed more progressive and open attitudes towards gays and lesbians, *unless* they were heavy viewers, in which case their attitudes converged with those of moderates and conservatives. Despite some obvious positive gains, television still marginalizes divergent or "deviant" groups, and the exact same patterns he found in 1984 still hold in current data from the GSS. Gross's groundbreaking work in this area shows that, although the mainstream appears to celebrate moderate, middle of the road outlooks, mainstreaming actually means more restrictive, prejudiced, and intolerant views about minorities,

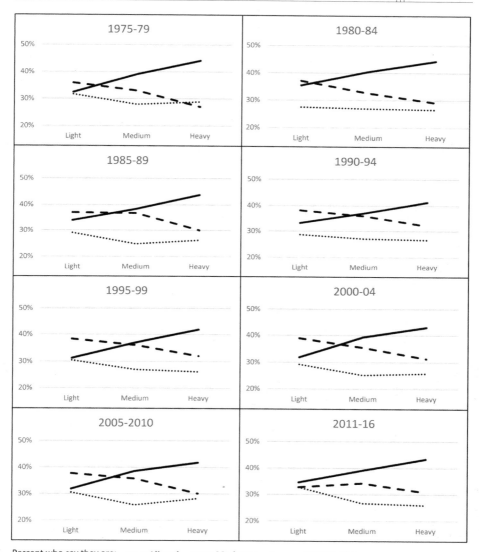

Figure 6.1: Television Viewing and Political Self-Designation, 1975–2016.

along with related attitudes that are highly conducive to authoritarianism (Morgan & Shanahan, 2017).

It is doubtful that either Gerbner or Gross could have imagined what their early "conversations" would generate. Building on the initial focus on violence and victimization, cultivation research expanded to examine many other aspects of life and society, including gender roles, aging, health, science, the family, educational and occupational aspirations, politics, religion, minorities, sexuality, materialism, authoritarianism, the environment, and more. Cultivation studies have been carried out in Argentina, Australia, Belgium, Brazil, Canada, Chile, China, England, France, Germany, Hungary, Iceland, Israel, Japan, Mexico, Nigeria, Russia, South Korea, Sweden, Taiwan, Thailand, Turkey, and elsewhere.

About 800 cultivation studies have been published in academic journals (not to mention the many dissertations, conference papers, and YouTube videos on the topic). Cultivation, along with agenda setting and uses and gratifications, is one of the three most cited theories in mass communication research published in key scholarly journals between 1956 and 2000 (Bryant & Miron, 2004). An analysis of nearly 1000 articles on media effects published between 1993 and 2005 found that cultivation was *the* most cited theory (Potter & Riddle, 2007).

With "cultivation," George Gerbner came up with a powerful and memorable metaphor for a new, challenging, and critical way to think about media effects. And Larry Gross put the meat on the bones of the theory. He expanded and sharpened the concept and gave us concrete and pragmatic ways to investigate it. Although their efforts were deeply intertwined, Gross's contributions to cultivation theory and research are distinct and fundamental. The dynamic synergy of their collaboration produced what has been a vital area of scholarship for more than 40 years, with no signs that it is going away any time soon.

Note

1. I appreciate the helpful comments of Fanny Rothschild, Nancy Signorielli, and James Shanahan on an earlier draft of this chapter.

References

Bryant, J., & Miron, D. (2004). Theory and research in mass communication. *Journal of Communication, 54*, 662–704.

Gerbner, G. (1966). An institutional approach to mass communications research. In L. Thayer (Ed.), *Communication: Theory and research* (pp. 429–445). Springfield, IL: Charles C. Thomas.

Gerbner, G. (1970). Cultural Indicators: The case of violence in television drama. *The Annals of the American Academy of Political and Social Science, 388*, 69–81.

Gerbner, G., & Gross, L. (1973a). *Cultural indicators: The social reality of television drama.* Annenberg School for Communication, University of Pennsylvania. Retrieved from: http://www.eric.ed.gov/PDFS/ED079390.pdf

Gerbner, G., & Gross, L. (1973b). *Abstracted from cultural indicators: The social reality of television drama.* Annenberg School for Communication, University of Pennsylvania. Retrieved from: http://web.asc.upenn.edu/gerbner/Asset.aspx?assetID=2020

Gerbner, G., & Gross, L. (1973c). *Violence profile no. 5: Trends in network television drama and viewer conceptions of social reality.* Annenberg School for Communication, University of Pennsylvania. Retrieved from: http://www.asc.upenn.edu/Gerbner/Asset.aspx?assetID=2767

Gerbner, G., & Gross, L. (1976). Living with television: The violence profile. *Journal of Communication, 26*(2), 173–199.

Gerbner, G., Gross, L., Morgan, M., & Signorielli, N. (1980). The 'Mainstreaming' of America: Violence Profile no. 11. *Journal of Communication, 30*(3), 10–29.

Gerbner, G., Gross, L., Morgan, M., & Signorielli, N. (1982). Charting the mainstream: Television's contributions to political orientations. *Journal of Communication, 32*(2), 100–127.

Gerbner, G., Gross, L., Morgan, M., & Signorielli, N. (1984). Political correlates of television viewing. *Public Opinion Quarterly, 48*(1), 283–300.

Gross, L. (1984). The cultivation of intolerance: Television, blacks, and gays. In G. Melischek, K. E. Rosengren & J. Stappers (Eds.), *Cultural indicators: An international symposium* (pp. 345–363). Vienna, Austria: Verlag der Osterreichischen Akademie der Wissenschaften.

Gross, L. (2009). My media studies: Cultivation to participation. *Television and New Media, 10,* 66–68.

Hammond, K. R. (1948). Measuring attitudes by error choice: An indirect method. *Journal of Abnormal and Social Psychology, 43,* 38–48.

Messaris, P., & Gross, L. (1977). Interpretations of a photographic narrative by viewers in four age groups. *Studies in Visual Communication, 4*(2), 99–111.

Morgan, M., & Shanahan, J. (2017). Television and the cultivation of authoritarianism: A return visit from an unexpected friend. *Journal of Communication, 67*(3), 424–444.

Potter, W. J., & Riddle, K. (2007). A content analysis of the media effects literature. *Journalism & Mass Communication Quarterly, 84*(1), 90–104.

Shanahan, J., & Morgan, M. (1999). *Television and its viewers: Cultivation theory and research.* London: Cambridge University Press.

7. Conjuring Religion in the Media Age and in Media Scholarship

Stewart M. Hoover

Twenty-Five years ago, on October 3, 1992, the Irish singer Sinead O'Connor shocked a *Saturday Night Live* audience with what proved to be an act so scandalous that it earned her widespread and loud condemnation. It also signaled a profound shift in the geography of American religion, a shift that had long been underway, largely unnoticed, and continues to the present. That shift is a recentering of religious authority and meaning-making away from its traditional sources in history, doctrine and clerical authority and toward a diffuse and dispersed circulation of "the religious" in the visual and material cultures of the media.

Sinead's gesture was simple. During her last slot on the show that night she sang Bob Marley's "War," ending it with a stark visual display. Holding up a color photograph of then-Pope John Paul II, she declared, "fight the real enemy," and tore the photo to pieces. The reaction was immediate and stark. There was no applause. The next day the press covered the incident intensely. The following week's host on *SNL*, the actor Joe Pesci, devoted his monologue to a misogynist tirade against O'Connor. Several weeks later, at a major star-studded concert in New York honoring Bob Dylan, she was booed off the stage. Her record sales plummeted. Her segment did not appear in the reruns of *SNL*. Her argument against the Pope and the Catholic Church was profound and heartfelt, and in the words of one reflection on her act on its 25th anniversary, is now well-justified by the way history has unfolded (Daily Edge, 2017). O'Connor's intent was to protest what has now been shown to be widespread abuse of children within the church, something she herself had experienced.

Her objective is linked to the argument I wish to develop, but is not the central point here. What is more significant to my purpose is the way she chose to protest (a specific act directed at a specific person), the place she did so (on a national television program which at the time had a significant younger demographic), and the reaction (immediate and widespread condemnation). The act and the object of the act are central. John Paul II was, by that time, widely-recognized as someone who had "modernized" the Papacy to the extent that he had made it much more accessible and media-friendly through the projection of a warm, accessible persona. He had humanized the office in an unprecedented way. This made him a human icon, and his attempt to thereby center the symbolic authority of the church in public discourse in his person may or may not have been successful. What was successful was his project of making himself a kind of global celebrity, the first time anyone in his position could have been thus described.

O'Connor intended to contest church practice and church authority, and rightly surmised that the most visible, iconic, representation of that for an audience that she presumed ought to have been amenable to her message, would be John Paul II. What she seems to have done instead was to have attacked an icon that had achieved a significant level of sacrality.

This controversy should have been deeply ironic given a wider context and the work of another raised-Catholic singer. Only three years before, Madonna had released her controversial "Like a Prayer" single and video. Widely popular, Madonna had for most of her career played with, and contested, the Catholic Church's authority. Many early photos of her, including her infamous appearance on the cover of *Penthouse Magazine,* depicted her exposed flesh adorned with crosses and crucifixes. Like O'Connor, she would say her purpose was to push back at what she saw as a repressive and damaging presence in her life and in the lives of other young people. The "Like a Prayer" video was in fact quite theologically incoherent, combining burning crosses with a Black Gospel choir and placing a Catholic Romanesque interior in a country chapel featuring a statue of an African-American corpus as a saint. In the most salacious gesture, she brings this corpus to life, is kissed by him, and cavorts lasciviously on the floor, all the while dressed in a filmy black dress. This could not have been a more focused attack on what she saw to be the main "sins" of the church: its exclusiveness and racism and its puritanical repression of women and sexual expression. At least one thinks that is what it was about.

The irony here lies in the fact that, while her project *vis a vis* Roman Catholicism was not without its critics from within the Church and in wider conservative circles, her career progressed more-or-less unabated. More significantly, by October of 1992, her whole *oeuvre* was "mainstreamed" among popular-music and media audiences. This presumably included the audience for *Saturday Night Live* on October 2 of that year and the audience at the Dylan concert several weeks later. She was not attacked by the tabloid press or her concert audiences. She was not booed off stages because of her approach to religion. The religion in Madonna was, simply, a big ho-hum. Her approach was met with what media theorist Larry Gross (1972) would call a "tacit" reading and thus reception by its publics.

This juxtaposition between O'Connor and Madonna reveals a subtle and layered set of social and cultural relations that point to a transformation, by then well underway, of the locus of religion. We can see this in the contrast between the locus of "sacrality" in the two examples. It seems that, by 1992, much of what Roman Catholicism had long held to be important elements of its symbolic repertoire were no longer visible in that way in broad media circulations. Instead, a new kind and locus of "sacrality" could be seen in the iconic media personhood and subjectivity of "the Pope" as a man. He had made himself accessible, and had introduced himself as such an icon, and that was his location and his basis of authority in that broader context. That was where religion mattered enough to fight about, to shout about, to boo about, and to exercise market power about. And, it is in that broader context that religion and spirituality have become more and more present and more and more profound, yet subtle and layered, in their presence in contemporary social life. They have become more symbolic, in a way, and thus their circulation as symbols and as expressions of symbolic power are also expressions of real power. This is more and more obvious all the time in contemporary politics.

To develop this argument further, we can see that two things are involved. First, the shift I have talked about and second, the interrelated development of a broader, mediated, commodified context of market exchange that has come to be the central location of contemporary cultural production. "Religion" and "media" have co-evolved at least since the Protestant Reformation, and we must not overlook that it was the political economy of publishing that is responsible for a great deal of that evolution. The existence of this context of exchange—which we in commonplace conversation refer to as "the media"— has become the determinative condition for much of social and cultural life. This broad and definitive view of the media has animated a range of culturalist media research for at least three decades (for an early and influential statement of this approach, see Gerbner & Gross, 1978). More recent work in the culturalist paradigm, including that influenced by the tradition of British Cultural Studies, has shared the underlying notion that the broader cultural marketplace is the place where important values discussions (in politics, gender, class, race and generational difference) have taken place. Curiously, this discourse has not included a substantive focus on religion. My object here is to address this in a small way by exploring what seems to be a major transformation in religion accomplished in relation to modern mediation.

In other work (Hoover, 2016), I have suggested the ways that traditional religious authority has felt the impacts of this shift. First, religious authority can no longer have a "private conversation." This has been profoundly felt by the Roman Catholic Church in relation to the issue that animated Sinead O'Connor a quarter-century ago. As much as a church might wish to hold matters within some kind of sacred boundary (a practice that Catholicism in particular had grown comfortable with), that is no longer possible. A broader mediated sphere of scrutiny and exposure (beginning with—but not limited to—journalism: see for example the fact that the film *Spotlight* won the Oscar in 2016) is now determinative. Second, religious authority can no longer control its own symbols. This is obvious in the case of Madonna and her cruciform bodily adornments, but also of course in Sinead's scandalous act. It is less obvious in religions—such as Protestantism—where pieties are less centered on legitimated symbols and objects (though there is a large and vibrant debate over whether it is a case of Protestantism being aniconic or simply focused on different kinds of objects). Third, media and media circulations necessarily differentiate and relativize religions. The fact that all symbolic and rhetorical claims today circulate in a central symbolic marketplace defined by the media means that all religions are necessarily accommodated in its inventories. They all sit on the same "shelf" as it were, and it makes them all subject to evaluation according to common standards. Some "win" some "lose," some are better "at media" than are others. Finally, recognizing that to exist today in the cultural marketplace it is necessary to exist in the circulation of cultural commodities we call "the media," religions must today "brand" themselves. They must find ways to make specific and attractive claims in ways that fit the logics of material circulations of the neo-liberal cultural market. Some are obviously better at this than others. The fastest growing branch of Christianity in Africa, Asia, and Latin America—the neo-Pentecostal movement—is significant for its active participation and branding in the media.

This gives some definition to my assertion that the Sinead and Madonna juxtaposition confirmed a shift—by then long underway—between "religion" and "media." It could be seen, as I said as a shift in the locus of "sacrality" in the culture. That Sinead's act mattered so much more than Madonna's many acts became an important "cultural indicator" (to quote Gerbner and Gross) of what mattered and what matters. And the case is a telling one. The

Catholic church has long been more focused on symbols, doctrine, and history, and the media sphere more focused on sensation and celebrity. Sensation and celebrity won out, and the church itself—and its Pope—were complicit in that they had actively sought to place him as an icon in media circulation, making him subject to its forces of sensation and celebrity.

Broader Trends

The 1990s became a watershed decade in relation to religion and media in ways far beyond Sinead O'Connor on *SNL*. It was the period when religion became much more explicit in television content. The two watershed programs were *Touched by an Angel*, in 1992 and *7th Heaven* in 1996. *Touched* was by far the more significant in that it was the first prime-time entertainment series that was actually about God, and that took God (and Angels) seriously. It became hugely successful, and served to convince a skeptical television industry that religion could sell (as long as it was a generic "golden rule" religion that did not get too specific about doctrine—it did not, for instance, mention Jesus even though the audience was predominantly Christian). Television had long avoided or compartmentalized religion, but after the 1990s, it became more mainstream, and in a wide range of frames, from traditional Judaism and Christianity to "new age" spirituality, to vampires, and beyond.

This is an important frame for the shift I have been talking about. As publics and audiences have become less and less subject to traditional religion (a fact confirmed almost weekly by one new survey or another), they have found a ready supply of religious and spiritual goods in the supposedly "secular" media. Those goods, by the way, involve both things focused on faith and spirituality (as was the case with *Touched*) and things focused on framing or commenting on religion (for example, in *South Park*, *The Simpsons*, or *The Colbert Report*).

Legacies of Scholarship—and of Protestantism

But how could this shift take place in a country that is so religious, so marked by religion? American social theory has long been committed to a theory of "secularization," whereby religion would gradually fade in influence as levels of education and economic development increase (Berger, 1967). While this theory is no longer widely accepted in its original form and there is a vibrant debate about its need for redefinition (see, for example, Calhoun, Juergensmeyer and Van Antwerpen, 2011 and Gorski, 2017) as a notion it still—in its most brittle form—tends to hold sway, particularly in the fields that constitute media studies. Among many scholars of the media it is unfortunately still thought that religion remains a residual concern of fading interest. The situation was put rather acidly by a leading scholar of religion who also chairs one of the most distinguished religion faculties in the American academy:

> For its part, media studies has happily presumed that religion expired somewhere between the French Revolution and Marxism's dismissal of religion as the opiate of the masses, a largely inert pacifier that was no match for more interesting distractions such as entertainment media. Secularization was supposed to mean that the nasty incursion of religion into public life would be no more and that the secular state, safely insulated from ecclesiastical control, would arise. Disestablishment happened, to be sure, but religion did not go away. There are far fewer practicing Christians in Europe today, but growing numbers of Muslims, Hindus, Sikhs, and Buddhists in London, Birmingham, Amsterdam, Paris, Berlin, and Hamburg. Indebted to Stuart Hall and the Birmingham School of Cultural Studies, media studies still by and large embraces the secularization thesis. You will not find many religion scholars housed in media studies departments. You will need to walk across campus to find them, and they may very likely give you an odd look when you knock on their doors and ask to be admitted to their seminars on Augustine or Paul or the Caliphate or the Babylonian Talmud. However, if you look carefully, you can find a growing number of seminars on "Religion and Media," "Religion in the Public Sphere," "Digital Religion," and the "Material Culture of Religions," where inherently interdisciplinary studies of what Jeremy Stolow (2005: 125) has aptly termed "religion as media" are quietly charting out an encounter of two neighbors who are only just meeting. (Morgan, 2013)

Morgan suggests several signposts significant to my inquiry here. First, that the idea of secularization has been too inartfully applied, particularly in the media studies field. Religion has not "faded" or "gone away," while it has in fact been changing in ways that are consistent with some of the architectures of secularization theory. Yes, social and demographic changes have led to changes in American religion, including the decline in participation in traditional religion. At the same time, though, entirely novel forms of religion expression, interest, and practice do seem to be emerging, many of them expressed and expressable in the media. The binary of "media" and "religion," where the important questions were about the effects on one another, now must be re-thought (Hoover, 2006). Stolow's formulation "religion *as* media" goes a long way to describing what I am talking about here. We need to understand how the media today are the definitive landscape of religious and spiritual exploration, expression, resistance, and struggle.

To interpret this in the American case requires a more complex historiography than a simple account of decline in religion. It is impossible to understand religion in America without understanding Protestantism and the

Protestant legacy (Gorski, 2017). In another work (Hoover, 2017) I have explored how the Protestant project evolved as an effort at implicit governmentality consciously articulated to emerging patterns of media circulation in the American context. This reality, where Protestantism became generically definitive as the cultural and moral center of the culture, is one that both American Catholicism, and American Evangelicalism, both prominent movements articulated to public mediation, are subject.

A vibrant recent scholarship (see, for example, Fessenden, 2008 and Hollinger, 2011) has been aimed at recovering a scholarly purchase on what Digby Balzell (1987) called "The Protestant Establishment." As Balzell described it, there existed at the heart of American culture in the Twentieth Century a tradition of Protestant institutional authority which resided at the center of cultural and state power, but did so implicitly, having positioned itself as the generic center. Its power was expressed through its interconnections with the levers of state, academic, and cultural institutions. But again, it had long since become "tacit" and largely invisible.

Tracey Fessenden (2008), a literary historian, has charted how this was accomplished, and the ways that what we might call "The Protestant Project" came to instrumentalize means of communications in pursuance of its aims. A detailed account of this history is beyond the scope of this chapter, but I'll provide an outline. In Fessenden's and Hollinger's (2011) accounts, Protestantism's transplantation to the American shores coincided with, and was marked by, the essential conflict and contradiction of religion in modernity: the problem of diversity and pluralism. In the earliest days of the republic, the puritan fathers saw the new land as a way of permanently marking a sacred geography (articulated by one of them—and misquoted by Ronald Reagan—as a "city on a hill"). It was to be a beacon to the world and its many religions and cultures. This earliest, more obviously hegemonic, Protestantism began to evolve with the immigration first of other Protestants such as Baptists, Quakers, and Anabaptists and later of Jews and Catholics.

This was of course articulated and codified first in the State Assemblies of the colonies, notably Virginia, and later the U.S. Constitution, as an arrangement that tolerated religious difference and pledged state non-intervention. As Fessenden notes, this was well within the intention and remit of Protestant authorities, who chose to interpret this situation, and their role in it, in a particular way. They were comfortable with any arrangement that it could interpret as its own hegemony over difference and diversity. It thus sought to mark the culture with an implicit Protestant frame.

In later years, this project became even more implicit and generic, Fessenden notes, as Protestantism came to focus its resources on the gendered domestic

sphere, and to do so through publishing (Hoover, 2017). The literatures of
the prodigious 19th Century "cult of domesticity" (DuBois & Dumenil, 2005)
were both deeply Protestant in their orientation to indivdiualism and the disciplines of everyday life, and generically influential on later publishing, including
of secular school readers. In this and in many other ways, the Protestant project
sought to mark the culture with its framings, but to do so tacitly and implicitly
through modern media. Protestantism had long been comfortable with several
features of emerging patterns of the media marketplace across the 19th and 20th
Centuries. First, its traditions of evangelism and circulation had instantiated the
notion, in American culture, that religion was in fact a "marketplace." Its commodities, in the form of books, tracts, and other artifacts bound adherents into
a growing material market. Second, it had long been comfortable with media,
with mediation, and with instrumentalizing media for both religious and secular
ends. Finally, its involvement with the urban evangelism of the 19th and 20th
Centuries had accommodated it to mediatic practices of publicity, promotion,
and—most importantly—sensation (Hoover, 2017).

Historical Roots

It of course goes without saying that Protestantism had coevolved with mediation from the time of the Reformation. Luther was a prodigious and successful pamphleteer and publisher. As Elizabeth Eisenstein noted in her definitive
history of printing (1978), the era also saw the rise of a new economy of
publishing, the earliest stirrings of what we today know as "the media." And
the roiling public discourses and controversies unleashed by the Reformation
provided ready markets. Thus the colonial pulpit was so integrated into the
logics and economies of publishing that it almost made no sense even in that
period to posit religion and media as a binary. Each had its own significance,
though, and that is where my account finds another thread. The emergence
of publishing as a political economy, as an economic activity that could "rest
on its own bottom," as it were, was a significant development. It meant that
in some fundamental sense, publishing was no longer necessarily subject to
the state or to the church, but was its own apparatus. Struggles of course
continue—over clerical and state control of journalism for example—but that
proves the point. Publishing needs to be controlled because it always has the
capacity to be autonomous, and increasingly in the context of neoliberal market globalization, is freed (in a conditional sense). This has of course deepened and broadened in the era of digital media.

Protestant authority has thus existed in an ambiguous and ambivalent relationship to media. The fact that mediation could develop its own autonomies

and its own logics meant that the Protestant project to mark the domestic with specific values and themes through publishing directed at the domestic sphere and women could be taken up autonomously by commercial enterprises. The values with which it aimed to invest the domestic sphere were in many ways more important than religious symbols, doctrines or artifacts. The enforcement of Protestant codes of conduct became the goal. The unique Protestant perspective was that daily life, worklife, the whole of practice in the civil sphere, are direct expressions of and markers of faith. These are explicit to the Protestant mind, traditional markers (signs and symbols that might matter to Catholics, for instance) need not be. For Protestants, faith was not something to be "topped up" on Sunday, but lived in concrete and material disciplines in the everyday. To Protestant leaders, media that articulate to the everyday should then be the object. The fact that they were not explicitly marking the culture with "religion" *per se*, did not mean they were not thus active. Their commitment to cultural hegemony remained, but was expressed in ways that gradually became accepted as generic markers of "American-ness." Thus the commonplace in the television era that the generic American audience was found in the Protestant Midwest (Rosenthal, 2008).

If this account is correct, then we can see some possible sources for the shift I have been talking about. First, this implicit Protestant legacy might be seen in the commonplace, tacit, and accepted ways that media are so integrated into domestic life, and in conditioning the domestic (Spigel, 1992; Johnson, 2008; Hoover, Clark & Alters, 2003). This has been the case since the 19th Century, when the Protestant project of the domestic first saw popular mediation as an important resource for the circulation of values and means of successful living. Second, we can see how, as an implicit and generic project, this focus on the domestic and on the private sphere might have emerged in its particular American forms as a generic task of state governmentality. Niklas Rose's account of state interest in regulation of the private sphere rings very close to the sound of 19th Century marketing of domesticity:

> In the name of social and personal wellbeing, a complex apparatus of health and therapeutics has been assembled, concerned with the management of the individual and social body as a vital national resource, and the management of "problems of living," made up of techniques of advice and guidance, medics, clinics, guides and counselors. (Rose, 1996, 37)

The capacities of mediated guidance to carry authentic moral and normative authority might well be rooted in a residual tacit acceptance that had long conventionalized such practices under a generic Protestant umbrella. That Protestantism long ago blessed the state as an expression of its will (through its interconnections to the state in the "Establishment era" described by

Balzell) could well have made it generally acceptable and generically plausible that so-called "secular" mediations could do that sort of work.

The Politics of Religion in the Public Sphere

This could as well be behind contemporary struggles over religious presence in the public sphere. It has been long and widely known that establishment Protestantism stood at the center of the culture well into the 20th Century. Yes, it exercised its power tacitly and generically, but it also became explicit and manifest at key moments, most notably in those moments framed as the main rituals of American "civil religion" (Bellah, 1992, Gorski 2017). Sessions of Congress, Presidential inagurations, sporting events, and other national moments were marked traditionally by the presence of Protestant clergy. Catholics and Jews were later allowed in, but at the sufferance of Protestant authority. Since the 19th Century, American Presidents have been Protestant—with one notable exception. The Supreme Court used to be dominated by Protestants (there is only one presently serving).

This cultural location for Protestantism, and its ability to mark and frame the culture's values and ideals, is also what lies behind much contemporary political discourse. As the Protestant establishment (in the form of the formerly dominant "mainline" groups) has faded in numbers and influence, others have aspired to achieve the centrality they imagine was the Protestant legacy. But they have chosen to do so in a different way. The two main pretenders are of course American Catholicism and the surging American Evangelical movement.

Each, of course, has a different history in relation to Protestantism and the public sphere. Roman Catholics quite rightly resent their elision in a cultural and political context where their numbers should have justified more of a presence near cultural and state power from the 19th Century onward. For Evangelicals, it is a more tangled history. Their roots, in turn-of-the-20th-Century Fundamentalism, are very much in a direct challenge to a Protestant establishment that they thought of as entirely too generic by the end of the 19th Century. The "social gospel" controversy of that time concerned the trend among mainstream Protestants to use their position of power and influence to social, rather than religious ends (Webb, 1994; Marty, 1991). The result was a fissure, with the Fundamentalist movement wishing to turn the instruments of cultural power amassed by dominant Protestantism toward more explicitly religious ends. The modern Evangelical movement is the product of a century of evolution of that movement into one that, while less marginal and more connected to mainstream culture and cultural values, nonetheless retains the desire to do public Protestantism differently.

Both conservative Catholics and conservative Protestants were jarred by the upheavals in the middle of the 20th Century. The campus, social, and sexual revolutions meant for them that whatever cultural power the establishment had was being squandered if such things were the result. A few signal events then became rallying cries. One of the earliest and most notable was the Supreme Court's 1962 School Prayer decision. It and other changes became important "markers" of the power and influence of religion, and a generic Protestantism was seen as lacking the vision and the power to actually promote such symbolic values and prosecute symbolic battles.

Contemporary political debates over "religious liberty" can then be said to be exactly about this issue. Outsiders tend to be confused by the claim among advocates for "liberty" exceptions in public services and accommodation. Shouldn't "liberty" actually be about opening markets, not closing them based on some religious or moral test? The issue is actually in a different register. For proponents of "liberty" the debate harks back to a narrative of how American Protestantism lost its way. For them, the actual "liberty" is less important than the fact that American culture used to be marked by certain conventions and ethics and values, and no longer seems to be. Cake bakers may never have thought of discriminating against some of their customers until the issue became framed in symbolic terms. And, most significant to my purpose here, this struggle over symbols is a struggle defined and conditioned and circulated by "the media." It is not confined to separated spaces of religious activism and action. It is not really a battle over liberty and exception, but over a desire for the culture to be marked in certain ways.

That "marking of the culture" is fundamentally a Protestant idea, and one that in the American context was long ago seen as powerfully expressed in the ability to reserve to itself generic, tacit authority. That it is now made to be explicit by Hobby Lobby on the Evangelical side and by the Little Sisters of the Poor on the Catholic side, is a sign of change in the nature of cultural geographies and markets. These advocates, though, will not succeed in their task of shifting the culture. The marketplace logics of contemporary media circulation remain the definitive force. Their implicit normative claims to be about individualism, individual flourishing and self-determination, and autonomous action in the private and domestic spheres (fundamentally Protestant ideals) continue to rule the day.

Religiously-distinct advocates such as the Catholic and Evangelical forces I've described will continue to find themselves subject to the same conditions that have long faced religious authority in the media age. They cannot control their own symbols or narratives. They find themselves relativized in a horizontal marketplace of supply. They are subjects to the logics of its mediations. The shift I have been speaking of continues, and there is little that any religious impulse can do about it.

Media Scholarship

That this is all a struggle over symbols and over social and cultural imaginaries (Taylor, 2004; Hoover and Coats, 2015) should long ago have made these relations ripe for culturalist media scholarship. Recent developments in politics, such as the rise of the "Trump phenomenon" in the U.S. and of ethno-nationalism in Europe reveal religion as a lacuna of media theory and research. As my discussion here has shown, religion is necessarily a complex and layered component of modern social and cultural change and stasis. But it is implicated across the whole range of issues traditionally of concern to media scholarship. It can be, at the same time, transparent and interpretable to a media project focused on the nature of symbolic practice (Gross, 1972) through careful analysis.

So why has it been missing? David Morgan, who I quoted earlier, provided a description, not an explanation. I have pondered this myself in the years since my doctoral advisor, Larry Gross, thrust a copy of Peter Berger's *Sacred Canopy* into my hands and urged me to take up a communicational focus on the social and cultural problem of "the religious" in contemporary culture. As I have pursued my research and sometimes struggled to find audiences for my work in my own field, I have come no nearer an answer, though I have my own critique. The efforts in the field have tended to focus first on media as instruments or religion as ideology. Both views rest on a binary of religion and media that is a conceptual dead end in an era when the media have come to occupy so much of the space of religion.

A more promising direction, for many, was laid out in another piece that Larry Gross once pointed me toward, James Carey's classic ritual theory of media (Carey, 2009, see also Hoover, 2017). But Carey remains unsatisfactory for the reason that he so essentialized both the categories of "ritual" and of "religion" that neither could work as a descriptor of contemporary cultural forms. Like many others (McLuhan most notably), he tended to see religion and ritual as hermetic to their fixed locations and conventions, rather than as symbolic capital that would circulate in a system of cultural and media exchange.

The field in general, then, has missed the emergence of new locations and systems of production of "the sacred" in contemporary media. To refer to commonplace Durkheimian categories, religion may have lost its ability to enchant, but enchantment remains possible, and thus a kind of religion persists, in the media. The irony of the case with which I began is that the image of John Paul II was enchanted in ways and to an extent that he may never have anticipated or imagined. This enchantment, though, was constituted by a complex and layered set of histories and relations in the circulations of the media marketplace. Its Protestant roots have framed its plausibility as a location where normative ideals, even religious and spiritual ones, can find a place. That same legacy has infused the marketplace with a logic that focuses on the individual and on sensation and on the normative value of action and relations in those terms. The decline of interest in settled religious authority—Catholic and Protestant—means that the image of the Pope as the leader of the Universal Christian Church with all the trappings of theological and social power that should imply was not the image that was being torn up. Instead, it was a symbol that referenced a long semiotic trail of references but was nonetheless accessible in, and framed by, the media.

References

Balzell, D. (1987). *The protestant establishment: Aristocracy and caste in America*. New Haven: Yale.

Bellah, R. (1992). *The broken covenant: American civil religion in time of trial*. University of Chicago Press.

Berger, P. (1967). *The sacred canopy: Elements of a sociological theory of religion*. New York: Anchor Books.

Calhoun, C., Jeurgensmeyer, M., & van Antwerpen, J. (Eds.). (2011). *Rethinking secularism*. New York: Oxford.

Carey, J. (2009). "A cultural approach to communication." In *Communication as culture* (pp. 11–28). New York: Routledge.

Daily Edge (2017). 25 Years On, here's why Sinead O'Connor deserves praise for ripping up photo of the Pope, Daily Edge online, http://www.dailyedge.ie/sinead-oconnor-pope-3632821-Oct2017/ (accessed October 3, 2017).

DuBois, E. C., & Dumenil, L. (2005). *Through women's eyes: An American history*. Boston: Bedford/St.Martin's.

Eisenstein, E. (1978). *The printing press as an agent of change*. Princeton: Princeton University Press.

Fessenden, T. (2008). Culture and redemption: Religion, the secular, and American literature. Princeton: Princeton University Press.

Gerbner, G. & Gross, L. (1978). *Cultural indicators: A research project on trends in television content and viewer conceptions of social reality*, (unpublished paper), The Annenberg School of Communications. http://web.asc.upenn.edu/gerbner/Asset.aspx?assetID=2597 (accessed October 4, 2017).

Gorski, P. (2017). *American covenant: A review of American civil religion from the Puritans to the present*. Princeton: Princeton University Press.

Gross, L. P. (1972). *Art as the communication of competence*. Paper presented at the Symposium on Communication and the Individual in contemporary Society. Rome.

Hollinger, D. (2013). *After cloven tongues of fire: Protestant liberalism in modern American history*. Princeton: Princeton University Press.

Hoover, S. (Ed.). (2016). *The Media and Religious Authority*. University Park: The Pennsylvania State University Press.

Hoover, S. & Coats, C. (2015). Does God make the man? Media, religion, and the crisis of masculinity. New York: New York University Press.

Hoover, S., Clark, L. S., & Alters, D. (2003). *Media, Home, and Family*. New York: Routledge.

Johnson, V. (2011). *Heartland TV: Prime-time television and the struggle for U.S. identity*. New York: New York University Press.

Marty, M. (1991). *Modern American religion, vol. 1: The irony of it all, 1893–1919*. Chicago: University of Chicago Press.

Morgan, D. (2013). Media and religion: A critical review of recent developments. *Critical Research in Religion, 1*(3), 347–356.

Rosenthal, M. (2008). *American Protestants and TV in the 1950s: Responses to a new medium*. London: Palgrave MacMillan.

Spigel, L. (1992). Make room for TV: Television and the family ideal in postwar America. Chicago: University of Chicago Press.

Jeremy, S. (2005). Religion and/as media. *Theory, Culture & Society 22*(4), 119–145.

Taylor, C. (2004). *Modern social imaginaries*. Durham: Duke University Press.

Webb, G. (1994). *The Evolution Controversy in America*. Knoxville: The University Press of Kentucky.

8. The 'Thing' About Music: Hearing Power at the Nexus of Technology, Property, and Culture[1]

ARAM SINNREICH

One of the more pernicious myths of our times is that music is a *thing*. This assertion, though easy enough to refute, is reinforced regularly by a broad variety of interests that are invested, for an equally broad variety of reasons, on insisting upon its thing-ness.

The most obvious example is the role of music as a commodity in the contemporary "music industry."[2] Producers, printers, recorders, sellers, licensors and distributors of musical scores and records have a longstanding economic interest in the thing-ness of music for the obvious reason that a thing can be manufactured, bought and sold. Of course, in order to achieve these economic ends, a social intervention is first required: A bait-and-switch operation in which the commodity is effectively substituted for the ineffable and very non-thinglike thing it commodifies, thus transforming the nebulous *participants* in the musical process into starkly opposed *producers* (those within the music industry's castle walls) and *consumers* (the vast majority of us who now find ourselves locked outside).

This process, in turn, requires that we justify the erection of such walls through the normalization of the concept that music is a *special* aspect of human culture, divorced from its other, more mundane aspects (e.g. eating lunch, taking a shower); that musicians are a *special* type of human uniquely suited to the task of producing these artifacts; and that the results of their labors are *scarce* and therefore *valuable*. This logic is so everpresent in contemporary society as to be invisible; consider pop music superstar Taylor Swift's 2014 op-ed in the *Wall Street Journal* (!), in which she opines that "Music is art, and art is important and rare. Important, rare things are valuable." Could there be a more straightforward, self-assured, self-interested summary of the reasoning behind music's commodification?

Larry Gross (1995) describes this sequestering of sanctioned cultural production in terms of art's banishment to a cultural "reservation," and argues compellingly that there is a direct causal link between our cultural understanding of art and artistry as a thing apart, and the economic (and political) ends this concept serves. In his words, it is "important to understand that the ideology of talent and individuality as the passport to the reservation is congruent with the institutional structure of the official, elite art worlds." (p. 14). Thus, the thing-ness of music may serve effectively as the foundation of a venerable multibillion dollar industry, but it does so at the cost of separating us from ourselves and from one another socially and culturally on a fundamental level.

Another set of stakeholders for whom music's thing-ness serves an important function are technologists, or, more specifically, those who benefit economically from the research, development and diffusion of new communication technologies. While these interests are often aligned with the "music industry" stakeholders discussed above, their agendas are separate enough to come into frequent conflict (as a brief glimpse at jurisprudential history will show), and the nature of music's thing-ness within this field is less related to its role as a *market commodity* and more related to its (equally arbitrary and historically determined) role as a *sociotechnical artifact*.

In point of fact, music—precisely because of its ubiquity and centrality in human culture—is often used as a test case for new communication technologies, or as a lure to bring new enterprises and customers to those platforms. Music is the original "killer app" that validates a communication technology, and, in so doing, reifies itself as a commodity to be transacted via that communication platform. This was true of print (where music publishing predated the rationalization and bureaucratization of Western society by a few centuries), radio (where music programming was a primary element in the industrialization and networking of the industry, following a robust period of peer-to-peer over-the-air communications), sound recording (where music soon superseded Edison's chief ambitions for the new technology, such as letter dictation, audiobooks and elocutionary instruction), and contemporary digital technologies ranging from the personal computer to the worldwide web to the smartphone. Even technologies with explicitly different purposes are often adapted to suit this end; for instance YouTube, which was originally launched as a platform for user-generated video (an original tagline for the service was "Broadcast Yourself"), is now one of the primary distribution channels for major label music; at the time of writing, 23 of the 25 most-viewed works on the service are commercial music videos (Pardee & Hubby, 2017).

Furthermore, the thing-ness of music is a central facet of the design and development of new communication technologies. Just as the commodification of this ineffable aspect of the human condition required that we swap what James Carey (2009) would call its "ritual" aspects for more transmissive ones, the development of formats and standards for the capture, editing, storage, transmission, and reception of music requires that we foreground certain aspects of it while ignoring or downplaying others. As Jonathan Sterne (2012) argues in his groundbreaking work on "format theory," the psychoacoustic modeling involved in creating the MP3 standard privileged certain types of listeners, and certain modes of listening, over others. More broadly, any technical intervention in musical culture requires a narrower definition of music than cultural history would suggest, and music often becomes a synecdoche for its method of containment or representation; thus, in a peer-to-peer file sharing network like Napster or BitTorrent, music is conceptualized as a "file," whereas in the context of print publishing, it is referred to as a "composition."

Finally, even the cultural analysis and critique of music can serve to reinforce its thing-ness. This is evident in the Cultural Studies tradition, for example, in which music (like other forms of cultural expression) is often treated merely as an empty and arbitrary signifier of political forces and social positions. In Stuart Hall's (in)famous formulation, popular culture "is the arena of consent and resistance … otherwise, to tell you the truth, I don't give a damn about it" (1988, p. 453). For those of us who both study cultural processes and *do* give a damn about music (even the popular kind), this last reification is the hardest to swallow. In this formulation, music is no more than a lifeless artifact, like a ventriloquist's dummy, sitting on a shelf waiting to be animated by the self-interested and manipulative efforts of some third party. Along similar lines, social and political movements frequently attempt to dragoon music into serving their symbolic bidding; consider Ronald Reagan's jingoistic use of Bruce Springsteen's "Born in the U.S.A." or Donald Trump's similar treatment of Neil Young's "Keep on Rockin' in the Free World," a generation later. In these cases, the songs aren't merely being exploited to speak to political agendas in polar opposition to the intended meanings of their authors, they are being reduced to sonic taglines for the granddaddy of empty signifiers, the brand of America itself.

Of course, despite these many pressures, there are alternatives to the doctrine of musical thing-ness, both inside and outside the world of cultural scholarship. In recent years, scholars across a dizzying array of disciplines seem to have discovered Christoper Small's 1998 book *Musicking: The meanings of performing and listening*, with about half of the book's roughly 2,500 citations occurring in the past four years, according to Google Scholar's current tally. Small's work is notable for a variety of reasons, chief of which is that he provides a new discursive lexicon for discussing music beyond its commercial, technological or symbolic role as a thing. Rather, Small emphasizes that music exists only as a situated practice, or set of practices, within the context of a broader set of social relations and cultural meanings. In his words, "to music is to take part, in any capacity, in a musical performance, whether by performing, by listening, by rehearsing or practicing, by providing material … or by dancing." (p. 9). Any ethnographic or humanistic exploration of musical cultures, anywhere in the world, will yield data that support this definition; despite the many reductive and reifying pressures placed upon music, it continues to swell beyond the boundaries imposed upon it from without, requiring industries, technologists, and researchers alike to adjust their expectations and practices accordingly. The fact that Small's book, and the perspective it embodies, have risen so drastically in prominence just as the market dominance of the MP3, embodied by Apple's iTunes Music Store, has begun to wane in favor of more fluid, less thing-y "streaming" models of music distribution, is one recent example of this complex dance.

The dialectical relationship between the thing-ifying capacities of markets, technologies and social ideation, and the musical aesthetics and practices they enable and constrain, is the subject matter of this chapter. In the pages that follow, I will elucidate what I believe are some of the key moments and turns in the cultural history of Western music, by tracing the coevolution of musical style with cultural notions of authorship, modes of production, and the legal regulatory framework surrounding music industries—specifically, transformations in the contours of copyright law, and in what are sometimes referred to as the "ethics of copying." Although the history explored briefly here is far from comprehensive, it does illuminate some compelling instances of the push-and-pull between thing-ness and musicking, and, more importantly, the "dance" is an aesthetically fascinating phenomenon in its own right.

A good place to begin our exploration is in the cultural moment that gave rise to the notion of music-as-a-thing. Although there were celebrated composers prior to the Renaissance, they tended to be either church musicians (such as Hildegard von Bingen and Petrus de Cruce) or court musicians and troubadours (such as Adam de la Halle and Guiraut Riquier). Like pre-Renaissance painters, these early musicians served a primarily functionary role, facilitating and commemorating religious and political events rather than expressing their individual perspectives apart from these functions. In other words, there was no meaningful distinction between musicking and the cultural practices in which the music was enmeshed.

This began to change with the rise of Ars Nova in the early 14th Century, "the first full manifestation of a pure musical art, freed from the service of religion or poetry and constructed according to its own laws." (Abraham, 1979; p. 72). With this liberation from institutional constraints, new Renaissance notions of individual authorship began to be applied to musical composition just as they were to painting and sculpture in the same era. This philosophical change bore aesthetic fruit; in some cultures, such as France, "mannerist" secular music began to outstrip religious music in complexity and sophistication by the turn of the 15th Century.

With the widespread adoption of the printing press in the 16th Century, European music began to see a formal division of labor between the creative, intellectual work of composing and the more mundane, physical work of performing—an articulation that, to this day, both reflects and naturalizes the social hierarchies inherent in the wealth and power gap between what today we refer to as "white collar" and "blue collar" labor. This helped to set composers—and their compositions—apart from the immediate circumstances of performance, and to spread their names and works broadly for the first time. The following century saw the birth of opera, the first musical form underwritten by bourgeois ticket-buyers in addition to wealthy court and church patrons. These two developments helped to accelerate the widespread demand for printed scores, laying the industrial and cultural foundations for popular music, and creating a marketplace primed for the introduction of copyright.

In the 17th and 18th Centuries, the Baroque and Classical eras were virtually defined by their "great" composers, who produced much of the music that we still venerate today. This was the epoch of J. S. Bach, Handel, Haydn, and Mozart. Although these composers were, and still are, revered for their ingenuity and originality, they also routinely engaged in the kind of creative "borrowing" that would today be considered grounds for a copyright infringement suit. According to the *Oxford History of Western Music*, "Every church and theater composer indulged in the practice," especially Handel, who copied "both his own works and those of other composers in unprecedented numbers and with unprecedented exactness," even recycling old material for two choruses of his best-known work, "Messiah." (Taruskin, 2009; p. 327).

Indeed, it's hard to find any composers in the Western classical tradition who did not make similar borrowings, even for their most celebrated compositions. In Mozart's "The Magic Flute," Papageno's signature song is lifted note-for-note from an aria written by his Viennese contemporaries for "The Beneficent Dervish," an opera whose libretto was even based on the same source material as Mozart's (Baer, 2002). Mozart himself was frequently copied by Beethoven, who used a series of arpeggios from "Don Giovanni" as a harmonic and rhythmic scaffolding for his beloved "Moonlight Sonata" (Tsur, 2000), and who lifted a theme from "Misericordias Domini" to form the central melody in his "Ode to Joy" (Hinton, 1998).

Although music historians today debate the degree to which these borrowings were considered ethical or plagiaristic by musicians and audiences at the time, they were clearly well within the scope of normal creative and commercial practice. This was partly because musical works didn't have the same aura of sacrosanctity and finality that they would acquire a few decades later, with Romantic notions of genius and authorship and the formalization of Gross' artistic "reservation;" for instance, it was common at the time for publishers to edit or "fix" the works of even the most celebrated composers before printing and selling their scores. (Sinnreich, 2010). But it was also due to the fact that there was no copyright yet for musical works, and thus neither the proprietary philosophy that justifies intellectual property (IP) nor the legal means or financial incentive to prosecute borrowings in court. The price of overstepping the line between influence and theft was reputational: a composer who borrowed too much "frequently drew sharp censure" from his peers (Roberts, 1987; p. 149).

Musical scores were granted copyright coverage decades before other "fine arts" like painting—probably because they were, like books and engravings, printed on presses by publishers, and because there was already an economic and political model for IP rights based on these analogous (and, to a certain degree, co-controlled) print industries. Although there had been a few very early examples of musical composers receiving monopoly rights for the publication of their own work, such as lutist Guillaume Morlaye's 10-year license from Henri II in 1552 (Annala & Matlik, 2010), comprehensive copyright coverage didn't apply to printed musical scores until 1777 in Britain,[3] 1793 in France, and 1831 in the United States.

It is no coincidence that copyright for printed scores emerged at the same cultural moment as musical Romanticism, characterized by an "emphasis on individuality and peculiarity, which became over the course of the nineteenth century an ever more pressing demand for originality." (Taruskin, p. 15). These two emergences did not occur contemporaneously merely because intellectual property and individualistic art share a common *philosophical* foundation, or because of some vague European zeitgeist (though it certainly played a role). Rather, with the ability to litigate, concerns about plagiarism became concerns about infringement, creating a *financial incentive* for composers to effectively distinguish their work from one another's. On the one hand, this is exactly the theoretical purpose underlying most modern copyright law—inspiring artists to create and share innovative work with the public. On the other hand, these new legal mechanisms upended centuries of established creative practice based on copying, which had given the world the innovative works of Handel, Mozart and Beethoven, among countless others.

Of course, musical composers in the copyright era didn't simply stop appropriating other people's work once these laws were passed—they just switched the focus of their appropriation from contemporary Western composers to non-copyrighted sources, such as Eastern and "folk" traditions. For the first hundred years of musical copyright, European and American composers exhibited a growing fascination with Eastern music, integrating melodies, rhythms and even instruments from a variety of Asian traditions into their work. Examples of this "orientalism" run the gamut from Mozart's 1782 opera "Die Entführung aus dem Serail" to Camille Saint-Saëns' "Samson et Dalila" a century later.

During this same period of time, Western composers also became increasingly interested in mining the public domain (technically, the remainder of the cultural archive unclaimed by copyright owners) for new material, integrating the ubiquitous, authorless, ownerless melodies from their local and national traditions into their own work. Sometimes, multiple composers would even recycle the same material, as when Beethoven and Mussorgsky both used the song "Slava" (published in a 1790 folk song anthology) for the "Razumovsky" string quartets (1806) and "Boris Godunov" (1868–73), respectively.

There are many reasons that Western composers chose to begin appropriating Asian and folk musics in the late 18th and 19th Centuries that have nothing to do with copyright or intellectual property. This was an era marked by expanding trade and conquest abroad, growing nationalism in Europe, and the development of a globalized culture, accelerated by new electronic communications networks in the form of first telegraphy and then telephony. In this context, it makes sense that Western artists and audiences would be interested in telling stories about, and reconciling their art with, the Eastern cultures and modes of expression with which they were confronted. Likewise, it makes sense that newly-unifying nations like Germany and Italy would look to folklore for some sense of national identity rooted in the premise of a common heritage. Whether these depictions of "Oriental" and "folk" were accurate—or even respectful—is almost beside the point; they were the musical manifestations of popular narratives, repeated and shared for purposes related to tectonic changes in the European sociocultural landscape at the time.

And yet, we cannot ignore the power dynamics inherent in intellectual property law, nor discount the role of copyright in inspiring and supporting these stylistic shifts. Just as the new democracies and republics of the modern era offered citizenship and enfranchisement to some while leaving others without rights or representation, the advent of copyright provided *protection to a privileged group of creators while simultaneously giving them free rein to appropriate from others.* To the classical composers of the 19th century, these unprotected works were simply a natural resource waiting to be extracted, like iron ore or coal. As Robert Schumann, a leading composer and musical scholar of the era, advised his peers and readers, "listen attentively to all folk songs. They are mines of the most beautiful melodies" (Schumann, 1946; p. 35).

This double standard became visible only in those rare instances in which it was violated. A classic example is George Bizet's 1875 opera "Carmen," for which the composer borrowed what he believed was a Spanish folksong in composing the melody of the "Habanera," one of the opera's signature arias and an instant international sensation. There was no shame in this; early printed copies of the score acknowledged frankly that the melody was "imitated from a Spanish song."

Yet it turned out that the melody wasn't a folksong at all—it was copyrighted in 1863 as "El Arreglito" by a contemporary Spanish composer named Sebastián Yradier. This revelation sparked years of international litigation and legal debate, further complicated when the Berne Convention copyright treaty—the first of its kind—was signed a decade later. Ironically, the legal wrangling was all undertaken by those with commercial interests in the sale of the sheet music, rather than by the composers themselves. Both had already passed away—Yriadier in 1865, and Bizet in 1875, a few months after the opera's premiere.

A final kink in this story: although he published and copyrighted the tune first, it is likely that Yradier himself was not its composer either. Prior to writing "El Arreglito," he had traveled from his native Spain to Latin America and "collected" the melodies he heard there for future use in creating "pseudo-folk" compositions with a Spanish flavor (McClary, 1992). Had Bizet done the same, going straight to the source rather than appropriating an appropriation, there would have been no lawsuit and no outcry. The original source of Yradier's musical inspiration has never been credited or compensated, nor was there any call for it.

Despite the "Carmen" imbroglio and the shifting ethics and aesthetics of appropriation, musical copyright in the 1800s typically wasn't used to police "borrowings" by one composer from another, but rather to prevent one publisher from selling wholesale copies of a song controlled by another. In the U.S., in fact, there appears to be only one case during the entire 19th Century[4] in which one song was found to infringe on another based on substantial similarity—and both songs in this case were essentially variations of the public domain tune "O Danny Boy."

This dynamic changed in the 20th Century, a far more litigious period in which the economic stakes grew considerably with the advent of the musical recording and broadcasting industries, as well as the revisions to copyright that both anticipated and reflected these technological and economic developments. During the early part of the century, there was a virtual gold rush among composers and publishers to lay ownership claim to melodies both old and new.

The epicenter of this frenzy in America was the popular music industry, exemplified by the publishing powerhouses of Tin Pan Alley, and the booming market for what was then called "race music"—African American styles such as blues, jazz and ragtime. Savvy composers of the time, such as W. C. Handy, Jelly Roll Morton, and George M. Cohan, published and copyrighted hundreds of songs, many of them minimally differentiated from the public domain material their work was drawn from, and others more or less lifted directly from less-savvy composers who lacked the expertise or means to file for copyright themselves.

By midcentury, copyright infringement cases were so common in the music industry that several prominent law firms specialized in this subfield. Although the vast majority of suits (as always) were settled privately, the number of judicial decisions increased drastically, from 15 in the first full century following the creation of American musical copyright to 30 in the next *quarter* century. After the creation of the phonographic "master" copyright in 1972 and the significant extensions to copyright coverage and power in the 1976 revision to the law, litigation went into overdrive: between 1975–2000, there were 56 judicial opinions on music copyright cases, many of them setting the bar for infringement lower and lower. One well-known example is *Bright Tunes Music v. Harrisongs Music*,[5] the infamous 1976 suit in which ex-Beatle George Harrison was found by a federal judge to have "subconsciously" plagiarized "He's So Fine," a song made famous a decade earlier by girl group The Chiffons, in his solo hit "My Sweet Lord."

Yet even as music copyright was becoming stronger, more assiduously policed, and consequentially more influential in shaping and constraining the sound of commercial music, composers and performers pushed back increasingly against these constraints. While visual artists like Hannah Höch, Pablo

Picasso and Marcel Duchamp were experimenting with new techniques like collage and readymades that undermined the philosophical foundations of authorship (and by extension, challenging the legitimacy of intellectual property), musical artists in both the U.S. and Europe began to apply similar principles to their own work.

In the years after World War II, innovators like John Cage, Pierre Schaeffer and Pierre Henry used the recording and copying capacities of newly-developed magnetic tape to develop *musique concrète*, a kind of sonic collage, while they and others experimented with chance-based, or "aleatory" composition, in which randomly-generated numbers are used to determine pitch, rhythm, and other aspects of the music. As with their painter and sculptor peers, these composers didn't typically risk facing a copyright infringement suit, but their work still served to highlight some of the central tensions surrounding the role of IP in their creative and commercial environment, by poking holes in the legal, technological and cultural constraints imposing thing-ness on musicking.

A generation later, the cutting-and-pasting techniques used in *musique concrète* began to filter into popular music. Early examples included The Beatles' self-consciously avant-garde "Revolution 9," and the brilliant, postcolonial experimentalism of Jamaican dub reggae innovators like Lee "Scratch" Perry and King Tubby. Yet these techniques remained somewhat arcane curiosities for most artists and audiences until the late 1970s, when a Jamaican-born DJ named Kool Herc based in the Bronx began to integrate these aesthetics into his live performances, building the musical foundations for what would soon come to be called hip-hop.

Within a decade, hip-hop had become a major musical force in American media culture and around the world. Innovative DJs and producers in this field soon expanded beyond turntable-based scratching and beat juggling, exploiting new technologies like the Roland TR-808 drum machine (released in 1980) and the Akai MPC series of digital audio samplers (released in 1988) to create dense, complex tapestries of sound, merging both recognizable and unrecognizable snippets of song, speech and industrial noise with sequenced beats and synthesized tones. Many artists, critics, and scholars hailed hip-hop both as a challenge to established, Eurocentric pop music aesthetics and as a slap in the face of the regimented, cartelized industry that promoted them—celebrating the new aesthetic as a promising avenue of liberation from thing-ness.

At first, as with visual collage, most hip-hop DJs weren't intentionally confronting copyright so much as ignoring it altogether. As Hank Shocklee, a founding member of the pioneering group Public Enemy, explained in an interview, "At the time, it wasn't even an issue. ... The copyright laws didn't really extend into sampling until the hip-hop artists started getting sued" (McLeod, 2004).

This was technically true; with neither legislation nor case law addressing the matter, music sampling existed in a legal gray area between fair use and infringement. Yet after two prominent hip-hop artists—Biz Markie and De La Soul—lost infringement suits for sampling in 1991, industry practice changed entirely, and every sample had to be pre-cleared and licensed from whichever label owned the rights to the source material. This had two significant effects. First, it consolidated this radical, independent new art form within the existing cartels; for the most part, major labels would only clear samples for and from other major labels, and at the rates they charged (thousands of dollars or more per sample), no one else could afford to use them. Second, it changed the music. As Public Enemy's Chuck D explained,

> Public Enemy's music was affected more than anybody's because we were taking thousands of sounds. If you separated the sounds, they wouldn't have been anything—they were unrecognizable. The sounds were all collaged together to make a sonic wall. Public Enemy was affected because it is too expensive to defend against a claim. So we had to change our whole style. (McLeod, 2004)

This wasn't merely a stylistic change. The inability to create sonic collage on the same scale and with the same freedom as before blunted the political and cultural bite of the entire genre. It profoundly changed the ways in which hip-hop was *musicked*. In Shocklee's words, "If you notice that by the early 1990s, the sound has gotten a lot softer" (McLeod, 2004). Music critics and historians have acknowledged this fact, as well; in the 2010s, this bygone era of uninhibited sampling in the 1980s and early 1990s is often referred to nostalgically as the "golden age of hip-hop," and spoken of with the same nostalgia and reverence that film historians use to describe cinema before the censorious constraints of the Hays Code were imposed.

The 1991 ruling against Biz Markie, in which Judge Kevin Duffy directly cited the 10 Commandments ("thou shalt not steal") as an "admonition followed since the dawn of civilization,"[6] effectively chilled "fair use" claims for sampling, shutting down any legal recognition of the right of samplers to transform copyrighted recorded material by constructing a false cultural narrative that privileged the myth of creation *ex nihilo* over the historical fact that musical creativity has always involved a degree of creative borrowing. A decade later, the decision in the *Bridgeport v. Dimension*[7] case against "gangsta" rap group N.W.A. established that *de minimis* claims (a legal precept holding that some uses of copyright material are so minor or negligible as to fall beneath the bar for infringement) could not even be made in the case of brief, unrecognizable samples. Today, though hip-hop is still a lucrative global market, the blunting of its force as a commercial and global vector for dissent, critique and innovation[8] has been lamented at least since Nas proclaimed in 2006 (the year following the *Bridgeport* ruling) that "Hip Hop Is Dead." This claim is, of course, debatable, and there are several reasons to believe that the genre may yet have some life in it.

First of all, in the late 2010s, some of the most popular and successful new hip-hop artists, such as Kendrick Lamar and Run The Jewels, use backing tracks that harken back to the dense, collagist soundscapes of De La Soul and Public Enemy (unfortunately, Lamar has also been sued for infringement for uncleared samples). Second, although sampling remains unaddressed in copyright legislation, there is evidence that today's courts, populated by many judges and clerks who have a cultural relationship to hip-hop, may be more sympathetic to fair use and *de minimis* claims than their predecessors in the previous generation.

In 2014, for instance, rapper and impresario Jay-Z successfully defended an infringement case for his song "Run this Town," which used a one-syllable sample from "Hook and Sling, Pts. 1 & 2," a 1969 funk hit by Eddie Bo. In his memorandum dismissing the suit, Judge Lewis A. Kaplan argued that the plaintiffs had "not stated a plausible claim" because the sample had "essentially no quantitative significance" to the original work, and because the complaint had "improperly conflate[d] factual copying and actual copying."[9] Thankfully, when it comes to hip-hop, today's judiciary exhibits a level of cultural and legal sophistication that far outstrips "thou shalt not steal."

As this brief history indicates, musicians have always "borrowed" from one another, from Bach to Bizet to Biz Markie. Copying is an essential element of musicking, and, by the same token, we can understand historical constraints on these practices as attempts to impose thing-ness upon music by institutional interests with commercial, technological or sociopolitical agendas. Yet the story is more than a Manichean battle between the forces of musical liberation and repression; rather, the push-and-pull between regulation and resistance is itself an engine of innovation. Without the looming threat of copyright infringement, would Western composers have invested as fully in Orientalism? Without the cartelization of sampling permissions, would hip-hop's underground, and the "mixtape culture" that characterizes it, have grown as influential or as prevalent? In short, the shape of our musical culture today is the result of centuries of battles, negotiations, and accommodations, an elaborate and ongoing dance between the thing-ifying pressures of markets, technologies and ideologies on one side, and the human drive to music on the other.

Notes

1. This chapter was adapted in part from my forthcoming, as yet untitled, book on intellectual property from Yale Press.
2. As Williamson and Cloonan (2007) have aptly argued, a more appropriate term given the diversity of economic and political interests at stake would be the plural "music industries."
3. This coverage was based on the landmark court case *Bach v. Longman*. Statutory coverage for music didn't exist in Britain until 1842.
4. Blume v. Spear 30 F. 629 (C.C.S.D.N.Y. 1887)
5. Bright Tunes Music v. Harrisongs Music 420 F. Supp. 177 (S.D.N.Y. 1976)
6. Grand Upright v. Warner 780 F. Supp. 182 (S.D.N.Y. 1991)
7. Bridgeport Music v. Dimension Films, et al. 410 F. 3d 792 (6th Cir. 2005)
8. "Underground" and non-commercial sample-based music, such as mixtapes and mashups, have very different standards and aesthetics, for a variety of reasons that are fascinating but beyond the scope of this chapter. For more information, see Sinnreich, 2010.
9. TufAmerica, Inc. v. Warner Bros. Music Corp., et al. 67 F. Supp. 3d 590 (S.D.N.Y. 2014)

References

Abraham, G. (1979). *The concise Oxford history of music*. Oxford: Oxford University Press.

Annala, H., & Matlik, H. (2010). *Handbook of guitar and lute composers*. Pacific, MO: Mel Bay Publications.

Baer, A. (2002, Feb 13). Wolfgang Amadeus Copycat: Did Mozart plagiarize? *Slate*. Retrieved from http://www.slate.com/articles/arts/culturebox/2002/02/wolfgang_amadeus_copycat.html

Carey, J. (2009). *Communication as Culture*. London: Routledge.

Gross, L. (1995). Art and artists on the margins. In L. Gross (Ed.), *On the margins of art worlds* (pp. 1–16). Boulder, CO: Westview Press.

Hall, S. (1988). Notes on deconstructing 'the popular.' In J. Storey (Ed.), *Cultural theory & popular culture: A reader* (2nd Edition). Athens, GA: Universty of Georgia Press.

Hinton, S. (1998). Not 'which' tones? The crux of Beethoven's Ninth. *19th-Century Music, 22*(1), 61–77.

McClary, S. (1992). *Georges Bizet: Carmen*. Cambridge: Cambridge University Press.

McLeod, K. (2004, May 31). How copyright law changed hip hop. *AlterNet*. Retrieved from: http://www.alternet.org/story/18830/how_copyright_law_changed_hip_hop/

Pardee, G., & Hubby, K. (2017, Aug 25). The 25 most popular YouTube videos of all time. Retrieved on September 14, 2017, from: https://www.dailydot.com/upstream/most-viewed-youtube-videos/

Roberts, J. H. (1987). Handel and Vinci's 'Didone Abbandonata': Revisions and borrowings. *Music & Letters, 68*(2), 141–150.

Schumann, R. (1946). *On music and musicians* (K. Wolff, Trans.). Berkeley: University of California Press.

Sinnreich, A. (2010). *Mashed up: Music, technology and the rise of configurable culture.* Amherst, MA: University of Massachusetts Press.

Small, C. (1998). *Musicking: The meanings of performing and listening.* Middletown, CT: Wesleyan.

Sterne, J. (2012). *MP3: The meaning of a format.* Durham: Duke University Press Books.

Swift, T. (2014, July 7). For Taylor Swift, the future of music is a love story. *Wall Street Journal.* Retrieved from http://www.wsj.com/articles/for-taylor-swift-the-future-of-music-is-a-love-story-1404763219

Taruskin, R. (2009). *The Oxford history of Western music, vol. 2.* New York: Oxford University Press.

Tsur, R. (2000, Jan 11). Metaphor and figure-ground relationship: Comparisons from poetry, music, and the visual arts. *PsyArt: An Online Journal for the Psychological Study of the Arts.* Retrieved from http://psyartjournal.com/article/show/tsur-metaphor_and_figure_ground_relationship_

Williamson, J., & Cloonan, M. (2007). Rethinking the music industry. *Popular Music, 26*(2), 305–322.

9. *The Emotional Politics of Populism, in Honor of Larry Gross*

Eva Illouz

One of the most enduring and pervasive clichés of political philosophy and journalistic discourse, is that enlightened politics and emotions are antithetical. One example among endless possibilities is provided by a recent *New York Times* comment about Trump: "Because of his victories in the Republican primary and then the general election, his campaign was hailed for its tactical genius. But it was driven by, and tailored to, his emotional cravings. All that time on Twitter wasn't principally about a direct connection to voters. It was a way to stare at an odometer of approval and monitor, in real time, how broadly his sentiments were being liked and shared" (Bruni, 2017). Here "emotions" are all the more vile that they are 'cravings,' as if the Churchills or Roosevelts of this world did not have emotional cravings or as if the search for justice itself were not an emotional craving. In common political parlance, "emotions" is a code word which stands for a rhetoric devoid of content which unites voters and their leaders through what is "base" and "primitive" in them.

There are compelling reasons for the normative argument against mixing emotions in politics. Political life is a public entity, emotions are private. Politics is about the collective good and rational consensus building; emotions are irrational, even self-destructive. Politics is the art of crafting self-interest, of lying, and winning. Emotions are the expressive, true, authentic part of the self, not the strategic one. Politics is displayed in public spaces and is a public performance while emotions are the silent way we have to share the world with ourselves, sometimes consciously, sometimes unconsciously. Where politics concerns the planned engineering of society for the well-being of a collective body, emotions are non-reflexive, spontaneous, private, known only by the individual. Emotions express a raw, immediate response to the world, while politics attempts to appeal to virtues and ideals.

The contrast between the two concepts is all the more striking that the public philosophy of liberalism is fundamentally based on the assumption of a double rationality: citizens usually choose leaders according to their best interests and the public sphere is the site of deliberation and debate (see Habermas, 1991; Ackerman, 1980). In its most naïve version, the liberal public sphere enables free circulation of ideas, debate with truth prevailing, and the smooth competition of various interests reconciled through fair procedures. For these reasons, emotions seem at best antithetical with politics and at worst a corruption of the democratic political process.

The systematic rejection of emotions from the political process has contributed to obscure and render unintelligible the nature of what we call the electoral process, in voters' stubborn loyalty to what Arlie Hochshild dubs "deep stories." In her recent book *Strangers in their own Land*, Hochschild (2016) addresses a question frequently asked by liberals: why do people (seemingly) vote against their interests? Her response is straightforward: to satisfy emotional needs. For Hochschild, both conservatives and liberals hold on to "deep stories" about who they are and which values they believe in. Deep stories don't have to be true; but they have to *feel* true. What makes them feel true is precisely the fact they capture and give a form to a variety of dominant emotions: anxiety, hope, disappointment, pride. In an in-depth ethnographic study of white working-class heterosexual people in Louisania, Hochschild suggests that for them, the American Dream did not work and that this social experience shaped the plausibility of the stories they tell to explain their life situations and their prospect.

Emotions not only inhere in the political process but cannot be expunged from it, which in turn means that to think about democracy is also to think about the kind of emotions that ought to be encouraged and present in the political arena. If we want to understand populism we must give up the dichotomy between high/rational and low/emotional politics. The point is not to contrast a rational to an emotional politics but to recognize two different emotional politics.

Emotions and Rationality

Far from being antithetical to rationality, emotions are often conducive to it. Famous research by the neuropsychologist António Damásio in a book that is already more than 2 decades old, *Descartes' Error* (Damásio, 1994) has showed that the deliberative rationality involved in decision-making must be rooted in emotions because only through emotions can one form an enduring and valenced attitude toward an object. That is, only through emotions can we hierarchize our preferences and figure out what is most urgent and most important. And it would seem that this would be crucial for the process for example of voting or forming a political attitude. Were voters entirely rational, they would have difficulties prioritizing their preferences: between foreign or domestic issues, between economics or values. To refer again to Antonio Damasio's study, a perfectly rational citizen would list attributes of each one of their candidates and then they would try to figure out according to the long list of attributes without a sense of the set of issues which s/he privileges. Thus the point here is not to figure out our well–understood interest but rather to be able to identify the set of core emotional issues that matter to us as social agents who think morally and imaginatively. Arlie Hochschild's *Strangers in their Own Land* suggests just that, namely that people vote according to some deep stories that organizes their social experience into stories shaped by some consistent set of emotions. Far from expressing a primitive part of the self, emotions organize one's social experience in a way that makes sense of one's position in a structured network of relationships. These emotions become enduring when they are encoded in stories (e.g., "corporations plundered the earth" or "gay marriage will destroy our families.")

Emotions are essentially eudaimonic, that is, they express one's point of view on the world from the standpoint of one's goals, values, and conceptions of the good life (Nussbaum, 2003). My grief, joy, or anger are all about my position in the world and about what is good for me in that world. "Emotions look at the world from the subject's own viewpoint, mapping events on to the subject's own sense of personal importance or value" (p. 33). Class resentment for example typically translates a complex set of emotions such as economic threat, fear of downward mobility and envy of other groups perceived to be successful. Social experiences are compacted into emotions that are translated and organized in deep stories.

If emotions can help us sort out and hierarchize our preferences and formulate some deep stories about who we are, voting according to family values is no less rational than voting according the economic interest. Liberal elites, steeped as they are in strategic thinking never fail to puzzle over the working classes' inability to think of their class and economic interests. Yet "family values" make perfect sense for voters for whom self-worth is more likely to derive from their ability to have and maintain a family than from their paycheck or managerial skills.

As another example of the role of emotion in the political process, we may evoke the case of anger in popular insurrections. The young Tunisian Mouhamed Bouazizi who set himself ablaze in Tunisia after a policeman wanted to close down his vending cart in the street set off a chain reaction of emotions and ultimately a popular insurrection. That chain reaction was acctivated by emotional identification, not by enlightened opinion. Commenting on the event a journalist in the *Guardian* suggested that:

> Watching events in Tunisia over the past few days, I have been increasingly reminded of an event in 1989: The fall of the Romanian dictator, Nicolae Ceausescu. Is the Tunisian dictator, Zine El Abidine Ben Ali, about to meet a similar fate?
>
> After 22 years in power, Ceausescu's end came suddenly and somewhat unexpectedly. It began when the government harassed an ethnic Hungarian priest over something he had said. Demonstrations broke out but the priest was soon forgotten: they rapidly turned into generalized protests against the Ceausescu regime (…) Twenty-six-year-old Mohamed Bouazizi, living in the provincial town of Sidi Bouzid, had a university degree but no work. To earn some money he took to selling fruit and vegetables in the street without a license. When the authorities stopped him and confiscated his produce, he was so angry that he set himself on fire. (Whitaker, 2010)

In all of the examples above, emotions are part and parcel of the political process, but they are made invisible, because they precede outcomes which liberals define as rational: the capacity to hierarchize one's preferences, using anger to demand public accountability, etc. Thus emotions not only inhere in the political process, but can also produce rational outcomes, as opinion formation or democratic governance.

Emotions inhere in the electoral process and are an essential aspect of the voter's orientations and motivation. Rather than being chaotic they are encoded in deep stories.

Political Climates

Emotions also constitute what we conventionally call somewhat fuzzily a "political climate," or the background which makes policy decisions and changes legitimate and acceptable. The great literary theorist Raymond Williams coined the expression "structures of feeling," which designate two opposite phenomena (Williams, 1977, see also Filmer, 2003). Structures of feeling point to experience that is inchoate, defined through who we are without being able to just say what is this "who we are." And the notion of structure also suggests that this level of experience has an underlying pattern that is systematic. Fear pervaded the Cold War policies as much as it pervades anti-Muslim policies presumably based on anti-terrorist policies. The fear "free floats" but has powerful institutional anchors. For example, during the Cold war fear was activated and maintained by development of nuclear weapons, proxy wars and constant struggle for dominance, massive anti-communist propaganda, rivalry at sports events, or technological competition (e.g., the space race). Similarly, the post 9/11 climate morphed into a free-floating fear located in the NSA power, surveillance procedures in airports, news stories about terrorists, policy speeches calling on citizens to be vigilant, social networks diffusing images of terror attacks, street police, and citizens' patrols. Such fear becomes a free floating climate, an "atmosphere," located in the interstices between and betwixt media stories, the state, and the citizens' own way of processing events and news stories into emotional narratives. Emotional moods or climates operate as non-conscious synthesizers of multiple media images, media stories, and affective registers located in politicians' speeches, policy making and ways of framing events. An emotional mood is thus not one single thing. It is many cultural codes in many institutional locations and evokes feelings through identification and metaphorical association. It spreads in the social bond through contagion (as when we say that "panic is contagious"), imitation (as when we shout at a rally because others do), and through identification (as when protesters identified with Mohamed Bouazizi). An emotional climate is made up of different threads: it is about the capacity of politicians to capitalize on ordinary citizens' emotional experiences and give that experience a name, a frame and a purpose; it is also about the capacity by political actors to instill and ongoingly produce specific emotions. Think for example of the general climate of humiliation in Germany after World War I and the 1919 Versailles treaty which demanded from Germany steep compensations for the War. Such humiliation was the compounded result of a variety of actions: loss of territory (Germany lost 13% of its overall territory); the war guilt clause which held the Kaiser and the German people morally responsible; the demand for reparations; the dismemberment of the German army, all of these events were interpreted by ordinary citizens as humiliating signs of defeat; these were integrated in a narrative and emotional frame of humiliation which started circulating in German society and was later be capitalized on by an obscure politician named Adolf Hitler. Humiliation and its narrative were the emotional ground binding the politician to his constituency. An emotional mood is thus the unconscious ground that provides the unconscious legitimacy of policies and political orientations.

An emotional mood is more diffuse, less conscious and more enduring than emotions *per se* which are typically short-lived, have a well-defined object and can be easily brought to the awareness of the subject. Emotions are individual and conscious while emotional climates are collective and operate at a sub-conscious level.

Emotional moods can be structural– embedded in the deep cultural traditions and institutions of a society—or conjunctural—generated by transient political events.

Dominique Moïsi provides an example of the first, with his broad mapping of world political geography of emotions. In his view, we may divide the world in zones with different emotions, as fear, humiliation, or hope as dominant emotions of entire civilizational blocks. He asserts that "The Western world displays a culture of fear, the Arab and Muslim worlds are trapped in a culture of humiliation, and much of Asia displays a culture of hope" (Moïsi, 2007). Whatever the usefulness of such broad-sweeping statements, they do point to the theoretical possibility that different political cultures provide different interpretive background which in turn shapes the emotional framing of political events. In a more nuanced and empirically documented way, Gerbner and Gross's famous "cultivation hypothesis" concurs with Moisi (Gerbner, Gross, Morgan, Signorielli, & Shanahan, 2002). Although it never explicitly referred to the sociology of emotions, cultivation analysis is in fact an analysis of the emotional mood that pervades the American media public sphere which, congruent with Moïsi's claim, they view as dominated by fear but which they view as a tool for social control.

Emotional moods are set by powerful social actors. That is, whatever emotions circulate in the social body, for these emotions to acquire a public status they must be solidified and stabilized in publicly displayed affective registers controlled by powerful actors. Elites, political actors, and citizens struggle over the frame of events and their struggles are as much about the interpretation as it is about the emotional meaning of events. Interpretive frames contain affective registers, stories, values that are implicitly structured by an "emotional pitch," a "deep story," and a dominant emotional imaginary to which an event will be connected. Emotions are produced by the strongest actor in liberal polities, namely the state and its elites, and are variously contested by political agents.

For example, the 2008 taxpayer bailout of the mega insurance company AIG elicited indignation in many citizens' organizations but was justified by its engineers as a measure to save the economy and instill hope. Alan Charney, program director of UsAction declared that its organization was organizing protest rallies and explained his position as: "because the American people are rising up and saying no, no, no," (Rooney, 2008). a position unambiguously motivated by indignation. In contrast, the head of the Federal Reserve, Ben Bernanke, announced the bailout estimated at 85 billion $ (See Karnitschnig, Solomon, Pleven, & Hilsenrath, 2008). The purpose of the bailout was to avoid a global financial crash (most mutual funds in the world owned AIG stocks) and to maintain a climate of economic trust, where trust and optimism are fungible emotional assets converted into economic performance.

The state is, along with media, the strongest actor in shaping emotional moods because its power is performative. When a state representative proclaims "we all mourn the victims of terror attacks" he is de facto producing a collective mourning. We can think also of the role of the state in the politics of memorialization which is organized around grief, guilt or forgiveness. The politics of memory is initiated by the state and memorializing something is a state-emotional act (for example taking responsibility for past discriminations or massacres). Engineering collective grief, guilt, or forgiveness is a political ritual whose purpose is to create performatively a collective emotion which represents at once the state and the collectivity. State-emotional ceremonies declare and perform emotions as grief, loss, guilt, forgiveness. Emotions can thus be moved from the private to the public sphere, they can be engineered publicly and made to pervade private concerns, or they can be performatively created in public spheres through collective movements or state policies.

Emotions can thus become public and collective through the performativity of powerful social actors.

A Normative Theory of Emotions and Politics?

The next step is to reflect on whether we want to distinguish between good or bad emotional politics. This is just what Martha Nussbaum has tried to do in her massive *Political Emotions* (Nussbaum, 2013).

To the question whether some emotions should be more privileged than others, Nussbaum's answer repeats some of our best established clichés: love and compassion are to be privileged; fear, shame, envy are to be banished from political arrangements. Putting to one side the surprising triteness of her suggestions, I will offer two objections. Negative emotions are deemed to be negative only from the standpoint of a subject who finds them unpleasant or threatening. But when viewed in structural terms, these negative emotions turn out to be quite crucial to the maintenance of groups and social arrangements. For example, the 17th century English political philosopher, Thomas Hobbes, suggested that "fear" was constitutive of the state of nature. More precisely, as Hobbes proclaims in *De Cive* (See Hobbes & Monti, 2004), it is not mutual love between men that makes them enter into a social contract and civil society, but rather their mutual fear. Fear, then, is at the heart of the social contract and civil society, with the power of the state lying in its capacity to create peace. Or to take another example, in his *Fable of the Bees* (See Mandeville & Harth, 2007), Bernard de Mandeville famously argued that greed and envy could generate positive social goods such as commerce and exchange. What made these negative emotions socially useful was their capacity to transmute themselves into a positive social good—economic activity, industriousness, competitive, gain—which, in turn created mutual interdependency and economic flourishing.

To offer yet another illustration: According to some historians, in the Middle-Ages, hatred was a useful instrument to test and display "one's ability to recruit kin, friends, and dependants." (Smail, 2001, p. 94). Not only were certain types of vengeful anger considered to be the sign of virtuous souls, but they were also ways to preserve one's social honor and reputation, thus suggesting that hatred was an important social institution and mechanism to maintain status and social structure.

My point thus should be clear enough: what may perhaps be true for individuals (namely that negative emotions decrease their well-being, success, or capacity for love) may not be true for collective bodies, as negative emotions play regulative roles in social life. Emotions then are not good or bad for society in the same way they are good and bad for an individual. Let me take this point further: in the same way that fear, envy, or anger are not only destructive passions, but can organize social and political bonds love and compassion are not the right candidates for the formation of a good political bond. Nussbaum thinks that the purpose of the political bond is to foster love. Reading Tagore in an exquisitely subtle way, the conclusion of her analysis is that "society must preserve at its heart, and continually have access to, a kind of fresh joy and delight in the world, in nature, and in people, preferring love and joy to the dead lives of material acquisition that so many adults end up living, and preferring continual questioning and searching to any comforting settled answers" (Nussbaum, 2013, p. 93).

I will again ignore the triteness of Nussbaum's conclusion and focus on her argument that "love and joy" should be preferred to the "deadness" of material possessions. We may easily retort to the naivete of such view that in her discussion of Augustine's notion of *agape*, Arendt famously wrote against the role of love in political affairs (Arendt, 1996). If love were to play any such role in politics, Arendt claimed, we could never have the power to forgive or judge. Arendt went so far as to suggest Augustine's love is "unconcerned to the point of total unworldliness" (Arendt, 2013, p. 242) with our particularities, reminiscent of the indifference of agape. That is, because love does not enable the act of judgment, such love does not allow human beings to make up their minds on their own and to engage into what Nussbaum thinks should be at the heart of society, namely justice and fairness. Moreover, far from not having enough love infused in it, liberal societies have created many institutions promoting love ad nauseam.

I suggest that religion or moral philosophy should **not** be our starting points and that we should keep intact the distinction between psychological and collective levels of analysis. Sometimes they indeed overlap, but sometimes they don't and a good analysis of emotions and politics should posit the epistemic difference between individual and collective levels. To use a psychoanalyst like Winnicott to make sense of social pathologies is bound not to yield any new or interesting insight, beyond those we already know about with regard to the psyche.

Traditional liberal theory of the public sphere as a politics that is governed by reason puts the moral philosopher and commentator in the trite position of constantly bemoaning and whining the fact that the politics is too emotional or too negative. Instead I suggest: (1) that rational politics is infused with emotions (2) that we cannot apply models of individual psychic and emotional health to the body collective, (3) that we cannot know always and in advance how negative and positive emotions will play out.

Populist Emotions

If democratic politics is infused with emotions, what then is the distinction between democratic emotional politics and so-called populist politics? I will offer the following hypothesis. A populist politics has 3 emotional characteristics: it makes fear and anxiety into the plausible collective horizon for the body collective. It appeals to fear to redraw the boundaries of the body collective and break old forms of social covenants; it uses resentment as a way to contest elites power, and to promote new social groups; and finally, it is able to recode hatred for others into love for the country and collective intimacy.

Fear, resentment and love are the three emotional structures I turn now to analyze.

Fear

As Corey Robin has argued, fear exists in 2 contrasted political traditions: one is the Aristotelian tradition in which fear is a civilized and adequate response to moral challenge; and the other is the Montesquieu tradition in which fear was a primitive passion subject to manipulation by tyrants (Robin, 2014). For Aristotle, fear is a way to instill virtue. For Montesquieu it is a regression, political and moral at once (see Gold & Revill, 2003). Modern polities have used fear widely especially in the area of crime (Gerbner, Gross, Morgan, Signorielli, & Shanahan, 2002). Think of the examples of the moral panics around pedophilia or the violence of marginal groups like African Americans. This kind of fear is instilled by the state, by the media, by elite groups defending access to their neighborhoods, and is viewed as a way to justify police power and the surveilling activities of the state. Its effect is to reinforce moral boundaries around certain social groups. Fear instilled by populist leaders aims to draw geographical and symbolic boundaries around the body collective, by invoking the threat of inner decay and the threat posed by the worm within and drawing a straight line with the external forces that threaten to bring down the economic and cultural strength of the nation as a whole. The "fear scape" of populist leaders aims at drawing a boundary between inner and outer groups. As aptly summarized by Tom Friedman: "The Trump doctrine is very simple: There are just four threats in the world: terrorists who will kill us, immigrants who will rape us or take our jobs, importers and exporters who will take our industries—and North Korea" (Friedman, 2017).

The following excerpts come from Ben Anderson's useful compilation of Trump's discourse in his article *The Affective Style of Donald Trump*[1] helps us get a sense of the various ways he appeals to fear.

> When we were all younger—many of you are my age and many of you are younger—but when we were all younger we didn't lose so much, right? We don't win anymore. As a country, we don't win. (…)

As Anderson put it In speeches, he [Trump] "raised the imminent threat of future economic losses dramatized through stories of broken lives in the present after jobs have moved abroad and people and communities have been left behind. Losing is not only confined to the economy, though, and far from only a matter of people's individual lives. For Trump, it's a generalised condition of the United States today. At a rally in Boca Raton, he asks his audience to: "Think about it: When was the last time the United States won at everything? We're losing at war, we're losing at trade, we're losing at everything." The result of this generalised, all pervasive, losing is, to quote the title of Trump's 2015 book/manifesto, a "crippled" America. Time and again the Trump campaign dramatizes this condition of being "crippled" through images of broken everyday infrastructure. Campaign videos feature clips of unidentified roads and bridges falling down in spectacular scenes that root ruin and destruction in ordinary American life. His unfocused, rambling comments during a Q&A after a victory speech on Super Tuesday are typical: "Our infrastructure is going to hell, our roads, our highways, our schools, our hospitals, our airports" (Anderson, 2017). Trump moves effortlessly from foreign to domestic internal enemies. "The illegal immigrants who have taken jobs that should go to people here legally, while over 20 percent of Americans are currently unemployed or underemployed" (Quoted in Anderson, 2017).

This fearscape intertwines economic and ethnic fears all in one. In a famous book on *Populism*, Ian Werner Muller claims that one of the main characteristics of populism is to name enemies from within (Muller, 2016). The most powerful fear articulated by populist leaders is the one that manages to articulate the fear that the geographical and cultural boundaries of the collective are under threat and that the threats from outside somewhat resonate with threats inside. This corresponds to the view of the political as articulated by Carl Schmitt in the *Stanford Encyclopedia of Philosophy*. Schmitt famously claims that "the specific political distinction ... is that between friend and enemy" (2008, p. 26). The distinction between friend and enemy, Schmitt elaborates, is essentially public and not private. Individuals may have personal enemies, but personal enmity is not a political phenomenon. Politics involves groups that face off as mutual enemies (2008, pp. 28–29). Two groups will find themselves in a situation of mutual enmity if and only if there is a possibility of war and mutual killing between them. The distinction between friend and enemy thus refers to the "utmost degree of intensity ... of an association or dissociation" (2008, pp. 26, 38). The utmost degree of association is the willingness to fight and die for and together with other members of one's group, and the ultimate degree of dissociation is the willingness to kill others for the simple reason that they are members of a hostile group. The enmity-friend divide which according to Schmitt is the hallmark and prerogative of the state can take place and reproduce itself only if it articulates such emotions as fear and hatred.

Resentment

In his book, *Ressentiment* written in 1912 (translated by Lewis Coser) Max Scheler defined the core emotional structure of resentment, (Sheler, [1912] 1992, 119):

> "Revenge, envy, the impulse to detract, spite, Schadenfreude, and malice lead to ressentiment only if there occurs neither a moral self-conquest (such as genuine forgiveness in the case of revenge) nor an act or some other adequate expression of emotion (such as verbal abuse or shaking one's fist), and if this restraint is caused by a pronounced awareness of impotence. There will be no

ressentiment if he who thirsts for revenge really acts and avenges himself, if he who is consumed by hatred harms his enemy, gives him 'a piece of his mind,' or even merely vents his spleen in the presence of others. Nor will the envious fall under the dominion of ressentiment if he seeks to acquire the envied possession by means of work, barter, crime, or violence. *Ressentiment can only arise if these emotions are particularly powerful and yet must be suppressed because they are coupled with the feeling that one is unable to act them out—either because of weakness, physical or mental, or because of fear.* Through its very origin, ressentiment is therefore chiefly confined to those who serve and are dominated at the moment, who fruitlessly resent the sting of authority. When it occurs elsewhere, it is either due to psychological contagion—and the spiritual venom of ressentiment is extremely contagious—or to the violent suppression of an impulse which subsequently revolts by 'embittering' and 'poisoning' the personality." (emphasis added)

In Scheler's view, *Ressentiment* is desire for revenge without the capacity to act on that desire for revenge.

The people Hochschild studied in Louisiana may be an illustration. Her interviewees claim that women, blacks, Latinos, or gays made great progress but did so illegitimately. These groups are perceived, in Hochshild's words, as "line cutters." These are exactly the conditions described by Scheler for ressentiment: these groups elicit envy but a powerless form of envy since they are protected by what those who feel they have been cut in line view as the legal apparatus and the liberal elites. This is exactly that kind of resentment Trump invokes: "[T]he system is rigged against the people—rigged by corporations, rigged by the media, rigged by the political elite, rigged by special issues, rigged by donors—and that your anger is legitimate, that there is a truth to it. And, importantly, the affirmation that you are not alone in that anger—other people feel it" (quoted in Anderson, 2017).

Love and Pride

Offering the hope of a 'rebuilt' America, Trump combines the promise of 'greatness' with another promise—that his supporters and America will start 'winning' again. At a rally, he invokes what this future full of 'winning' might feel like: "We're going to win so much. You're going to get tired of winning. You're going to say, 'Please Mr. President, I have a headache. Please, don't win so much. This is getting terrible.' And I'm going to say, 'No, we have to make America great again.' You're gonna say, 'Please.' I said, 'Nope, nope. We're gonna keep winning'" (quoted in Anderson, 2017). Pride is here the emotion that is obviously tapped by this discourse. Pride is the affirmation of the self and its worth, all the more affirmed that for the working-class portion of Trump's voters, worth is incessantly challenged by chronic unemployment and work-related anxiety. Once people are empowered through pride, they can be united through love. Pride and love constitutional a key emotional syntagm of the right.

Indeed, Trump refers to the people who attend his rallies in a way that explicitly refers to his love for them: "Believe me, they're all over the place. I see them. I talk to them. I hug them. I hold them. They are all over the place" (quoted in Anderson, 2017).

The recoding of hate as love is a phenomenon that occurs across the political spectrum. In her analysis of an Aryan website Sara Ahmed illustrates just this. This is a quote from the white Aryan Nation supremacist website:

> The depths of Love are rooted and very deep in a real white nationalist's soul and spirit, no form of "hate" could even begin to compare. At least not a hate motivated by ungrounded reasoning. It is not hate that makes the average white man look upon a mixed race couple with a scowl on his face and loathing in his heart. It is not hate that makes the white housewife throw down the daily jewspaper in repulsion and anger after reading of yet another child molester or rapist sentenced by corrupt courts to a couple of short years in prison or on parole. It is not hate that makes the white workingman curse about the latest boatload of aliens dumped on our shores to be given job preference over the white citizen who built this land. It is not hate that brings rage into the heart of a white Christian farmer when he reads of billions loaned or given away as "aid" to foreigners when he can't get the smallest break from an unmerciful government to save his failing farm. No, it's not hate. It is love. (Aryan Nations Web site, quoted in Ahmed, 2004, p. 117)

Commenting on this website, Sara Ahmed suggests that:

"The average white man feels "fear and loathing"; the white housewife, "repulsion and anger"; the white workingman, "curses"; the white Christian farmer, "rage." The passion of these negative attachments to others is redefined simultaneously as a positive attachment to the imagined subjects brought together through the repetition of the signifier, "white." It is the love of white, or those recognizable as white, that supposedly explains this shared "communal" visceral response of hate. *Together we hate, and this hate is what makes us together* (Ahmed, 2004, p. 118). The capacity to recode hate as love is a powerful way to jolt the participation in populist politics. As Sara Ahmed put it: "In such affective economies, emotions *do things*, and they align individuals with communities—or bodily space with social space— through the very intensity of their attachments" (p. 119). Populist politics intertwines so-called negative and positive emotions.

Conclusion

Liberal and left-wing politics have been based on the useful fictions of progress and rationality. These fictions could guide the political imaginary of liberalism as long as industrial capitalism and nationalism seemed to deliver on their promises, that is, as long as they were able to expand the social covenant by integrating excluded social groups in economic production, providing them with the possibility of steady economic progress and the privileges accrued to national membership. As long as these useful fictions were aligned on a social order that seemed to accompany them, the notion of rationality and progress that were at the cornerstone of liberal states and nations could guide policy-making and voting. The crumbling of these fictions does not mark the polluting irruption of emotions in the body politic, but rather the victory of a global capitalism which has undermined the plausibility of national membership, economic progress, or rationality as narratives for the self or for the collective. Until liberalism finds new useful fictions, liberalism and left-wing politics are well-advised to tap into the vast emotional reservoir of the disquieted citizens for whom neither capitalism nor nationalism do not provide promises of a better life anymore.

Note

1. http://societyandspace.org/2017/02/28/we-will-win-again-we-will-win-a-lot-the-affective-styles-of-donald-trump/

References

Ackerman, B. (1980). *Social justice in the liberal state* (Vol. 401). New Haven, CT: Yale University Press.

Ahmed, S. (2004). "Affective economies." *Social Text, 22*(2), 117–139.

Anderson, B. http://societyandspace.org/2017/02/28/we-will-win-again-we-will-win-a-lot-the-affective-styles-of-donald-trump/, accessed 5.15.2017

Arendt, H. (1996). *Love and Saint Augustine*. Chicago: :University of Chicago Press.

Arendt, H. (2013). *The human condition*. Chicago: University of Chicago Press.

Bruni F. (2017, Aug 18) The week when President Trump resigned. *The New York Times.* Retrieved 10.9.2017: https://www.nytimes.com/2017/08/18/opinion/sunday/president-trump-resignation.html?

Damasio, A. R. (1994). Descartes' error: Emotion, reason and the human brain. New York: Putnam.

Filmer, P. (2003). Structures of feeling and socio-cultural formations: The significance of literature and experience to Raymond Williams's sociology of culture. *British Journal of Sociology, 54*(2), 199–219.

Friedman T. L. (2017, 31 May). Trump's United American Emirate. The New York Times. Retrieved 9.10.17: https://www.nytimes.com/2017/05/31/opinion/trumps-united-american-emirate.html?

Gerbner, G., Gross, L., Morgan, M., Signorielli, N., & Shanahan, J. (2002). Growing up with television: Cultivation processes. *Media effects: Advances in theory and research, 2,* 43–67.

Gold, J. R., & Revill, G. (2003). Exploring landscape of fear: Marginality, spectacle, and surveillance. In *Capital and class, summer,* special issue on *The Geographies and Politics of Fear,* pp. 27–47.

Habermas, J. (1991). *The structural transformation of the public sphere: An inquiry into a category of bourgeois society.* Massachusetts: MIT Press.

Hobbes, T., & Monti, C. (2004). *De cive.* Vol. 2. Kessinger Publishing.

Hochschild, A. R. (2016). *Strangers in their own land: Anger and mourning on the American right.,* New York: The New Press.

Karnitschnig, M., Solomon, D., Pleven, L., & Hilsenrath J. E. (2008, September 16). U.S. to take over AIG in $85 billion bailout; Central banks inject cash as credit dries up. *The Wall Street Journal.* Retrieved 9.10.17: https://www.wsj.com/articles/SB122156561931242905

Mandeville, B., & Harth, P. *The fable of the bees.* UK: Penguin, 2007.

Marcus, G. E., & MacKuen, M. B. (1993). Anxiety, enthusiasm, and the vote: The emotional underpinnings of learning and involvement during presidential campaigns. *American Political Science Review, 87*(3), 672–685.

Moïsi, D. (2007). The clash of emotions: Fear, humiliation, hope, and the new world order. *Foreign Affairs, 86*(1), 8–12.

Muller, J-W. (2016). *What is populism?*Philadelphia: University of Pennsylvania Press.

Nussbaum, M. C. (2003). *Upheavals of thought: The intelligence of emotions.* Cambridge: Cambridge University Press.

Nussbaum, M. C. (2013). *Political emotions.* Cambridge MA: Harvard University Press.

Plato. (1996). *Gorgias.* (W. D. Woodhead, trans.). In E. Hamilton H. Cairns, & L. Cooper (Eds.), *The collected dialogues of Plato.* New York: Bollingen Foundation.

Robin, C. (2004). *Fear: The history of a political idea.* Oxford: Oxford University Press.

Rooney, B. (2008, September 25) Bailout foes hold day of protests. *CNN-Money.* Retrieved 9.10.2017: http://money.cnn.com/2008/09/25/news/economy/bailout_protests/?postversion=2008092517

Scheler, M. (1994). "Ressentiment, Marquette studies in philosophy." Milwaukee: Marquette University Press.

Schmitt, C. *The concept of the political: Expanded edition.* University of Chicago Press, 2008.

Smail, D. L. (2001). "Hatred as a social institution in late-medieval society." *Speculum*,
    76(1), 90–126.

Whitaker, B. (2010, December 28) How a man setting fire to himself sparked an upris-
    ing in Tunisia. *The Guardian*. Retrieved 9.10.17: https://www.theguardian.com/
    commentisfree/2010/dec/28/tunisia-ben-ali

Williams, R. (1977). *Marxism and Literature*. London: OUP.

10. The Community in Community Media: Islands and Interactions in a Digital Universe

CINDY HING-YUK WONG

Twenty plus years now have passed since I completed my dissertation on Scribe Video Center in Philadelphia under the direction of Larry Gross (Wong, 1999, 2002). In this work, I conducted an ethnographic study of Scribe, an organization devoted to making the tools of film/video-making available to members of its community. In subsequent years, while many of the social issues that underpinned my work and Scribe's mission have continued to challenge Philadelphia and American society—racism, inequality, education, prejudice, loss of place and memory—the changes in the wider media environment have constituted a veritable 21st Century Gutenberg revolution. Looking back to the 1990s, I grappled with hand-held video and 2 GB non-linear editing suites as novel wonders. Even e-mail seemed new and exciting, and the possibilities of social media and constant access were hard to grasp when the virtual and flexible scarcely had been imagined outside of sci fi (the original *Blade Runner* 1992 does not even envision cell phones). At the final stage of writing of the dissertation in 1996–67, I was in Hong Kong, Larry and I corresponded via email; that felt like a real milestone. Yet even on this information pre-highway, one of the most important points Larry stressed for me was to articulate what made Scribe media *community* media: what exactly did Scribe participants mean by "community," in theory and practice? This paper, based on continuing relations and follow-up visits and interviews with those involved with Scribe, asks how today's new media and media ecologies have affected Scribe's mission and what we may learn from Scribe's choices in terms of evolving practices, products and community.

As historians and teachers of media and digital immigrants ourselves, it is important to remember that in the 1990's, there was no Facebook, Google, or Instagram, and Amazon was a new small book seller online. Today, most people, especially young people, receive as well as produce information very differently than their peers 20 plus years ago. Connection has become immediate, multi-layered and portable with a good data plan. There also has been monumental growth in the sheer amount of media content available alongside changing possibilities of distribution and access. On the surface, all these changes seem to have the potential to foster the growth of community media and for everyday communities to use media to their advantage. Indeed, many scholars have argued that the new digital media environment has changed social relations. (Bowman & Willis, 2003 in Burgess, 2006). Others, like Barış Çoban, see social media as a solution for progressive social movements, buoyed by the use of social media in activist protest movements around the globe (2016). At the same time, with the U.S. elections, we can see that new media, especially social media, can be used by people of all political orientations, sometimes forming virtual "communities" serving or propagating very particular agendas, attacking civil society.

In this essay, I analyze today's Scribe Video Center and its projects to understand how new media ecologies have affected these programs while keeping my eye on *what community means,* especially visions of community as face-to-face, place-based social constructs that may renegotiate media. To do so, we must understand the relationship between media technologies and environment and the specific vision of community media embodied by the practices of Scribe Media Center. Hence, I first explore briefly the context within which Scribe was established and the mission of Scribe as a community organization. Scribe video practices have emphasized a few core repeated characteristics: a stress on access, valuation of process/participation as much as or more than product, a commitment to community self-expression/storytelling, a non-profit ethos and a dedication to subject matters oriented toward the greater Philadelphia region. While some of these converge with possibilities of new media, others embody a power of resistance that still defines Scribe as a rare urban institution. Here, then, I want to read Scribe's continuing production through the prisms of both new media and continuing quests for community.

Defining Scribe by Community and Media Worlds

Scribe Video Center is *itself* a community organization, bound together with the residents and Geo-ethnic media that constitute the three major components of the model of Neighborhood Storytelling Network within concrete geographical locations (Kim & Ball-Rokeach, 2006). From its formation to the present, its members have interacted with the other groups around it as well as other local media within a living environment that encompasses the daily lives of people embedded within the larger national as well as global environment. Scribe itself is a media *community* organization as well in that the community service Scribe provides is media. Scribe, in particular, engages in producing stories from diverse communities, a practice similar to Jean Burgess' digital story telling where "'ordinary people' create their own short autobiographical films that can be streamed on the Web or broadcast on TV" (Burgess, 207). Scribe videos, however, demand collective efforts, cutting across professional/grassroots divides and using the process to reinforce community. Hence, to understand Scribe's community media, we need to understand what are the structural elements of the larger media landscape that make community media a compelling practice Scribe wants to engage.

Mass media in the United States have always meant big businesses. Before the arrival of Web 2.0, the technology largely meant that "average" persons could not produce media that could reach large audiences. Big movie studios and television networks dominated production, distribution, and exhibition. When cable television, and subsequently VCR started to arrive in major markets in the 1980s, the players expanded; however, despite public access (the subject of one of my first papers for Larry) there was little the consumers could do beyond choosing to watch some programs and not others and, eventually, to consume at different times. Production remained expensive if not prohibitive, although "accessible" video production equipment slowly expanded the possibilities of wider participation.

Filmmaker Louis Massiah established Scribe Video Center in 1982 "to explore, develop and advance the use of electronic media, including video and audio, as artistic media and as tools for progressive social change" (http://www.scribe.org/mission-and-history-scribe). Scribe was founded on a basic belief that, in a democracy, the media belong to the people and the people need to be empowered to participate in the media world. Scribe's organizers wanted everyday people to participate in this media landscape, to break the exclusivity of privately-owned media. Specifically, they felt that mass media contents did not represent diverse populations: the image and history of Philadelphia should expand beyond Independence Hall, *It's Always Sunny in*

Philadelphia, and *Rocky*. More importantly, they knew as media workers that most people did not have the tools to use the audio-visual media to articulate their ideas, thoughts and lives.

At a basic level, this need was met through various production classes, workshops and equipment rental offered at Scribe. Founder-director Louis Massiah was very clear in articulating to me in the 1990s that even with relatively accessible video equipment, most video makers came from the middle or upper middle classes; however, all people should have the same access to this technology. This statement articulates the gaps in video production literacy, and access to the hardware of video making that continue within a contemporary universe of "open access." The Scribe web page in 2017 still offers opportunities ranging from workshops on fund-raising and planning a documentary to "How to Write, Shoot and Share your 'Love' Story." Additional workshops focus on master global figures on master filmmakers like Moustapha Alassane. This range of opportunities, including the past as well as new techniques and practicalities, responds to the stated goals of Scribe to assist "emerging video makers and members of community groups in learning the craft of videomaking [while] Scribe also offers opportunities for experienced media makers." Scribe, however, does not offer any virtual online classes.

The Scribe model of community was not simply built on top down pedagogy and isolated individuals, but on people who share common goals and actions in concrete places of life, work and action and could cooperate with others to tell stories. Obviously, the internet has allowed many people to share and form like-minded communities that do not require geographic proximity. This technological capability also allows isolated individuals to produce "more individualized forms of activism," like electronic fanzines in transnational feminist alternative media (Reitsamer & Zobl, 330–332). Yet the creation of new diffuse and imagined communities was never Scribe's goal so much as collective expressions built on history, memory, and place.

Place almost seems anachronistic as we adapt to a virtual world where we are constantly told that space and time are overcome by multiple connections. Nevertheless, Scribe was—and remains—a grassroots media center that sees its mission as producing alternative media for local, placed-based communities. Unlike a community of Star Trek fans (Jenkins) that is connected through a placeless mass media product, Scribe has always looked at community first as a collective based on physical association with place and experience and Scribe sees media as a tool to further the goals of such communities. This brings us back to Kim and Ball-Rokeach's model that privileges physical spaces that differs from Reitsamer & Zobl's more individualistic cultural citizenship which free the individual citizen media producers from geography. This poses an important distinction in how community is defined, privileging community as physical places with people over community based primarily on media content or social issues, available in different channels of distribution. Physical space continues to be a key factor because people in physical communities share characteristics of that space, its living context—housing, schools, recreational facilities, social services, and trasportation (Kim & Ball-Rokeach, 176)—with their fellow community members. In practice, Scribe focuses on *under-served* communities which commercial media tend to ignore; the majority of Scribe projects are on racial, ethnic and gender minorities and on places that are often forgotten.

In addition to classes related to the production and distribution of moving images, then, Scribe has promoted a range of "community based" projects that link collective efforts to wider visions of community, bringing together professional videographers and other facilitators as experts with wider groups of grassroots citizens telling their stories. My dissertation focused on *Community Vision* (1990-), where facilitators worked with specific groups on videos they could use in training, argument/propaganda, or group-building. Subsequent programs have included *Precious Places* (2002-), the *Documentary History Project for Youth* (2005-) and recent one-time multi-video projects that include *Muslim Voices* (2014) and *Great Migration* (2017). All of these projects are based in Philadelphia and its suburbs, including southern New Jersey. In *Precious Places*, humanities advisors from the academy, video professionals, and citizens involved with particular groups constitute community over several months for pre-production and focus on a single day of shooting and editing of a short video. *Muslim Voices* was designed to "provide instructions and media tools to traditionally underrepresented Muslim groups in Philadelphia so that they can research and share the stories, significant events, achievements and issues" (http://www.scribe.org/muslim-voices-philadelphia). It has facilitated and shared projects from a wide variety of Islamic groups in the city ranging from older Black Muslims to recent transnational groups. *Great Migration* is perhaps the most diverse collection, ranging from an evocative elegy directed by premiere African-American filmmaker Julie Dash to more traditional community visions of institutions and groups in the city. New media have changed technologies in these projects but community media for Scribe in today's digital age retains its relationship to physical and sociocultural place.

The divergence between new media worlds and old definitions of community also shape distribution. Scribe has never been interested in producing mass media products that garner a great deal of attention outside its communities, in becoming a general content provider. In the digital age, this can be translated into likes and hits, but Scribe has not paid much attention to these numbers. Back in the 1990s, when asked how Scribe could compete with mass media, Louis Massiah flatly explained to me that I was comparing apples and oranges. Scribe helped produce media that are made by "the community" and for the community that controls its non-profit distribution. Therefore, Scribe has never subscribed to rules that dominate the mass media, from ratings to profit. It is largely funded by foundation grant money. By not participating in the for-profit structure of the media system, Scribe video makers were not striving to be major players who change the capitalist media landscape. We learn to understand media in all its manifestations by paying attention to this form of interventions that are not dominated by dollars and viewership.

At the same time, Scribe has not engaged in what is normally termed activist media. Scribe wants to change the world by fostering diverse voices, expressing challenges encountered by communities, not necessarily seeking open confrontations. Scribe subscribed to more gradual and deliberative process of media empowerment. Videos were used for screenings in schools, recruitment of clients, training of mediators, or not used at all as community groups disbanded. This narrowness has opened space for more activist media collectives as well in Philadelphia such as the Media Mobilizing Project, founded in 2005, whose slogan is "Movements Begin with the Telling of Untold Stories" (https://mediamobilizing.org/). The fact that the worlds of media production and distribution have expanded, after all, have never meant that Scribe sought to dominate community production either; pluralism may be possible in new ways that actually allow Scribe to reinforce its practices and mission. To understand these practices, we must turn to community and media as process.

Community Media and Community Processes

Recruitment: Finding Communities

The processes by which Scribe solicits community projects have scarcely changed since the 1990s. Each year, Scribe hires a coordinator with diverse ties in Philadelphia to go to different area groups to ask if they are interested in making a video to tell their stories. While groups also may have contacted Scribe through its website, this agent visits community organizations personally and will explain the possibilities and values of the project. This process, by itself, restricts the locations of production: the openness of digital communication is balanced by projects that only become viable with knowledge and commitment of the human community, including its space and members, based on frank and intimate face-to face conversations. Community media here start with community, not with media. Moreover, while a robust internet solicitation may result in more applicants, Scribe has finite human and physical resource to make roughly ten videos per year. Digital technology, obviously, facilitates dialogue in planning and recruiting but resources also exist in physical space.

Within this geographic orientation, Scribe projects do not envision the mediated community as free of spatial dimensions, either. *Community Vision* projects have dealt with ethnic, class, cultural and other organizations, interesting people who have contributed to their communities, social services that provided essential services and problems faced by residents across neighborhoods. The projects ranges from *Books through Bars* (1997) about an organization that provides books to the incarcerated to *Ione Nash: Her Life, Her Art* (2013) by Arthur Hall Afro-American Dance Ensemble Alumni, which highlights Nosh' contributions to African dance in Philadelphia. Participants work together to articulate and celebrate their achievements; oftentimes, projects also involve older people as archives of memory and training for new generations. The rationale of their existence, though connected to wider social issues, is their proximity to their life and goals.

Precious Places, as the name suggests, is even more spatially oriented, documenting different sites, institutions and neighborhoods in Philadelphia, from the affluent Main Line (*Ardmore, A Village at Risk* 2006) to the older industrial mill town of Tacony (*Bridging Yesterday with Tomorrow* 2005) to inner city neighborhoods like the South Philadelphia Cambodian community (*Bra Buddha Ransi Temple* 2009). Taken together, these projects have raised larger questions about the increasing gentrification of Philadelphia that has demanded responses from neighborhoods vulnerable to development. However, the texts remain centered around specific spaces and their primary concerns is to showcase the place the community loves. *El Centro de Oro: The Golden Center* (2010), for example, is produced by three community organizations—Raices Culturales Latinoamericanes, Taller Puertoriaueno and HACE DCD (5th and Lehigh District) to "confront mainstream media stereotypes through the imagery of this beloved central street" (http://www. scribe.org/catalogue/el-centro-de-oro-golden-center).

The Documentary History Project for Youth projects focus on a different broad topic every year; the topic for 2015 was "Policed" and 2016, "Justice." Here it is the imagined community of Philadelphia youth, embodied in volunteers who learn the tools for researching history and producing media products expressing their concerns with their lives, school, voting, fashion, food, and even poetry. Students are recruited and taught through Philadelphia high schools and youth classes after school, on weekend and in summer programs. *Healing Words* (2014—theme "Poetic Justice"), for example, documents how diverse youths in the city use words to express their joy, fears and anxiety. While these projects are grounded in Philadelphia, they reflect youth as a segment of the city and are also adamantly collective projects with different youths taking different roles for the project. Here, the youths experiment not only with videos, but also with audio and websites. In this sense, these projects seem to resemble the content we associate with individual production in Web 2.0. Yet, Scribe projects are grounded in training and discussions of media and media literacy and are made by peers in concrete communities, either in school or in their neighborhoods. Moreover, the resultant videos are situated within a range of uses that define them as products for concrete audiences rather than elements for an impersonal media universe.

Thus, this very initial process of solicitation establishes face to face interaction that builds on *and* builds communities. Even though the Scribe website solicits projects, the level of informed commitment the final projects will need demand frank discussion of the actual time and effort involved, which will dissuade some groups. New digital technology should facilitate at this early stage of planning and recruiting but it is a gateway *to* the process of community building that starts with the interviews and commitments.

Production: Remaking Community

Given the opportunities to make a video about themselves, many Scribe participants are initially quite eager to participate. However, making a linear narrative video requires a great deal of work from people who are not professional video makers and have other obligations; only those organizations who can muster a reliable cadre of enthusiastic members and volunteers complete the projects. Burgess' idea about "autonomous citizen producers" (209) is an apt concept here that understands most of these part-time community video producers as citizens who live within specific communities, with concerns beyond video making. While Scribe sees video making as a cultural competency, few of these participants see the act of video making as occupying a privileged position in their lives; that is, Scribe community video makers rarely pursue media professionalization in their subsequent lives.

Digitization and the spread of cell phone and social media seem to have made everyone with a cell phone a producer of moving images. However, to make a coherent collaborative video piece of a certain length, between five and fifteen minutes, that conveys a message to concrete publics demands a great deal more coordinated and committed time and effort. Scribe demands that work be done collaboratively, from planning to scripting to basic tasks like filming, sound and interviews as well as final editing. While professional consultants are in place, they are there to advise and help, not to replace participation from community members.

The shared production process, in turn, becomes extremely important in community building where the facilitator possesses the familiarity—continually updated by new technology—on how to turn ideas into video images, while people in the community organizations own the knowledge of what their lives are all about. They are the content. The Scribe model basically sees the facilitator as an outsider who is there to provide a helping hand to the real maker of the video, members of the community, who know the needs of the community, its people and what it wants to say and to whom. This entails a great many meetings between facilitator and the production teams. Substantive decisions are made in face-to-face interactions and it is these social decisions that bring technologies into play.

In the late 1990s, I worked on several projects including an AIDS organization—We, the People (*New Faces of Aids* 1994)—and Asian American high school students working with Asian American United (*Face to Face* 1996). In 2007, I was involved again in a similar project with the Asian Arts Initiative that eventually produced *I Come from a Place*. The first few meetings with each of these groups were spent brainstorming ideas about what they wanted the video to say—a process that initially requires building some kinds of trust. In the 90s, there was a great deal of stigma and misunderstanding about AIDS; at We, the People, the core group wanted to make a video to challenge this hegemonic representation, to show the audience that people with AIDS are not any different from anyone else. A handful of participants made a video that primarily features talking heads, witnesses who explain as human beings how they contracted AIDS, were diagnosed and how they have learned to live with AIDS. The video ends with a wedding among two participants, and, in a moment both joyful and painful, its credits remember a participant who died during months of filmmaking.

Face to Face showcases youths talking about their different experiences being Asian American in Philadelphia. The young videographers are also the subjects of the video. Here, an established organization, Asian Americans United, worked with Scribe to recruit and train younger high school students who chose the issues and conducted interviews to deal with problems

of school, media stereotypes, police and other issues of day to day life. Repro-
ducing/recruiting community was thus built into the process, but the students themselves *made* the film. They felt that many people did not see them
beyond the Asian stereotypes but they also wanted to speak to others in urban
immigrant communities caught in multiple questions of identity. Again,
today this might be the stuff of YouTube posting but the process involved
sharing, planning, working together in interviewing, shooting and editing,
and thinking about how such products could speak for Asian-American
youths, to them and to others.

In production it becomes clear that these groups are primarily interested
in speaking to those whom analysts would define as their "own" community,
with the added potential benefits of showing other neighbors in Philadelphia
who they are or how they deal with an issue. The videos are monuments
of who the community videographers are and why they are important. In
production meetings, we rarely discussed wider distribution or envisioned
audiences much until the final stages of preparation. When Scribe showcases
public screening of new releases, audiences are not the impersonal or con-
sumerist component of the worldwide web but those who see semblances of
themselves in the works and share concerns with the media makers themselves,
including many they know personally or encounter in everyday interactions.

Products: The Visions of Community Visions

Looking back over many years of Scribe production, even with the move from
analog to digital, the images and structures have not changed too much. Most
of them rely heavily on talking heads, oftentimes situated in readily-known
spaces, at least for community members. We see faces of people talking about
their work, their neighborhoods and communities. Location shots, like street
signs or buildings, situate the community in a concrete geographical context.
The familiar faces and places take on more meaning through personal knowledge. Events are often incorporated into the videos, a baseball game or celebration or even young Asian American filmmakers fooling around, mocking
Kung Fu movies that later became part of the record of community as lived
experience.

Clearly, these texts involve thought and selection about "who" community is. The interviewees in *New Faces of Aids* are diverse, with people of
different ethnicities, genders and sexual orientations although they all looks
very healthy. In *Face to Face,* the youths and their families comes from different Asian countries, but all grew up in Philadelphia. Their origins are
expressed by their words and their looks which forces the audience to see that
Asian Americans are diverse, bringing very different histories to a complex,

socially-constructed category they must deal with. As part of this text, the youth provide concrete lived examples of how they learn to confront stereotypes and turn them around.

The *Muslim Voices* and *Great Migration* series also feature clear patterns of speakers intercut with scenes of places known to the audience. Here, Scribe curates works that is tied to Philadelphia;. Scribe sees the series as "part of both the history of Islam in Philadelphia and the history of the city itself." (http://www.scribe.org/muslim-voices-philadelphia) Similarly, in the videos for the Great Migration, all the stories tied to Philadelphia, including the Pennsylvania Railroad, the United Negro Improvement Association of Philadelphia, Mother Bethel A.M.E. church and the black newspaper the *Philadelphia Tribune*.

Form is subservient to function. Many videos are traditional linear narrative and are formally mundane, relying on a central subject matter and showcasing people who have experience, thus authority, as they express their story and ideas to support the central statement. Scribe videos have adhered to linear storytelling, still a dominant form of video, while generally avoiding experimentation associated with new formats found in other online moving pictures that which can be ephemeral, extremely short, and done without much editing. While some Scribe products are lyrical and beautiful, especially among the professionally-made Great Migration projects—Scribe community videos do not generally aspire to be cinematic masterpieces.

New media have enabled forms of audio-visual story telling which are non-linear, primarily through internet and web pages with hyperlink which allows the audience to navigate the directions of the narrative. Yet, that does not mean that this is the only choice a collaborative group will make, nor that it serves their vision of needs and interactions. Do Scribe Community Media products, mostly 10-minute long linear documentary narratives, "compete" with the new media forms or complement them in different patterns of use? While Scribe video has remained resolutely linear and non-interactive, interactivity and collaboration permeate the production and exhibition ends of the endeavors: where the videos are made collectively and shared in non-anonymous settings. Let me now turn to that final stage.

Distribution: Reproducing Community?

As I observed in the dissertation two decades ago, the distribution of community media remains a daunting task, involving another world after the travails of production that many groups simply did not want to learn and enter. If we focus on the ease of dissemination that has become characteristic of the world of Web 2.0, distribution can seem almost automatic. Yet as the product and property of communities, Scribe videos from their very beginning have different goals and meanings based on community ownership and use.

Some general public distribution has been in place for decades. Scribe organizes free public premiers of *Community Vision*, *Precious Places* and most programs at Philadelphia's International House, a combination dorm and community center on the campus of the University of Pennsylvania. Oftentimes, these events celebrate the achievements of the community filmmakers as they can share their works with others in their communities. Some Scribe videos are also shown on local public and cable access TV stations and some have been screened in small film festivals with specific social themes, such as Asian American film festivals. Scribe also contacts colleges and other Philadelphia area institutions offering programs like a selection from *Muslim Voices* or *The Great Migration* that can be linked to education or community events. Nevertheless, wider screening opportunities remain limited and rarely are videos shown to people who may not have much connection with the communities involved or Scribe.

Distribution, as I showed in 1997, is a right and responsibility of organizations. Some used them in lobbying or outreach. Some used them to familiarize new participants with history or even goals. And, over time, some lovingly-made products fell into disuse, as even community organizations themselves disappeared from the Philadelphia landscape. The videos became archival, yet still perhaps inspirational for new generations or groups.

Scribe nonetheless facilitates new links between community media and place within its network of collaborators. Many of these videos, for example, are showcased in a summer *Street Movies!* series at sites around the metropolitan area, where Scribe, together with other local community organizations, host public screenings. While I had attended these in the 1980s and 1990s, it was interesting to revisit the Street Movies on Thursday August 24 at Disston Recreation Center, hosted by the Tacony Civic Association & Historical Society. Taking over a parking lot and green space around a school that now serves as community center, the evening event began with live music before the three videos were shown. The first video, *Bridging Yesterday with Tomorrow* (2005), created by the host Tacony Civic Association, chronicled the origin of the neighborhood itself, a "milltown" structured by the presence of former Disston ironworks that is now reinventing itself. The two other videos screened, however, dealt with very different facets of Philadelphia, reviving past projects: *Giant Steps* (1994) by the John Coltrane House Film Committee in Strawberry Mansion and *Music Education at the Clef Club* (2016), a school for Jazz, in South Philadelphia. While there were fewer than twenty people in attendance, the event itself was about community building. Members of the historical society were there to talk and free pretzels were distributed to welcome the audience including strangers like me and my family. The people who introduced the video expressed genuine ownership and pride in the 12-year-old work linking past and present.

In April 2017, I had attended a larger event for a wider public at Philadelphia's African-American History Museum. Entitled "Tone Poems & Light Stories," this exhibit combined artifacts from a changing Philadelphia in the early 20th century with selections from Scribe's films of migration stories and people. In the exhibit and at the reception, I was drawn into conversations with people who wove their own experiences and recollections into these films, creating community around shared media and experience. Once again, place, media and interactions were the building blocks of mediated community.

The availability of distribution channels from social media to YouTube and Vimeo clearly offers new opportunities and Scribe participates in them. Scribe's website lists over 200 videos, arranged alphabetically (http://www. scribe.org/). Most are shorts. Some entries on the list only provide textual information about the video; others have direct links to the video themselves. Some offer excerpts of the videos on YouTube and some have hyperlinks that link to the websites of, for example, Books Through Bars. Summaries may also include biographical materials and links about the facilitators and filmmakers. Scribe website also has another link that leads to New Releases, which offers 8 completed videos with live video links; interested visitors can purchase some of the collections although few sales have been made through these online channels. Like every practitioner of new media, Scribe also uses cross media platforms, even though this is just one aspect of its approaches to dissemination. This site, in a sense, is as much about representation of Scribe as a community organization and *archiving* its own history and vision as in producing new audiences, much less revenue. Ultimately, the product belongs to the producers, in this case, the community, and they decide how they are going to use the videos.

Again, is Scribe using the latest media technologies to further its goals? Obviously the projection of videos has gotten less complicated with high quality portable digital projectors. On the other hand, not much has changed at Scribe. Considering how the consumption of video has changed in the last twenty years, one might ask how Scribe could use the new tools. Most young people, for example, consume their videos on line via their mobile devise. Should Scribe try to capture this type of audience with an app?

To answer such questions, we must consider the different ways videos are consumed and their relationship with community building. Could the organizations put the video on their website and get a bigger audience, thereby attracting them to support or engage with the organization? Yes, if *they* wish to. However, these works have to share an immense and crowded internet space. If we associate Web 2.0 with young people as digital natives, we might learn from the ways they select and share their favorite video with their group of online friends and encourage community media producers to do the same. Yet, this would require more extensive discussion and even training in wider platforms for organizations that are often short on resources. It also would sever the consumption of the videos from specific screening in real places but it could potentially lose the opportunity for face to face interaction, for recognition of self and neighbors, as well as Scribe's initial commitment of extending media literacy and access across digital divides. Community needs have not been erased by contemporary media ecologies. Alternative networks formed on line, or at least instigated by online sharing do not replace the core practices of community in these media so much as supplement them. Scribe offers a lesson in permanence amidst a world in change.

Conclusions

These short reviews and reflections on Scribe Video two decades after my original research repose the relationship between community media and new technologies by reassessing the categories of my initial work on context, production, product and distribution. Community media outlets, in the nearly 40 years of Scribe's work around Philadelphia, have been created to challenge the dominance of commercial mass media. Community media processes associated with Scribe are accessible, participatory, and low cost. New technologies are there for easier production, upload and viewing; however, Scribe's focus throughout has been less on media and technology than on community building including media literacy and reinforcing community through media practices. New media certainly have expanded the potential for everyone to be media producers and distributors and new worlds within which such projects can be created and distributed locally and globally. However, as Scribe has insisted, community also relies on the ability of people getting together and working towards their common goals. Within this framework, place, participation and process continue to be the most important elements in their important vision of the community in community media.

Within new worlds of mediation, Scribe Media Center continues to strive to use media to build communities and many communities that have been served by Scribe have learned to use media to express themselves, articulate their visions and using videos to communicate with their constituents.

Of course, Scribe now also has its own Facebook, Instagram and Twitter accounts and a fairly robust website in order to reach interested parties; nevertheless, most deep relationships still depends on the close, personal interaction taking place in real spaces to thrive. Scribe uses new media more to make initial contacts with new members, to enhance production and to use the web to better distribute its works, so more people can learn about what they do. Clearly, it might also choose to do more. Yet, these, too, are choices for Scribe to make as a community organization itself. As Scribe continues to evolve in the digital age, it has embraced thoughtfully some digital technologies and opportunities, yet only to better serve its place based orientation in community building. Ultimately, is that not the definition of community in community media?

References

Atton, C. (2014). Alternative media, the mundane, and "everyday citizenship". In M. Ratto, M. Boler, and R. Deibert (Eds.), *DIY citizenship: Critical making and social media* (pp. 343–359). Cambridge, MA MIT Press.

Bowman, S. & Willis, C. (2003). WeMedia: How audiences are shaping the future of news and information, The Media Center at the American Press Institute, Reston, VA.

Burgess, J. (2006) Hearing ordinary voices: Cultural studies, vernacular creativity and digital storytelling. *Continuum, 20*(2), 201–214.

Çoban, B. (Ed.) (2016). Social media and social movements: The transformation of communication patterns. Lanham, MD: Lexington Books.

Jenkins, H. (1988). Star Trek rerun, reread, rewritten: Fan writing as textual poaching." *Critical Studies in Mass Communication,5*(2), 85–107.

Kim, Y. C., & Ball-Rokeach, S. J. (2006). Community storytelling network, neighborhood context, and civic engagement: A multilevel approach. *Human Communication Research, 32*(4): 411–439.

N. A. Participatory Community Video, Scribe Video Center, and Place by Louis Massiah https://www.ithaca.edu/fleff/tropianoandzimmermann/massiah/?platform=hootsuite

Ramasubramanian, S. (2016). Racial/ethnic identity, community-oriented media initiatives, and transmedia storytelling. *The Information Society, 32*(5), 333–342.

Reitsamer, R., & Zobl, E. (2014). Alternative media production, feminism, and citizenship practices 328–342 In M. Ratto, M. Boler, & R. Deibert (Eds.), *DIY citizenship: Critical making and social media*. Cambridge, MA: MIT Press.

Wong, C. (1999). Understanding grassroots audiences: Imagination, reception, and use in community videography. *Velvet Light Trap* #42, 91–102.

Wong, C. (2002). Grassroots authors. In D. Gerstner & J. Staiger (Eds.), *Authorship and Film* (pp. 213–231). New York: Routledge.

11. The Tacit Dimension of Communication: Symbolic Competence and Symbolic Power

DAVID W. PARK

The field of communication has made numerous important contributions to understanding the context around culture. Critical political economists of communication have amply demonstrated how the features of media systems can shape content. Scholarship concerning media reception has instructed us about the extent to which audience response cannot be explained entirely through reference to message characteristics. Marshall McLuhan and the other so-called medium level theorists have addressed how the introduction of a medium provides the impetus for cultural change. Media effects researchers have given us countless valuable insights into how different messages can affect audience members' beliefs, attitudes, and behaviors. In almost all of this work one finds scholars drawn to the idea that that intelligibility reigns and that, for the most part, messages are meaningful. There is a tacit centering of the academic project—within and beyond the field of communication—on the idea that messages are intelligible, that our responses to them stem from our being able to understand them to some extent, and that this is an important part of how the media come to matter. After all, why would we care about messages if they were not meaningful?

Larry Gross gave us a most compelling argument for understanding how intelligibility should not always be taken for granted. By so doing, he explained one of the most important means by which communication comes to work. He did so by arguing that communication often does not work, that messages often do not wind up meaning anything to wide swaths of would-be audience members. Regardless of any cognitive complexity on the audience's part, any opportunities for resistance to a dominant ideology, any public-mindedness on the part of those who operate media organizations, messages can be unintelligible. This oft-overlooked element in the communication process derives from Gross's focus on a tacit dimension of communication: the audience member's symbolic competence.

In this chapter, I will explain the basic idea of symbolic competence, put the idea of symbolic competence into a broader context in communication and other fields, and conclude with some notes regarding why it is that the symbolic competence project never came to occupy the place on center stage I think it deserves.

The Tacit Dimension of Intelligibility

In the DNA of Gross's concern for symbolic competence one can find him digging around, isolating how messages come to be meaningful. There is a sense that—to many people—messages come off more or less as white noise, or as meaningless chatter, or perhaps as an overheard conversation in a language one does not speak. Symbolic competence is the thing that allows us to decode a message at all, and appreciation for symbolic competence requires us to attend to something tacit.

When Gross teaches symbolic competence, he does so with reference to the tacit. It was two books—Eugen Herrigel's *Zen in the Art of Archery* (1953) and Michael Polanyi's *The Tacit Dimension* (1966)—that I recall him using to explain the workings of symbolic competence. Both books emphasize the exuberance of the human condition and our inability to capture the human condition completely via reference to referential symbols. In other words: content fails us all the time. Even more directly relevant to my discussion here, both books address the content-less 'click' that occurs in between ignorance of how an act is performed and fluency in the means of accomplishing the act. They do this in strikingly different contexts.

Zen in the Art of Archery (1953) finds German philosopher Eugen Herrigel telling the story of his own tutelage in archery, under the guidance of Master Kenzo Awa. Herrigel uses archery as an exemplar of what Dhyana Buddhism—or Zen—can teach those unfamiliar with it. It functions as a terrific introduction to the principles of Zen, especially for westerners. Herrigel emphasizes how his studies of archery and the Zen approach led him away from the kinds of theoretical or rationalist concepts that one might expect out of Western philosophy. He came to find that "all right doing is accomplished only in a state of true selflessness, in which the doer cannot be present any longer as 'himself'" (1953, p. 44). His archery master warned him that he should "not practice anything except self-detaching immersion" (1953, p. 49). Concluding notes address how archery can be compared to other skills, such as sword fighting, where "[t]he more" [the sword fighter] tries to make the brilliance of his swordplay dependent on his own reflection, on the conscious utilization of his skill, on his fighting experience and tactics, the more he inhibits the free 'working of the 'heart'" (1953, pp. 72–73). A similar point can be made regarding the practice of ink-painting, where mastery "is only attained when the hand, exercising perfect control over technique, executes what hovers before the mind's eye at the same moment when the mind begins to form it, without there being a hair's breadth between" (1953, p. 77). In this manner Herrigel assembles a model for practice that emphasizes not the individual agent but the context in which the agent becomes immersed. The attainment of no-mind points us away from content-based or intellectualized discussions of how we go about doing things, and toward a fuller understanding of fluency and competence as embodied and unconscious practice.

In *The Tacit Dimension*, the philosopher chemist Michael Polanyi begins from "the fact that *we can know more than we can tell*" (1966, p. 4 [ital. in orig.]). What he develops is a powerful critique of the positivist approach to science, and the assumptions about knowledge that positivism carries with it. Polaynyi builds much of his critique on ideas from Gestalt psychology. Gestalt psychology instructs us that we recognize a familiar face "by integrating our awareness of its particulars without being able to identify these particulars" (1966, p. 6). It is "[t]his shaping or integrating I hold to be the great and indispensable tacit power by which all knowledge is discovered and, once discovered, is held to be true" (1966, p. 6). Polanyi links this kind of knowing to the phenomenon called subception, wherein we acquire knowledge without explicitly knowing what we know (1966, pp. 7–8). Polanyi offers a profoundly embodied understanding of knowledge, where, "by elucidating the way our bodily processes participate in our perceptions we will throw light on the bodily roots of all thought, including man's highest creative powers" (1966, p. 15). As Polyanyi elucidates in his *Personal Knowledge*, the "aim of a skillful performance is achieved by the observance of a set of rules which are not known as such to the person following them" (1958, p. 49). Polanyi's central focus in *The Tacit Dimension* was scientific knowledge, but he plainly understood that once science had been demonstrated to rely on inchoate and unnoticed psychological and social phenomena, the same tacit dimension could be extended to all realms of human experience.

All of this focus on the tacit might frustrate a student of communication. One might ask: what is it that happens in these countless silences that helps us understand communication? Especially given Gross's close identification with the Cultural Indicators project—with its systematic consideration of broad patterns in television messages—this focus on silence was most striking. Of course he uses these texts to establish conceptual scaffolding for the idea that symbolic competence is always part of communication. Symbolic competence takes its place as the tacit dimension of the communication process.

Symbolic Competence

After arriving at the Annenberg School of Communications in the fall of 1968, Gross found himself "making a sudden, unplanned sideways move from social psychology" (Gross, 2009, p. 66). In the years just before he and George Gerbner launched the Cultural Indicators project into very high gear, Gross published a number of works concerning the quiet things that make communication possible. In 1973 through 1975, Gross published "Art as the communication of competence," (1973a) "Modes of communication and the acquisition of symbolic competence," (1973b) "Symbolic strategies" (with Sol Worth, 1974), "How true is television's image?" (1975a), and "Yes, but is it communication?" (1975b). When I studied with Gross, the Herrigel and Polanyi books were combined with "Modes of Communication and the Acquisition of Symbolic Competence" and "Art as the Communication of Competence" to explain how messages in art came to be meaningful.

Throughout these writings, Gross presents a careful argument regarding how this quiet part of the communication process—symbolic competence—comes to matter, and why something as seemingly uncontroversial as fluency in a symbolic code—an ability to receive a message qua message—can help pry open much of what we need to understand about the workings of media. The successful performance of a communication act requires that the audience have symbolic competence.

The opening salvo in this approach to communication comes in "Modes of Communication and the Acquisition of Symbolic Competence," where Gross begins by sketching out one of the precepts that underwrites much of his subsequent scholarship: the idea that "[m]eaning can only be understood or purposively communicated within a symbolic mode, and some minimal level of competence is the basic precondition for the creation or comprehension of symbolic meaning within such a mode" (1973b, p. 189). Symbolic competence requires

(1) knowing the range of symbols and the range of referents to which they apply, (2) some awareness of the operations and transformations involved in coding such messages and activities, (3) the ability to store and retrieve information coded in the proper mode, and often, if not always (4) some awareness of the results of prior performances (by oneself or others) that may serve as the basis for evaluating the quality of the encoded behavior/message. (1973b, p. 194)

This is not very complex, but already one finds a refreshing acknowledgment of the fact that messages do not contain meaning and do not demand response and may in fact not even be recognized as messages if the recipient lacks the necessary symbolic competence.

Of course, like Herrigel learning archery, we attain symbolic competence indirectly, through immersion. When learning our native tongue, Gross writes, "[w]e begin to hear meanings instead of sounds, and we do so involuntarily" (1973b, p. 197). We can acquire symbolic competence in a variety of different modes, including the social-gestural, iconic, logico-mathematical, and musical modes (1973b, pp. 197–200). Gross finds great significance in the existence of this breadth of modes of symbolic competence. He describes a "verbal fallacy" at work in many considerations of how we think, learn, and communicate. This fallacy involves taking it as given that "thinking is primarily linguistic," and thus that "readings and writing is a precondition for all meaningful learning" (1973b, p. 202).

This focus on competence found a more focused outlet in Gross's article titled "Art as the Communication of Competence." Here Gross extended the idea of symbolic competence to the arena of art. The interdependence between the roles of communicator and audience member becomes a keynote in this discussion. Gross notes that, according to his definition of artistic communication, "it is necessary that" artist and communicator "share a common symbolic code" (1973a, p. 115). For an audience member to decode an artistic work, the "work must be perceived by the audience *as the result of purposive acts of choice*, and responded to in terms of the audience's sense of taste and quality" (1973a, p. 116, [ital in orig]). Again it is a silent and invisible component to this that sets everything in motion. He considers how "the actual operations involved in the act of skillful performance"—the pianist's technique, the painter's brushstroke—"come to be tacit and transparent" (1973a, p. 125). With this then established, Gross explains how different criteria come to be "applied in the evaluation of the competence of the creative performance" (1973a, p. 126).

Much the same philosophy of symbolic competence can be found in Sol Worth and Gross's *Journal of Communication* article titled "Symbolic Strategies" (1974). Here we see the idea of symbolic competence broadened

significantly, used to address not just art but the very fundaments of significa-
tion. Worth and Gross start about as broadly as possible, addressing the question
of how "we distinguish 'natural' from 'symbolic' events, and how … we assign
meaning to them" (1974, p. 27). They explain that the difference between natural and symbolic events can be found not in the events themselves, but in the
interpretive strategy we employ when faced with them. Worth and Gross sort
meaning situations into three categories: existential, ambiguous, and communicational (1974, p. 28). Communicational meaning situations are those "we
clearly 'know' to be symbolic and communicative," as when we read a book,
converse with friends, surf the web, or watch television (Worth & Gross, 1974,
p. 28). In a gesture back to the idea of symbolic competence, they note that
"meaning is not inherent within the sign itself, but rather in the social context,
whose conventions and rules dictate the articulatory and interpretive strategies
to be invoked by producers and interpreters of symbolic forms" (Worth &
Gross, 1974, p. 30). What follows is a description of how Worth and Gross
envision the process whereby humans come to develop symbolic competence.

Gross's focus on symbolic competence gets connected to broader and
more socially-oriented themes in communication study in the capstone for
this era, a chapter titled "How True is Television's Image?" (1975a). Here
Gross deftly explains the general idea of communication processes depending
on the social process of distributing symbolic competence. Instead of laying
out the kinds of broad outlines one finds in his other writings on symbolic
competence, here Gross begins with a blistering critique of "Western industrial
civilization" (1975a, p. 23). This is then linked to a brief and by now familiar description of the modes of human communication. Gross argues that,
as a result of the "non-equalitarian, exploitative social structure" in Western
industrial societies, these societies "have tended to narrow the range of commonly available and culturally valued symbolic competencies." These societies
are thus "characterized by a low level of *social synergy*" (1975a, p. 30 [ital. in
orig.]). Drawing on the ideas of anthropologist Ruth Benedict and psychologist Abraham Maslow, Gross explains that the "underlying psychology of a low
synergy social system is that of an economy of scarcity, in which the important resources are so limited that one man's wealth must inevitably reduce the
amount that is available to others" (1975a, p. 31). The unequal distribution of
wealth—and its attendant psychology—comes to shape even the "potentially
inexhaustible" resources such as "knowledge and information, art and beauty,
love and affection" (1975a, p. 31). This argument culminates in sections titled
"Asocial knowledge" (1975a, p. 34) and "Asocial art," where Gross explains
how this low synergy means of organizing a society results in horribly fore-
shortened understandings of how knowledge and art can operate.

Gross concludes the chapter by returning to broader arguments regarding what all of this means for how Western industrial society functions. The question we face, he concludes, is "whether an industrial system will be capable of providing its members with values and skills which are less maladaptive and more productive of self-sufficiency and meaningful social interaction" (1975a, p. 45). In a turn that brings this exercise closer to more familiar questions from media studies, Gross considers whether the mass media provide any way out of these dilemmas he has outlined. He finds little cause for optimism, pointing to two dysfunctions resulting from mass media: first, "the cultivation of false consciousness and biased images of reality," and second, the mass media's creation of "conditions in which our exposure to symbolic events is fundamentally passive and non-interactive" (1975a, p. 45). And so the mass media come to be implicated in the perpetuation of the low synergy aspects of Western civilization.

Throughout this work Gross emphasizes something media studies has habitually ignored: how it comes to be possible for communication to happen. Recurrent themes in this work include the idea that symbolic competence is necessary for message decoding, that there are numerous modes through which communication can operate, and that significance and meaning are not natural categories. It is the workings of this application of symbolic competence that makes communication happen. The wildly uneven distribution of this skill—which is itself made possible in large part by our lack of interest in there even being a skill at work—arranges things so that communication frequently functions as a curiously closed-off and inaccessible prospect. A low synergy social structure is reproduced via the uneven distribution of symbolic competence.

Note that in all of this work, Gross focuses squarely on the tacit dimension, on the very possibility of a message being received qua message. This focus on competence means that Gross was not looking at any of what have emerged as normal sites of data gathering for the communication scholar. One is tempted to compare this to Marshall McLuhan's dictum that the 'medium is the message,' or perhaps more appropriately to the symbolic interactionists' focus on how signs come to accumulate meaning only in particular social contexts. As with McLuhan and the symbolic interactionists, Gross pries back the message itself to see what makes it work. Both McLuhan and symbolic interactionism have been criticized for not clearing sufficient theoretical space for the workings of political and symbolic power. Gross's concern for power is easy to notice; power is implicated and reproduced in the uneven distribution of symbolic competence in the low synergy social systems of Western industrialized civilization. Though it takes a few different forms in the writings from this period of Gross's work, the basic structure of Gross's arguments here follows a path that starts with the establishment of the importance of symbolic competence, moves on to an explanation of different varieties (modes) of symbolic competence, and then concludes with an emphasis on how those of us in the industrialized West live in a system where these competences are unevenly valued and poorly distributed.

The central issue at work in all of this is how symbol systems and their component symbols come to be intelligible. A symbol system for which we lack competence will strike us as being so much static. The idea is reminiscent of Norbert Wiener's consideration of "'To-whom-it-may-concern' messages," (1954, p. 70) wherein messages being ultimately decoded in *any* way requires the individual (as audience receiver) to be able to apply some symbolic competence. The uneven distribution of symbolic competences across the social field that Gross describes puts this broad point into stunning social-political relief. Gross casts a net across social theory that puts the psychology of perception in touch with a leftist political imagination. Put in the deadpan of statistical analysis, we find a non-random distribution of symbolic competences, one that would seem to match closely the other inequalities in our society.

A crucial implication of Gross's work on symbolic competence is that the circuit between communicator and audience member is not always completed. Even when an audience member has the message right in front of them, there is a not-negligible possibility that it will mean nothing or nearly nothing to this person. "I don't get it" and "this isn't for me" are common, revealing, and important responses to messages. Unintelligibility such as one would find amongst individuals who lack symbolic competence is important because it is not uncommon and it is not randomly distributed. It is not a fluke, but is instead an indication that there is a major societal imbalance between those who do and do not possess symbolic fluency. Certainly John Durham Peters (1999) and Amit Pinchevski (2005) have philosophized communication as normally incomplete. Their interventions have cast light on our tendency to presume communication usually 'works.' Constructivists and cyberneticists have commented widely on communication breakdown. What Gross offers that can be distinguished from many other ideas of communication breakdown is an explanation of how intelligibility relates to social phenomena, and thus to power.

Symbolic Competence's Broader Application

Gross's description of symbolic competence owed something to Noam Chomsky's linguistics. Much as Chomsky has assumed that symbolic competence in a language was the same across all of those who are fluent in it, Gross takes symbolic competence in a mode to be more or less standard across those who have it.

Pierre Bourdieu developed a criticism of Chomsky that can be used to critique and extend Gross's ideas. Bourdieu tells us that Chomsky credits "the speaking subject in his universality with the perfect competence which the Saussurian tradition granted him tacitly" (1991, pp. 43–44). Bourdieu takes issue with the fact that Chomsky presumes that we can either be competent or not competent. The problem is that Chomsky's version "sidesteps the question of the economic and social conditions of the acquisition of the legitimate competence and of the constitution of the market in which this definition of the legitimate and the illegitimate is established and imposed" (1991, p. 44). In other words, Chomsky presumes that competence in a symbolic mode is much the same across the social formation. It can be acquired or not. This critique of Chomsky's model can be extended to Gross's understanding of symbolic competence in that Gross does not distinguish between different types of symbolic competence within the same communicational mode. In Gross's terms from the 1970s, one either does or does not have competence in a symbolic mode. Recall that it was the uneven distribution of who does and does not have symbolic competence that concerned Gross.

In a sense, all Bourdieu does is extend a version of Gross's critique of Western industrialized civilization into a model that takes heed of how not all competences within the same mode are the same. On the level of linguistic competence, different people are given access to different versions of the same codes and modes. Bourdieu warns us that "[t]o speak of *the* language, without further specification, as linguists do, is tacitly to accept the *official* definitions of the *official* language of a political unit" (1991, p. 45 [ital. in orig.]). Elsewhere, he applies this to the situation of competence in the codes of political commentary, where he asserts that one problem with the idea of public opinion polls is that they presume that "producing an opinion is available to all" (1993, p. 149). Bourdieu's argument is that symbolic competence in the codes of public affairs is not universally distributed. In a move that strikes me as being decidedly Grossian, Bourdieu even links the issues of symbolic competence that undermine public opinion polling to issues related to art, where "people must first think of the work of art as a work of art, and once they have done so, they need to have perceptual categories in order to construct and structure it" (1993, p. 152). In a parallel to the world of art, in order to respond to a political question, one must "be capable of seeing it as political," and also "to be capable of applying political categories to it" (1993, p. 152). In this manner, Bourdieu can be seen effectively extending Gross's concerns regarding the distribution of symbolic competence in modes into the world of symbolic competence in the dominant codes within these modes. Again, much as Gross would have it, the symbolic competence that Bourdieu describes is very unequally distributed amongst the population. In other words, as Bourdieu and Alain Darbel have argued: "[o]bjects are not rare, but the propensity to consume them is" (1990, p. 37).

There are countless ways to apply this concern for symbolic competence and its distribution to the study of the media. One relatively straightforward application of the concern for how well modes of understanding are distributed concerns media technology. We can understand fluency in media technology as a kind of symbolic competence, one that is not evenly distributed. Certainly this is one of the implications of Carolyn Marvin's description of how "technological literacy" functioned "as social currency" as media were introduced to the U.S. in the 19th and 20th centuries (1988, p. 9). Electrical engineers and other experts in telephone and telegraph technology asserted their own superiority over against "those suspect in electrical culture and perhaps dangerous to it, in terms of their textual competence" (1988, p. 15). Lots of kinds of technical knowledge can function as cultural capital separating different groups based on their access to symbolic competence of a particular kind. Of course this is reminiscent of the digital divide, the idea that different groups are separated in part by their different levels of access to and different understandings of how new media operate.

The idea of differing types of symbolic competence on the level of the communicative code can be pushed further. Indeed, if we are truly seeing niche audiences take the place of the mass audience, it will likely follow that divides in symbolic competence will become a more pressing issue. Rodney Benson tells us that as "cable television leads to the proliferation of news channels and programs, television may begin to operate more as an agent of class differentiation, as it already has in the United States" (1999, p. 485). In the language of Gross's symbolic competence, we are seeing the emergence of niches developed around divergent codes, each involving parallel but mutually distinguishable competences for meaningful audience response. The fragmentation of the media audience likely subtends the extension of the same kinds of problems in the distribution of competences that Gross described in "How True is Television's Image."

Most broadly, symbolic power can itself be understood largely in terms of the kinds of divergences of symbolic competence that Gross called to our attention in his work. Bourdieu argues that the symbolic power of a communicator "depends on their symbolic capital, i.e. on the *recognition*, institutionalized or not, that they receive from a group" (1991, p. 72 [ital. in orig.]). The symbolic power of utterances depends upon the differentiation of the spheres of human activity—an important part of what makes our society low synergy. The power of words becomes the "*delegated power* of the spokesperson, and his speech is no more than a testimony and one among others ... of the *guarantee of delegation* which is vested in him" (Bourdieu, 1991, p. 107 [ital. in orig.]). The uneven distribution of symbolic competence thus creates the grounds for symbolic power through the recognition of different levels of competence. In essence, we accept symbolic power because we recognize the different fluencies in play and accept the guarantee of delegation that comes from proper use of a code. Journalism speaks in its codes, politicians speak in theirs, musicians perform (and speak) in theirs, and so the social formation continues to reproduce itself. One under-explored corner of this idea is the extent to which symbolic power can break down as a result of profoundly diverged social conditions (I am tempted to suggest 'extremely low synergy societies'), where the guarantee of delegation Bourdieu posits is no longer recognized because the bridge between the authority and the public is too vast. Perhaps this is yet another case where we have over-estimated the power of messages to prompt some kind of response, to cue anything meaningful at all. This may give us even more motivation to concern ourselves with the conditions that support symbolic competence.

Conclusion

It is worth pausing to consider why Gross's concern for symbolic competence never became a more prominent school of thought in the field of communication. Gross's influence in the field is tremendous, and Gross himself would return occasionally to the theme of symbolic competence, but it must be admitted that the tacit dimension of symbolic competence never became the kind of towering influence in the field that other ideas of his eventually would. I think there are many reasons for the field's relative lack of pickup on the issue of symbolic competence.

Some of the reasons for symbolic competence's relatively marginal position in the field of communication derive from the features of the work that Gross published about symbolic competence. For instance, Gross described symbolic competence in terms that were drawn from wide and interdisciplinarity influences. Freshly plucked from the field of psychology by the Annenberg School of Communications at the University of Pennsylvania, Gross was still a transplant, a margin walker willing to engage with ideas from almost every part of academe. One can still read his work on symbolic competence and marvel at its creativity, its foresight, its critical edge, and its lucidity. But this interdisciplinarity, this connection to almost everything, seems also to have prevented symbolic competence from becoming a more broadly pursued project in communication. Certainly there was no pre-existing school of thought that stood ready to pick up Gross's ideas and develop an institution around them. It was too social scientific for the nascent cultural studies movement, and too humanist or too closely connected to critical theory for many in the social sciences.

Additionally, Gross's scholarship about symbolic competence did not come with research methods linked to the idea's broader application. The contrast with many other more methodologically ready-made ideas is instructive. Agenda-setting theory, the two-step flow of media influence, and cultivation theory all had methodological programs that filled in many of the spaces for those who hoped to adopt them for a research project. Gross presented symbolic competence more as an argument than as a research program.

Third, Gross's own focus moved on from symbolic competence to cultivation theory. Though he certainly never abandoned symbolic competence, by the late 1970s the Cultural Indicators project Gross worked on with George Gerbner had begun to define more and more of his scholarly output. Though cultivation theory certainly shared a great deal with the ideas laid out in Gross's considerations of symbolic competence, Gross's focus on symbolic competence per se had diminished markedly by 1980. The issue of symbolic competence would continue to play a role in Gross's scholarship concerning visual communication and art, but it would not occupy such a central role as it did from 1973–1975.

Fourth, the approaches to communication associated with 'cultural studies' came to touch on some of what Gross described in his considerations of symbolic competence. The concern for culture and for art that Gross exemplified here would find a home in much of the work done in cultural studies. Conceptualized as it often was as a kind of force in opposition to media effects research, cultural studies embraced an approach to culture that emphasized dominant, negotiated, and oppositional readings of culture to the neglect of concerns related to intelligibility. Methodologically, the cultural studies tradition in communication was identified largely in opposition to social scientific modes of understanding that Gross himself found to be perfectly apposite to his own work. On a disciplinary level, Gross's work on symbolic competence was too social scientific, and too disconnected from the work of the Birmingham Centre for Contemporary Cultural Studies and the work of James W. Carey to take its place among the British and American waves of cultural studies that had already begun to reshape the field of communication.

The history and sociology of science has repeatedly reminded us that it is not the quality of an idea that determines its level of prominence in a field of study. Gross's work on symbolic competence gives us a terrific example of an approach to communication scholarship that pries open how almost all communication works, connects divergent strands of communication-relevant ideas, and presents an important critical perspective on how inequalities reign in many communication contexts. The field of communication needs as many good ideas as it can find, and thus we ignore these ideas at our own peril.

References

Benson R. (1999). Field theory in comparative context: A new paradigm for media studies. *Theory and Society, 28*(3), 463–498.

Bourdieu, P. (1991). *Language and symbolic power.* Cambridge, UK: Polity Press.

Bourdieu, P. (1993). *Sociology in question.* London: Sage Publications.

Bourdieu, P., & Darbel, A. (1990). *The love of art: European art museums and their public.* Stanford: Stanford University Press.

Gross, L. (1973a). Art as the communication of competence. *Social Science Information, 12*(5), 115–141.

Gross. L. (1973b). Modes of communication and the acquisition of symbolic competence. In G. Gerbner, L. Gross, & W. Melody (Eds.), *Communication technology and social policy* (198–208). New York: Wiley.

Gross, L. (1975a). How true is television's image? In *Getting the message across* (23–52). Paris: UNESCO Press.

Gross, L. (1975b). Yes, but is it communication? *Journal of Communication, 25* (1), 191–194.

Gross. L. (2009). My media studies. *Television and New Media, 10*(1), 66–68.

Herrigel, E. (1953). *Zen in the art of archery.* New York: Vintage.

Marvin, C. (1988). *When old technologies were new: Thinking about electric communication in the late nineteenth century.* Oxford, UK: Oxford University Press.

Peters, J. D. (1999). *Speaking into the air: A history of the idea of communication.* Chicago: University of Chicago Press.

Pinchevski, A. (2005). *By way of interruption: Levinas and the ethics of communication.* Pittsburgh, PA: Duquesne University Press.

Polanyi, M. (1958). *Personal knowledge: Towards a post-critical philosophy.* Chicago: University of Chicago Press.

Polanyi, M. (1966). *The tacit dimension.* Chicago: University of Chicago Press.

Wiener, N. (1954). *The human use of human beings: Cybernetics and society.* Boston: Houghton Mifflin.

Worth, S., & Gross, L. (1974). "Symbolic strategies." *Journal of Communication, 24*(4), 27–39.

Part Three

Towards Inclusion

12. The Thread of Concern: Wildlife Films, Art, and Representation

Derek Bousé

Wild animals and motion pictures have always been a good match—the bigger the better. The acclaim in recent years received by such big-screen wildlife spectacles as *Kedi* (2016), *Monkey Kingdom* (2015), *Bears* (2014), *Chimpanzee* (2012), *The Last Lions* (2011), going back to *March of the Penguins* (2005), might make it hard for some audiences to recall a time when wildlife films were the exclusive province of television, where, in the words of the philosopher Dangerfield, they got *no respect*. Yet the years spent on the small screen (when it was still small) were a time of great ferment for the wildlife film genre. Storytelling models were finely tuned, new themes were explored, techniques were perfected, technology improved, budgets increased, and, above all, the audience was greatly expanded.

All of this went on right under the noses of scholars and critics, yet somehow escaped their notice. The Cinema Studies world had barely ever acknowledged the existence of wildlife films; *genre* theorists, in particular, had ignored them altogether. Even in the broadly based world of Media Studies, which had long been more television-friendly, the same held true. Soap operas, sit-coms, mini-series, music videos, animated cartoons, and even talk radio had all begun filling the pages of communication journals, but wildlife films, despite a growing global audience, continued to be overlooked.

Such was the state of affairs when, as a graduate student in the late 1980s, I approached Larry Gross to discuss the idea of doing an M. A. thesis on wildlife films. I feared at the time that I would be told to go back and find a subject with more *gravitas*, but I couldn't have been more wrong about Gross, and about what he believed and valued.

The significance of that moment might be understood in relation to a radio interview Gross gave three decades later. When asked if there were any one theme running through all of his work, Gross responded, "there is a thread that runs through my concerns ... I suppose, for justice, and for ... equal treatment for all."[1] Once again I was wrong about him, for I anticipated his answer would be a concern with *injustice*, but Gross put it in the affirmative—it was what he was *for*, rather than what he was against, that defined him.[2]

Expanding on this modest self-assessment, three themes emerge from Gross's writing and teaching that informed that early study of wildlife films he commissioned all those years ago, that have continued to inspire in the decades since, and that provide a map of the present discussion: (1) his concern with fair treatment, respect, inclusivity, and the undoing of neglect and disenfranchisement of all sorts; (2) his egalitarian view of culture, particularly in the realm of of art, as reflected in a concern with *who* gets to define it, who gets to say what is and what is not art, as well as who can and cannot be considered an artist; (3) his concern with the power to represent others (in media images), and with the real-world consequences of that power (and of those images).

Us and Them

Gross extended the principle of "equal treatment" as broadly as possible. It didn't apply just to ethnic or sexual minorities, or even just to human beings, for that matter, but to just about anyone or anything outside *mainstream* opinion. This meant, simply, that perspectives, ideas, and research subjects that might otherwise be dismissed deserved a fair hearing. He saw no reason why wildlife films shouldn't be taken seriously and accorded some scholarly respect. His immediate support for the idea even suggested there was a wrong that needed to be righted.

From a film-historical standpoint, there surely was. Major works by noted film historians had all failed to deal adequately, if at all, with wildlife films.[3] Yet motion picture cameras had been turned toward wild animals from the very beginning—and even before, if one recalls the animal images of Muybridge and Marey in the pre-history of cinema. In the earliest years of moving pictures, even before the refinements that led to the codification of narrative cinema as we know it today, filmmakers discovered what YouTube cat videos showed many decades later: the camera loves animals, and audiences find the images irresistible. So many early films depicted animals that it seems fair to say that the origins of wildlife film are inseparable from the origins of cinema itself.

What made animals so fascinating to viewers, however, was the very thing that later led critics and scholars to turn away: *they aren't us*. The presumption seemed to be that images depicting animals said nothing about us, about who we are, or about the human condition, with the implication that they could never, therefore, be taken seriously. Wildlife filmmakers have tended to see it otherwise. One producer wrote that he saw wildlife films as helping us "make order out of the seeming chaos around us ... and out of the greatest mystery of all—ourselves."[4] Or, as another put it,

> Whether by design or by default, most of our nature films, in my view, are intended to serve as fables or moral tales, in which animals are employed as surrogate humans, manipulated by the filmmakers to enact contemporary culture myths, which serve the primary purpose of defining and reinforcing social values.[5]

No humanist bias had prevented the earliest filmmakers from traveling to the ends of the earth to film wild species, nor the crowds from turning out to see the images they brought back. Early films were short, and a typical night's program might include a number of them depicting a wide range of subjects, including animals and nature. In that sense, cinema in the early twentieth century was an equal-opportunity entertainer. It had not yet sorted itself into content genres, the audience had not yet fragmented, and the critical establishment was still unbiased.

Early camera teams in the UK found success filming what was right in their own backyards, producing revealing close-up studies of birds that wowed audiences at the time, and that are still impressive today. One of the leading teams in this area was that of the Kearton brothers, Richard and Cherry. In 1908 President Theodore Roosevelt invited Richard Kearton to the White House to screen for members of the U.S. Biological Survey some of the films they had made depicting British birds and mammals. Roosevelt was already convinced that wildlife motion pictures could be of value to science. He would later invite Cherry Kearton to film him on safari in Africa. In 1913, when some of Kearton's films were screened in New York, Roosevelt was on hand to give them an enthusiastic introduction.

What happened to diminish the respect wildlife films seemed to be acquiring in those early years, and put them on the downslope toward marginalization?

There is, of course, no simple answer—beyond the obvious humanist preference already mentioned. There are two historical points, however, that may help explain wildlife films' expulsion from the mainstream. It is worth recalling that many of the early wildlife-related films actually did include people as an essential part of the scene or the action, or at least as audience surrogates. There was room for them in the frame, as nearly everything was filmed in long-shot. They were shown feeding animals, viewing them, stalking them, capturing them, and, too often, killing them.

The adoption of telephoto lenses, however, meant that close-up images could be made even of dangerous or otherwise unapproachable animals in wild settings. These could easily be edited with shots of other animals to produce "built up" dramatic scenes just as in mainstream movies.[6] In this way, animal stories could be told on film that no longer required humans in the picture. The animals themselves could be the dramatic center. This was, in a way, the evolutionary branching-off point that led to the emergence of the true 'wildlife films' as we know them, as something distinct from documentary films, including those depicting safaris, research expeditions, and conservation efforts—all wildlife related, but all essentially human endeavors, which was the difference that made a difference.[7]

Second, wildlife films were late in organizing as an industry with a solid institutional base. The Charles Urban Trading Company formed in 1903 to produce educational and scientific films, including "The Unseen World" series of films about nature and animal life, but ended production after less than fifteen years. British Instructional Films formed in 1919, and although it produced the highly regarded "Secrets of Nature" series, it was not devoted exclusively to nature or wildlife production, and the series itself was discontinued in 1933.

Hollywood, Babelsberg, Rome, the great filmmaking centers of the world, did not absorb the nascent wildlife film genre and give it an institutional home. Warner Bros and MGM both had in-house animation units producing cartoons, but no such dedicated structure existed for wildlife film production until Disney set up shop to make its "True Life Adventures" at the end of the 1940s. Arguably, the fact that the majority of people making wildlife films had for so long been freelancers, without formal studio affiliation, led to the misperception that they were mere *amateurs*, and to their work not being taken seriously by scholars.[8]

Hollywood's attitude was different. It may not have created space at the studios for wildlife films, but it was still fraternal in its outlook toward those who made them. This can be seen in the surprising number of Academy Awards given to wildlife films, starting in 1938 with the British import *The Private Life of the Gannetts*.[9] Yet the preponderance of awards went to Disney for the "True Life Adventures" it produced between 1949 and 1960. Significantly, three were for "Best Documentary Feature."[10]

Looking at these films today it is hard to believe they could be seen as such. The narration is often tendentious, no scientists or researchers are included, and no 'science advisors' are credited.[11] Films in the series were as heavily edited, scored, manipulated, and nearly as fanciful as Disney's animated films, mainly because they were produced and written by the same people.[12] Yet they effectively codified wildlife film as a coherent film genre, and prefigured the 'blue chip' model of wildlife filmmaking that emerged as dominant in later decades.[13]

Eventually the "True Life" series title, with its pretensions to documentary and truth, was dropped. Disney moved into producing fictionalized wildlife movies that often included human actors and scripted dialogue, yet oddly continued to employ a 'voice-of-god' narrator to explain the animals' behavior and motivations. Some of these films were adapted from animal novels, but all were clearly aimed at younger audiences. After theatrical release, they were slotted nicely into the weekly Disney television program, which at that time was the reigning paragon of 'family' entertainment in America, which meant the content was suitable for children, which in turn meant, essentially, *children's programming*. It was another unfortunate setback for wildlife films in America, nearly cementing their marginalization.[14]

At about this time in the early 1960s, National Geographic began producing documentaries for television. Many of these dealt with wildlife content, but usually centered on the research or conservation efforts of scientists—which is what made them *documentaries*.[15] Eventually, however, NatGeo discovered that when films did not include humans or current issues they could be re-sold for repeated broadcast without appearing dated. As a result, many of their productions began to shed documentary pretensions and moved more firmly into the mold of true wildlife films. Nevertheless, from the mid-1960s on, NatGeo generated so many high quality productions that American-made wildlife films began the long march toward de-Disnification.

What they could not undo, however, was the fact that these films were all still made for television, where they were not seen as 'films,' but as episodes in ongoing series, such as the BBC's *Wildlife on One*, or PBS's *Nature*. At a time when dawn was just breaking for the VCR, this meant that wildlife films fell by default into the category of ephemeral mass entertainments, to be seen once and quickly forgotten—down the memory hole.[16] Apart from the occasional newspaper review, little or no critical ink was spilled on their behalf.

In the UK the situation was different. Since the early days of the "Unseen World" series, wildlife content had never been regarded as trivial. The BBC had already been producing it for both radio and television when, in 1957, it formed its Natural History Unit (BBC-NHU) in Bristol, devoted exclusively to wildlife and natural history television production. In 1961 competing broadcaster Anglia Television launched its own wildlife program, *Survival*, making films with an even stronger narrative drive, and which soon rivaled the NHU in output and quality. Oxford Scientific Films and a few others soon entered the mix, all adding to the yield of high quality wildlife programs, and altogether attracting a sizable and loyal audience.

Wildlife films in the English speaking world had thus at last established institutional bases that made it possible to collect and pool talent, to share and concentrate resources, to refine techniques, and to produce films of consistent high quality. An *industry* was coalescing. During the 1970s British wildlife films were repackaged for broadcast in the U.S., and in the 1980s new American wildlife series were launched, quickly gaining a foothold in the prime-time lineup (on PBS, anyway). In 1982 "Wildscreen" launched in Bristol, quickly becoming the premier *industry* film festival, where buyers and sellers came to together shape the market. Its awards ceremony became the wildlife film industry's version of the Oscars.

Still, in the 1980s, wildlife films were produced mainly for television, with the predictable result of exclusion from 'serious' critical and scholarly discourse—but not for long. Larry Gross's greenlighting of an early, minor contribution to the research was one of the first gestures that started the momentum in the other direction.

But Is It Art?

Gross's egalitarian sensibilities were manifest well beyond his concerns with matters of equal justice and fair treatment. They extended deep into the realms of culture (elite and popular), all the way to wildlife films, and well beyond.

Most notable was his reconceptualization of art. For him the arts were "media of communication through which members of a culture create and share knowledge, belief, and feeling," because the sender and receiver share some sort of symbolic code.[17] The emphasis, obviously, is on sharing. As often taught in schools, however, art became another system of inclusion and exclusion; artistic competence and performance became the exclusive "province of the exceptional."[18] Gross's position was a profound departure from the notion, dominant since the Renaissance, that a work of true art had to be unique, original, and highly individual—something of which only the gifted were capable.[19] Twentieth-century Modernism added to this the idea that art also had to be radically innovative, a break with the past, as well as with existing standards for judging and evaluating art.[20] The value of a work of art came to be determined, therefore, by the degree to which it was *difficult*. Incomprehensibility became modern art's guarantor. If it could not be understood, then it must be art – but of course that would mean it communicated nothing. By contrast, if it could be easily grasped and interpreted, if it were comprehensible, if it communicated a clear meaning or message, then its status as art would be in question, as it clearly has been in relation to various kinds of folk, popular, and mass arts—which have often been demoted to the status of 'entertainments.'[21]

Gross's conception of art was egalitarian, although not necessarily democratic.[22] He did not call for art to be made more available or more accessible. His project was reconceptualization, not redistribution. He saw the contradiction inherent in the ideology of radical innovation, in the idea that *real* art outstripped standards for evaluation, and therefore communicated nothing to the present because it was seen as being *ahead of its time*. Its alienated, misunderstood creator, therefore, was effectively exiled to the future. Essentially, this anti-communication position was *message not received*. In the age of abstraction, in which art had lost its 'aboutness,' it was presumed there was no message. The content, if anything, was the form—but here, precisely, was what allowed it to be understood as communication.

Cubism provides an instructive example. Since the Armory Show in 1913 American audiences have found Cubist art difficult. Yet take any ten Cubist paintings from that period, line them up in a row, and one can immediately see the pattern, the theme and its variations. Pattern recognition is the first step toward deducing a code, and is therefore the basis of communication. It allows us to distinguish signal from noise, and then to make even finer distinctions among variations on the theme. This allows us to form expectations, to enjoy the anticipation of their fulfillment, and the pleasurable tension when that fulfillment is delayed or deferred.[23] The Russian Formalists called this *retardation*—a regular feature of the experience of poetic meter and rhyme.[24]

This *aesthetic experience* (Gross's preferred term in place of *art*) can be had apart from full comprehension of poetry's linguistic content (aesthetic codes being less precise than linguistic codes, but codes nonetheless). In recognizing the pattern, we can infer that it was intentionally ordered for the purpose of implying meaning, that it is therefore a 'symbolic event.'[25] The same is obviously true of orchestral music, which has no content at all in the traditional sense. The 'meaning' is largely in the pattern, the experience of the compositional structure. It can be argued that something like this is the basis of the *auteur* theory of film, which allows even the lesser works of directors such as Hitchcock, Welles, or Peckinpah to be appreciated for the stylistic signatures or regular thematic concerns that transcend any one of their films.[26]

As the study of wildlife films began, the guiding assumption was only that there must be some sort of artistry in their making—that is, the application of some sort of conventions, some realization of creative intentions, and some tacit grasp or appreciation of these by audiences. Gross warned against any approach involving hypothesis testing. His advice was simply to see first what was happening systematically in wildlife films, to discover their patterns of action, to see what sort of conventions governed them—in a word, to crack their code.

It didn't take long to detect enough regularities to indicate that this was a coherent film genre in its own right, operating by its own formal codes and conventions. Chief among these were narrative codes—storytelling conventions that ultimately had more in common with Hollywood features than with documentary. In the years since, documentary theorists have also begun talking about the need for a strong narrative, often using the same terms as Hollywood screenwriting manuals,[27] but at that time no one outside the wildlife film industry was writing about the storytelling conventions of wildlife films, or even acknowledging them as a narrative form.[28]

Those inside the industry knew very well they were in the storytelling business. Longtime BBC producer Jeffery Boswall noted in the early 1970s the relationship between artistic legitimacy and conforming to storytelling conventions:

> The need for a compelling storyline presses home most compellingly. Wildlife films may be fact and not fiction, but there are ways in which they need to be artistic without being unscientific. The most vital part of these ways, in my opinion, is in the devising of the storyline.[29]

American wildlife filmmaker Marty Stouffer was even more succinct, admitting that all of his years of filmmaking could be wrapped up in a single word: "storytelling."[30]

History shows that the move from *actualité* to story film, that is, the turn toward narrative in cinema generally, including films about animals and wildlife, came in the earliest years of the twentieth century.[31] As wildlife films later began to branch off from mainstream cinema, especially in the sound era, a number of basic storyline models emerged, leading eventually to the genre's codification in the 1950s. By the 1980s, wildlife filmmakers had already been working within a set of well defined narrative conventions for decades.[32]

By the 1990s, newcomers and wannabes at wildlife film festivals and symposia were being urged by commissioning producers not to perfect their technical filmmaking skills, but rather to go out and *find new stories*. One could make the academic argument here that a story is an artificial construct imposed on nature, not found in it, and so on, yet in the end it made no difference. Producers were exhorting aspirants to see in 'natural events' their potential as 'symbolic events,'[33] and to find in them something that could be *told*, that could be dramatized, put into a familiar dramatic format or structure that audiences would recognize. In this sense (and in Gross's), their approach was *aesthetic* in its very conception. Wildlife films long ago abandoned any pretense of conveying reality directly and unambiguously, relying instead on the application of conventions in which the audience was already competent, in which they had achieved some degree of *tacit fluency*.

Although in the earliest years wildlife depictions may well have been enjoyed for the beauty of the animals and faraway landscapes, they came to be experienced aesthetically when they were appreciated in the context of other films like them, against a background of viewers' experience of those other films, and therefore as creative variations on recognizable themes. The expectations viewers formed likely evoked pleasure when they were fulfilled, or, as mentioned earlier, when they were delayed or deferred. This may not have qualified wildlife films as great art in the traditional sense, but at the very least it meant that they could no longer be dismissed as artless science inscription practiced by filmmaking amateurs. Watching them had become a fully articulated aesthetic experience.

Representation and Power

Lastly was the possibility that the very mode of representation in wildlife films might be one of systematic *mis*representation, that they might in some way be failing to represent their subjects accurately, and, more importantly, with fairness. Gross's years of involvement in Cultural Indicators research had already made him alert to that possibility. He understood only too well the real world consequences for minorities and marginalized groups (which would include animals) of systematic misrepresentation. "How we treat others," the critic Richard Dyer noted, "is based on how we see them."[34] For Gross this was both an ethical and a political concern. It had to do with the distribution of power in society, with who got to represent others, who got to shape their media image, who got to 'tell their story,' and of course to what ends.

In the case of wildlife films, that 'who' had rarely been anyone with a formal wildlife protection or preservation agenda. Most wildlife films had, over the years, been produced for the commercial marketplace by run-for-profit production companies and broadcasters in business, mainly, to provide mass entertainment. The situation seemed to illustrate the oft-repeated refrain of Gross's longtime associate George Gerbner that our modern storytellers were not people with something to tell, but corporations with something to sell.[35]

Still, many individual wildlife filmmakers had expressed deep, personal concern for the welfare of wild animals, if not a moral obligation to 'speak' for them, or to 'tell their story.' "If we take any side," reflected one, "it is that of the wild creatures who otherwise would have no voice."[36]

The ethicist Peter Singer had already put the duty to speak for animals in terms linking it to the struggles of other (human) minorities, noting that animals

> cannot make an organized protest against the treatment they receive. ... We have to speak up on behalf of those who cannot speak for themselves. You can appreciate how serious this handicap is by asking yourself how long blacks would have had to wait for equal rights if they had not been able to stand up for themselves and demand it. The less able a group is to stand up and organize against oppression, the more easily it is oppressed.[37]

Yet speaking for them is one thing, and telling their story quite another. It meant getting inside their heads, understanding their motivations and behavior. We humans had been presuming to do that for thousands of years, and, for the most part, getting it wrong—even in Academy Award winning 'documentaries.'

That, however, had begun to change. The post-behaviorist 'cognitive revolution' in psychological sciences had spilled over into research on other species, producing a wave of insights into animal cognition and behavior.[38] It did not wash away all misconceptions, some of which still go unquestioned, but it was at least eroding their foundations. The last fifty years have seen groundbreaking findings in areas such as tool formation and use, language skills, symbol recognition, self-awareness, perspective taking, moral awareness (a sense of fairness), theory of mind (the ability to recognize the mental states of others), and even meta-cognition (the ability to reflect on one's own thought processes, including assessing the strength of one's own memories).[39] It has been shown recently that some bird species, especially parrots and corvids (crows and ravens) have "higher neuron packing densities" in their brains, and are therefore capable of cognitive feats that rival those of the great apes. As a recent study noted,

> They manufacture and use tools, solve problems insightfully, make inferences about causal mechanisms, recognize themselves in a mirror, plan for future needs, and use their own experience to anticipate future behavior of conspecifics, or even humans, to mention just a few striking abilities.[40]

All of this has directly challenged the 'rational' doctrine put forth by Immanuel Kant that animals have neither self-awareness nor the ability to make moral judgments, and therefore "exist only as means, and not for their own sakes, in that they have no self-consciousness, whereas man is the end."[41]

Research on animal cognition is still in its infancy, yet it has already led to a sobering realization of how shortsighted the Kantian doctrine was, and how much (as well as for how long) we had underestimated animal minds, misunderstood animal behavior, mischaracterized animals in fables, tales, and stories, and, in our own time, misrepresented them in film and television.[42] There are undoubtedly many more revelations still to come. Just as certain, however, is that there will be a great deal of deeply entrenched resistance from powerful interests for whom changing public perceptions of animals may spell a threat to business as usual.[43]

The onset of this revolution in scientific understanding can be dated roughly to 1960, which, as already indicated, also marks the beginning of the ascendancy of wildlife films on television, and their expansion as an industry.[44] In what might now be called the 'post-Disney' era, there was an ongoing industry-wide effort to *get it right* with regard to scientific accuracy. By the mid-1980s David Attenborough could say firmly that he felt "a great obligation to make it as right as we possibly can."[45] By that time also, the large international film festival Wildscreen had already begun serving as a de facto peer review process and semi-formal gatekeeping mechanism acting to promote higher standards. Today, wildlife films' complicity in the more obvious forms of misrepresentation and misunderstanding of animals may largely be a thing of the past.

More subtle forms persist, however, in the form of over-and under-representation—whether in the depiction of certain aspects of behavior, or in the portrayal of overall population numbers. With motion pictures and television favoring visual dynamism, action, and compelling narrative, animals in wildlife films lead intensely speeded-up and dramatic lives. The under-representation of hours spent in restful 'down time,' which for lions can amount to about twenty hours per day (or about 80% of their lives), becomes a kind of distortion or misrepresentation in its own right, revealing the inadequacy of commercial film and television for conveying the slow, often uneventful reality of life in the wild (this is now the province of the many un-edited nature webcams found online).

'Blue-chip' wildlife filmmaking, moreover, with its market-driven bias toward spectacular, *charismatic mega-fauna,* has led to over-representation on screen of big cats, apes, bears, wolves, elephants, sharks, whales, and so on.[46] At first glance, this list of audience favorites might look like a page from the annual "Red List" of threatened species.[47] One could argue that this is a good thing, bringing much needed attention to the plight of species whose numbers have been plummeting—provided that attention translates into action (which remains questionable). Yet it might also be that over-representation could lead to *desensitization*, or, in other words, familiarity could breed complacency. Seeing so many of some rare species on television, on a regular basis, might create a false impression of plenitude, and reduce the sense of urgency about real declining numbers. It is conceivable that in the not-too-distant future one might be able to see more individuals of some species on television, over a period of a few years, than any longer actually exist in the wild.

At the same time, species at even greater risk, such as the *Araripe Manakin* (a colorful bird native to Brazil), or the *Leaf-scaled Sea Snake* (which lives on coral reefs in the Timor Sea, west of Australia) remain largely unknown to the viewing public because they have not been the subject of decades of repeated wildlife film depiction. Their 'under-representation index' cannot be precisely calculated, but there is no doubt that these and other species, perhaps especially ants, who greatly outnumber human beings, have suffered disproportionate representation, if not outright 'symbolic annihilation' in wildlife television.

Such terms, borrowed from the 'Cultural Indicators' research that Larry Gross helped pioneer, remind us that representation in the media is best understood in terms of broad patterns of occurrence and non-occurrence, and that ultimately no single film or genre can be understood in isolation from its medium and its institutional setting.

Coda

Does it matter? In the past twenty-five years academic scholars have awakened to the creative and expressive potential in wildlife films, elevating them to a secure place among the narrative and visual arts. Yet the real question regarding wildlife films may be: *have they made a difference in the welfare of wild animals and the protection of species?* Sadly, the answer must be *no*—at least, not in the way, for example, that the increased number of sympathetically portrayed gay characters in mainstream television seems to have helped pave the way for acceptance of same-sex marriage.

As already noted, the ascendancy of wildlife films on television and the expansion of the global audience occurred during the very same years in which many wildlife populations experienced precipitous decline. Despite steady film output by the BBC and others, the Royal Society for the Protection of Birds (RSPB) reported an overall 67% decline in abundance of "Priority Species" in the UK since 1970.[48] Globally, the World Wildlife Fund (WWF) reports an overall 52% decline in the total population of wild animals since 1970.[49] Marine populations in the world's oceans are down 49% since 1970.[50] In each case, the data come from the years in which the wildlife film industry ascended and reached its peak. As production increased, the audience expanded, and worldwide exposure triumphed, actual wildlife population numbers fell.

What explains this striking inverse correlation? At one level, the failure of wildlife films to 'save' wildlife may just be another nail in the coffin of 'direct effects' theories of media. There had been occasional cases in which a wildlife film had generated outcry, or had been linked in some way to public action, but the evidence that the wildlife genre as a whole has been a force for good in relation to real wildlife preservation has remained anecdotal.

Further, it is likely that no amount of wildlife filmmaking, including persuasive, celebrity-studded wildlife documentaries, can possibly counteract the effects of a ballooning human population, which has more than doubled from 3.7 billion to 7.5 billion—again, since 1970.[51] The effects of this on wildlife populations, whether by fragmenting or destroying habitat, warming and acidifying the oceans, polluting waters, and just changing the planet's climate, are impossible not to see.

Add to this such sad developments as the industrialization of wildlife poaching in Africa, where the use of drones, light aircraft, high tech communications, and automatic weapons exceed the resources authorities have to combat it. As a result, some of the most widely filmed and most beloved of wild animals, including *four* of Africa's 'Big Five' (elephant, lion, leopard, and rhinoceros) now seem on the path to oblivion, where the ghosts of the Passenger Pigeon, the Dodo, the Moa, the Great Auk, the Stellar's Sea Cow, and others, await them.[52]

Given that some endangered species have been over-represented in wildlife film and television, and hypothesizing that this may have led to some degree of desensitization (as opposed to provoking anxiety) regarding the health of these species, then one achievement of the wildlife genre may ultimately be to lessen the psychic impact of confronting our own culpability in having driven them to the brink of extinction (words like 'needlessly' and 'wantonly' almost beg to be included in such statements).[53]

Wildlife filmmakers have long understand that what they are doing is in part a sort of 'salvage zoology,' making a visual record of something that is disappearing.[54] This is a very different agenda, however, from 'speaking for' the animals, or seeking to arouse public interest in preserving them *in the flesh*, and may ultimately signal a kind of sad capitulation to the reality principle. Despite all the acclaim received by the films mentioned at the beginning of this discussion, or by the BBC's spectacular, high-definition 'mega-series' *Planet Earth* (2006), *Planet Earth II* (2016), and *Blue Planet II* (2017), there is often an unmistakable elegiac quality to them. It can be little consolation to the filmmakers that their work has finally been taken seriously by academic scholars, when their living subjects continue to be hunted, fished, finned, trapped, and poached to the point of literal, biological, not symbolic, annihilation.[55]

Yet despite the impossibility of proving a negative, it may be that had there been no active wildlife film industry in the past fifty years bringing wildlife images to the public, and doing so in a way that communicated meanings and values that audiences shared, wildlife around the world might be in an even worse state than it is today.

Notes

1. From the public radio program *Scheer Intelligence*, July 7, 2016 (http://www. kcrw.com/news-culture/shows/scheer-intelligence/larry-gross-and-the-formation-of-the-gay-community).
2. It occurred to me in writing this sentence that I could not recall ever hearing Gross speak dismissively about anything. His intellect is so wide ranging, his sensibilities so egalitarian, that almost nothing was without interest or value.
3. Those historians include Paul Rotha, Basil Wright, Lewis Jacobs, Erik Barnouw, Kevin Brownlow, and Charles Musser, among others. For an elaborated discussion of the failure of film historians to deal adequately with the subject, see my *Wildlife Films* (Bousé, 2000), pp. 20–23.
4. Stouffer (1988: 368).
5. Writer-producer Barry Clark, in private correspondence (1997).
6. BBC producer Christopher Parsons (1971) devotes an entire chapter to 'building up' wildlife sequences. For a detailed analysis of the use of the close-up in this regard, see Bousé (2003).
7. An example of the failure to distinguish between a wildlife film and a documentary with wildlife content can be seen in the critical response to Werner Herzog's *Grizzly Man* (2005). Although clearly a study of the disturbed mind of Timothy Treadwell, reviewers often discussed it in the context of wildlife films, sometimes in relation to *March of the Penguins*, although the two films had little in common other than a 2005 release date. For an example of how they were nevertheless reviewed together, see Porter (2006).
8. We may have been witness to two similar 'amateur' phenomena in recent years: 1) the case of political bloggers, whose being awarded press credentials at the 2004 Democratic national convention was greeted with some skepticism by mainstream news sources, and 2) the case of 'citizen journalists' armed with smartphone cameras and live-streaming capability, whose work has often been used in reporting by mainstream news sources, but almost always with qualifiers attached to indicate their outsider and amateur status.
9. *The Private Life of the Gannetts* was produced in England in 1934, but only released in the U.S. in 1937, hence the 1938 Oscar for "Best One-Reel Short Subject." It benefitted from having Alexander Korda's name attached as a stamp of quality.

10. These were: *The Living Desert* (1953), *The Vanishing Prairie* (1954), and *White Wilderness* (1958). Five other Disney wildlife films won the Oscar for "Best Two-Reeled Short Subject."

11. An exception is *Secrets of Life* (1956), which includes a credit for "consulting biologists."

12. I have written elsewhere in more detail about the cross-pollination between Disney's animated and live-action animal films (Bousé, 1995, 2000).

13. "Blue chip" is an industry term (apparently borrowed from the world of stock trading) to refer to a solidly ratings-reliable model of wildlife filmmaking characterized by the following tendencies: (1) the depiction of mega-fauna—big cats, bears, wolves, sharks, crocodiles, elephants, whales, etc; (2) visual splendor—magnificent scenery, suggesting a still-unspoiled, primeval wilderness; (3) a dramatic storyline—a compelling narrative, often centering on a single animal, with a dramatic story-arc intended to engage viewers emotionally; (4) the absence of science—perhaps the weakest and most often broken of these rules, but the discourse of science often comes with its own narrative of research, technical jargon, and arcane methodologies, all of which can shift the focus onto scientists and spoil the fantasy of pristine nature; (5) the absence of politics—little or no reference to controversial issues, which are often seen as doom-and-gloom themes, and no overt propaganda on behalf of wildlife conservation issues; (6) the absence of historical reference points that would date the film, or ground it in a specific time, and thus diminish future rerun sales; 7) the absence of people, which may also spoil the image of a timeless realm, untouched and uncorrupted by civilization (see Bousé, 2000).

14. This is a severely encapsulated recounting of these historical developments, which are explored more fully in *Wildlife Films* (Bousé, 2000).

15. The first of these was "Miss Jane Goodall and the Wild Chimpanzees" (1963), which was filmed by Hugo van Lawick, who would go on to become one of the premier wildlife filmmakers in the world. During the years he and Goodall were married, they produced a series of wildlife television programs portraying the lives a number of other wild animal species, mostly in Africa.

16. Gross himself reported that in 1980, "fewer than 5% of U.S. households had VCRs and less than a quarter had cable" (Gross, 2001: 114), although his original source was a chart depicting the shift to home video between 1975 and 1997 in Butsch (2000: 269).

17. Gross (1983: 75). Writing a decade earlier, he put it this way: "Artistic communication is a form of culturally determined symbolic behavior in which an artist creates or arranges object(s) and/or events, purposefully, so as to imply meaning(s) and emotion(s) according to the conventions of a symbolic code, and these object/events elicit meaningful inferences in the artist himself and/or in others who possess at least minimal competence in the same cultural mode ... For artistic communication to occur it is not necessary for the artist and the audience to co-exist in either time or space. However, according to this definition, it is necessary that, to a significant extent, they share a common symbolic code. ... appreciation of artistic performances involves sufficient knowledge of the code and the style to be able to infer correctly the implied meanings and to perceive and evaluate the skill of the artist in choosing, transforming and ordering elements in order to articulate and convey these meanings and emotions (Gross, 1973: 115).

18. Gross (1983: 75).

19. As Arnold Hauser once put it, "The fundamentally new element in the Renaissance conception of art is the discovery of the concept of *genius*, and the idea that the work of art is the creation of an autocratic personality, that this personality transcends tradition, theory and rules" (1992: 61).

20. This has been referred to elsewhere at the "cult of novelty." See Perl (2014).

21. Noël Carroll, who has written extensively on mass art, summarizes the difference between its ease of comprehension and the difficulty of art at the other extreme as follows: "Avant-garde art is designed to be difficult, to be intellectually, aesthetically, and often morally challenging, to be inaccessible to those without certain backgrounds of knowledge and acquired sensibilities. Mass art, in contrast, is designed to be easy, to be readily accessible to the largest number of people possible, with minimum effort … Ideally, it is structured in such a way that large numbers of people will be able to understand and to appreciate it virtually effortlessly. It is made in order to capture and to hold the attention of large audiences, while avant-garde art is made to be effortful and to rebuff easy assimilation by large audiences" (1997: 190).

22. It should not be confused with the idea of 'democratized' art of the sort linked to mass production (Walter Benjamin) and commodification (Herbert Marcuse), and that was seen by some as a threat to traditional 'high culture' because it would ultimately lower standards and herald the "reign of the rabble" (Ortega y Gasset). The acerbic critic Dwight MacDonald remarked that Mass Culture is "very, very democratic" because of its refusal to make distinctions between 'high' and 'low' quality (1962: 12).

23. The art historian E. H. Gombrich once remarked, "Our whole sensory apparatus is basically tuned to the monitoring of unexpected change. Continuity fails to register after a time, both on the physiological and psychological levels" (1994: 108). The pleasurable experience of unpredictability he describes has been studied in relation to the neurotransmitter *dopamine*, which is released in the brain not so much with the achievement of pleasure, as previously thought, but rather in the *anticipation* of pleasure, especially when there is a degree of uncertainty or unpredictability. This would seem to explain the addictive quality of slot machines, as well as cellphone obsession. See Mirenowicz and Schultz (1994); Berridge and Robinson (1998); Berridge (2006); and Alter (2017: 126–127).

24. Shklovsky takes the concept beyond poetry, and applies it to narrative fiction in his *Theory of Prose* (1929, 1991). Especially delightful is Chapter 5, "Sherlock Holmes and the Mystery Story."

25. The concept is elaborated by Worth and Gross (1974).

26. The idea may also be implicit in Raymond Chandler's famous remark that, "The ideal mystery was one you would read if the end was missing," suggesting that narrative resolution and comprehension are less important than the aesthetic experience of the author's style (Chandler, 1988: vii). Yet the argument here cannot be reduced to individual style alone, because that can only be appreciated against a background of convention.

27. "To make good documentaries," writes Alan Rosenthal, "you need a strong narrative thrust and a tale that can be recounted in the most compelling, dramatic way possible" (Rosenthal, 2002: 10). In another how-to-make-documentaries text, readers are reminded of the importance of such things as character development and transformation, and that "conflict is considered to be the central feature that drives the

development of all stories" (Knudsen, 2012a: 98). This is followed by a discourse on the applicability of the "classic narrative" to Documentary filmmaking, employing terms such as *protagonist, antagonist, journey, quest, turning point, subplot, character motivation, dramatic irony, climax,* and *resolution* (Knudsen, 2012b: 119–124).

28. There had, however, been some scholarly analyses of the related genre of television science documentaries, such as those shown on the BBC series *Horizon*. See Gardner and Young (1981), and Silverstone (1984).

29. Boswall (1973: 593).

30. Stouffer (1988: 368).

31. See, for example, Thompson and Bordwell (2002: 42–50), Musser (1990: 337–369), and Salt (2009, chs. 8 & 9).

32. Nørfelt (1993) has pointed to no less than *fifteen* distinct models of "natural history film," although some, in my view, are science documentaries distinct from wildlife films in their focus on human activity.

33. Worth and Gross explain that 'natural events' are those we encounter in the course of our daily lived reality, and to which we might respond by asking *what should I do?* When the same event is presented on film or television, however, it becomes a 'symbolic event;' we can now only ask *what does it mean?* That is, what are the intentions behind it ? (implying the presence of an author) What is its significance in this context, relative to other events already shown, as well as to those anticipated, such as the conclusion one knows is coming before the end of the hour? One may not know what it means, yet still recognize it as part of a vaguely familiar structure that is clearly deliberately ordered, by someone, for some purpose, according to some shared system of rules (Worth and Gross, 1974: 134–136). See also Gross (1985).

34. Dyer (1993: 1).

35. Even the films in the highly regarded "Undersea World of Jacques Cousteau" series, that ran in prime-time on American television in the 1960s and '70s, did not depict legitimate scientific expeditions undertaken for actual research. The voyages were instead *pseudo-events*, mounted purely to be filmed and broadcast.

36. Stouffer (1988: 131).

37. Singer (2015: 24).

38. Howard Gardner (1985) has written the definitive historical exploration of the 'cognitive revolution' that occurred during this period, but confines his attention to the *human sciences*, omitting discussion of discoveries related to cognitive capacities in other species, with the exception of a brief passage dealing with Wolfgang Köhler's research on chimpanzees in the early 1920s (pp. 112–113).

39. On moral behavior among non-human animals, a good starting point is Bekoff and Pierce (2009), who do a good job of addressing the philosophical question of whether moral awareness necessarily entails moral responsibility. On 'theory of mind,' see de Waal (2006: 69–73) for a short critique of biases that have been built into research in this area. On meta-cognition, see Foote and Crystal (2007), Brown, et al (2017), and Templer, et al (2017), which are noteworthy because they find the phenomenon not among the great apes, but in rhesus monkeys and rats.

40. Olkowicz, et al (2016).

41. Kant (1997: 212). The "Lectures on Ethics" were not written down by Kant himself, but come to us as notes made by his students. Translations vary. In his book *Animal Liberation*, Peter Singer cites the 1963 Infeld translation, which yields this more succinct version of the Kantian position: "Animals are not self-conscious, and are there

merely as a means to an end. That end is man" (Singer 2015: 203). This position was recently (perhaps unwittingly) echoed by the ultra-conservative BBC commentator Claire Fox in a broadcast discussion of veganism and animal rights: "I suppose as a humanist I think animals are useless unless humans can make use of them, and if anything what I am worried about is enthusiasm for animal rights, because we've lost faith in an intellectual commitment to the exceptionalism of humans. I am a humanist, and animals are beneath us." (from the BBC radio program Moral Maze, August 3, 2017 (www.bbc.co.uk/programmes/b08zcbv5).

42. As well as, of course, inflicting on them catastrophic, if not apocalyptic levels of suffering, depredation, and industrialized slaughter. In his story, "The Letter Writer," Isaac Bashevis Singer, speaking through his character Herman Gombiner, laments that, "For the animals it is an eternal Treblinka."

43. The current struggle to gain legal 'personhood' for chimpanzees held captive in research facilities challenges the right to claim them as 'property' by the medical establishment, as well as by the zoo industry. There are legitimate fears that such changing perceptions of animals will spread. In the UK, where the number of vegans is now estimated at over half a million, the dairy industry is in crisis, and fears a "*demographic time bomb*" as younger consumers turn away, often citing shocking "*dairy is scary*" images and videos as the reason. In the US, resistance to such changing sensitivities is illustrated by the passage of corporate driven 'ag-gag' laws that criminalize the act of making surreptitious videos depicting animal abuse and suffering in slaughterhouses. Idaho's S. B. 1337 (2014) is a good example.

44. Miller (2003) dates the inauguration of the 'cognitive revolution' to 1956. Howard Gardner provides some additional background on the rationale for this dating (1985: 28–29). In this context, it is noteworthy that Russell M. Church's groundbreaking study of moral behavior among rats was also published right at about this time at the end of the 1950s. Significantly, Church's research preceded by two years the famous Milgram experiments in 'obedience to authority,' and showed the *opposite* effect— that is, that rats were reluctant to administer a painful electrical shock to their peers, showing sympathy for them even at the expense of foregoing a food reward to themselves (Church, 1959).

45. Burgess and Unwin (1984: 102). Attenborough continued: "If someone shows us that we have been inaccurate in the programme we will go to a lot of trouble to put it right before the programme is repeated—even though it may cost quite a lot of money."

46. Lekan (2011) reports a similar bias in African wildlife tourism, where attention to ecological diversity is often reduced to the 'big five' crowd-pleasing species (and traditional favorites of hunters)—Lion, Leopard, Rhino, Elephant, and Cape Buffalo.

47. The 'Red List' is maintained by the International Union for Conservation of Nature (http://www.iucnredlist.org).

48. From the RSPB's 2016 "State of Nature" report for England (http://www.rspb.org.uk/Images/StateOfNature2016_England_updated%2020%20Sept%20pages_tcm9-424986.pdf). Separate reports exist for Scotland, Wales, and Northern Ireland.

49. From the WWF's 2016 "Living Planet Report" (http://wwf.panda.org/about_our_earth/all_publications/lpr_2016/)

50. From the WWF's 2015 "Living Blue Planet Report" (http://assets.wwf.org.uk/custom/stories/living_blue_planet/).

51. "World population since the mid 20th century has grown by about 2% per year, a rate that doubles the population in roughly 35 years" (Marchetti, et al, 1996: 1). Several other things have doubled since 1970: the number of U.S. federal laws for environmental protection, the amount of government spending on pollution abatement, and the number of cars and trucks on American roads.

52. "Our generation is witnessing a disastrous decline among many of the world's best-known animals" a recent book concludes, as if to underscore the fact that screen time and fame have not been able to save these species. See Ceballos, Ehrlich, and Ehrlich (2015: 241).

53. One way of summarizing the *desensitization* hypothesis that seems especially relevant here is, "With repetition of the exposure, the stimulus progressively loses its ability to evoke anxiety." See Ardila (2015: 408).

54. Thirty years ago Stouffer wrote of his efforts to "document all the mammals and birds on the Endangered Species list" in America, presumably before they disappeared (1988: 86). More recently, photographer Joel Sartore has been waging a multi-year effort to photograph rare species for National Geographic's "Photo Ark" project, described at its website (apparently without irony) as "saving species through the power of photography" (https://www.nationalgeographic.org/projects/photo-ark/about/).

55. After reviewing population data for 177 vertebrate species from 1900 to 2015, one study concluded, "Earth is experiencing a huge episode of population declines and extirpations, which will have negative cascading consequences on ecosystem functioning and services vital to sustaining civilization. We describe this as a 'biological annihilation' to highlight the current magnitude of Earth's ongoing sixth major extinction event." See Ceballos, Ehrlich, and Dirzo (2017). In opposition to this admittedly gloomy scenario are the so-called "New Optimists," one of whom has argued that nothing is really changing, because "humanity has always threatened wildlife and other species, and we do that now as well," adding in support of this, "the world is estimated to be home to something like five to fifteen million species," and that "the International Union for the Conservation of Nature lists no more than 709 species as having become extinct since 1500." He concludes that it is "difficult to find hard proof of a mass extinction" (Norberg, 2016: 96). This sort of hyper-rational argumentation-from-the-numbers calls to mind a scene in the film *Dr. Strangelove* (1964), in which a hawkish general rationalizes a nuclear attack on the USSR: "I'm not saying we wouldn't get our hair mussed. But I do say … no more than ten to twenty million killed, tops!" Given a US population of 192 million in 1964, that translates into a 90–95% survival rate. No problem.

References

Alter, A. (2017). *Irresistible: The Rise of addictive technology and the business of keeping us hooked*. New York: Penguin Press.

Ardila, R. (2015). Behavior analysis, applied. *International Encyclopedia of the Social & Behavioral Sciences* (2nd ed., Vol. 2), 407–411 (available online at: http://dx.doi.org/10.1016/B978-0-08-097086-8.22002-3).

Bekoff, M., & Pierce, J. (2009). *Wild justice—the moral lives of animals*. Chicago: University of Chicago Press.

Berridge, K. (2007). The debate over dopamine's role in reward: the case for incentive salience. *Psychopharmacology, 191*(3), 391–431.

Berridge, K., & Robinson, T. (1998). What is the role of dopamine in reward: hedonic impact, reward, learning, or incentive salience? *Brain Research Reviews, 28*(3), 309–369.

Boswall, J. (1973). Wildlife filming for the BBC. *Movie Maker* (September), 590–632.

Bousé, D. (1995). True life fantasies: storytelling traditions in animated features and wildlife films. *Animation Journal, 3*(2), 19–39.

Bousé, D. (2000). *Wildlife films*. Philadelphia: University of Pennsylvania Press.

Bousé, D. (2003). False Intimacy: close-ups and viewer involvement in wildlife films. *Visual Studies 18*(2), 123–132.

Brown, E., Templer, V., & Hampton, R. (2017). An assessment of domain-general meta-cognitive responding in rhesus monkeys. *Behavioural Processes, 135*, 132–144.

Burgess, J., & Unwin, D. (1984). "Exploring the living planet with David Attenborough. *Journal of Geography in Higher Education 8*(2), 93–113.

Butsch, R. (2000). *The making of American audiences—From stage to television, 1750–1990*. Cambridge: Cambridge University Press.

Carroll, N. (1997). The ontology of mass art. *The Journal of Aesthetics and Art Criticism, 55*(2), 187–199.

Ceballos, G., Ehrlich, P., & Dirzo, R. (2017). Biological annihilation via the ongoing sixth mass extinction signaled by vertebrate population losses and declines. *PNAS, 114*(30), E6089–E6096. Available online at: http://www.pnas.org/content/114/30/E6089.full.pdf

Ceballos, G., Ehrlich, A., and Ehrlich, P. (2015). *The annihilation of nature: Human extinction of birds and mammals*. Baltimore: Johns Hopkins University Press.

Chandler, R. (1988). Introduction. *Trouble is my business*. New York: Vintage.

Church, R. M. (1959). Emotional reaction of rats to the pain of others. *Journal of Comparative and Physiological Psychology, 52*(2), 132–134.

de Waal, F. (2006). *Primates and philosophers—How morality evolved*. Princeton: Princeton University Press.

Dyer, R. (1993). *The matter of images: Essays on representations*. London and New York: Routledge.

Foote, A., & Crystal, J. (2007, March 20). Metacognition in the rat. *Current Biology, 17*(6), 551–555.

Gardner, C., & Young, R. (1981). Science on TV: A critique. In Bennett, et al (Eds.), *Popular Television and Film* (pp. 171–193). London: British Film Institute.

Gardner, H. (1985). *The mind's new science*. New York: Basic Books.

Gombrich, E. H. (1994). *The sense of order: A study in the psychology of decorative art* (2nd ed.). London and New York: Phaidon Press.

Gross, L. (1973). Art as the communication of competence. *Social Science Information, 12*(5), 115–141.

Gross, L. (1983). Why Johnny can't draw. *Art Education, 36*(2), 74–77.

Gross, L. (1985). Life vs. art: The interpretation of visual narratives. *Studies in Visual Communication,11*(4), 2–11.

Gross, L. (2001). The paradoxical politics of media representation. *Critical Studies in Mass Communication, 18*(1), 114–119.

Hauser, A. (1992). *The social history of art, Vol. II: Renaissance, mannerism, baroque.* London: Routledge.

Kant, I. (1997). *Lectures on ethics,* (Peter Heath, trans.). Cambridge: Cambridge University Press.

Knudsen, E. (2012a). The nature of stories and narratives. In W. De Jong, E. Knudsen, & J. Rothwell. (Eds.), *Creative documentary, theory and practice* (pp. 89–96). London and New York: Routledge

Knudsen, E. (2012b). The classic narrative. In W. De Jong, E. Knudsen, & J. Rothwell, (Eds.), *Creative documentary, theory and practice* (pp. 118–130). London and New York: Routledge.

Lekan, T. (2011). *Serengeti shall not die*: Bernhard Grzimek, wildlife film, and the making of a tourist landscape in East Africa. *German History, 29*(2), 224–264.

MacDonald, D. (1962). *Against the American grain.* New York: DaCapo.

Marchetti, C., Perrin, S., & Ausubel, J. (1996). Human population dynamics revisited with the logistic model: How much can be modeled and predicted? *Technological Forecasting and Social Change, 52*(1), 1–30.

Miller, G. A. (2003). The cognitive revolution: a historical perspective. *Trends in Cognitive Sciences, 7*(3), 141–144.

Mirenowicz, J., & Schultz, W. (1994). Importance of unpredictability for reward responses in primate dopamine neurons. *Journal of Neurophysiology, 72*(2), 1024–1027.

Musser, C. (1990). *The emergence of cinema, Vol. I: The American screen to 1907.* New York: Charles Scribner's Sons.

Norberg, J. (2016). *Progress—Ten reasons to look forward to the future.* London: Oneworld Publications.

Nørfelt, T. (1993). A model for natural history films. *Image Technology, 75,* 222–224.

Olkowicz, S., Kocourek, M., Lucan, R., Portes, M., Fitch, W., Herculano-Houzel, S., & Nemec, P. (2016). Birds have primate-like numbers of neurons in the forebrain. *Proceedings of the National Academy of Sciences (PNAS), 113*(26), 7255–7260. (*http://www.pnas.org/content/113/26/7255.full*).

Parsons, C. (1971). *Making wildlife films: A beginner's guide.* Harrisburg: Stackpole Books.

Perl, J. (2014). The armory show made modern art something you love to hate: Against the cult of novelty. *The New Republic* (February). https://newrepublic.com/article/116502/armory-shows-centenary-reviewed-jed-perl

Porter, P. (2006). Review Section. *Society and Animals, 14*(2):201–208.

Rosenthal, A. (2002). *Writing, directing, and producing documentary films and videos* (3rd ed.). Carbondale and Edwardsville: Southern Illinois University Press.

Salt, B. (2009). *Film style and technology: History and analysis* (3rd ed.). London: Starword.

Shklovsky, V. (1929, 1991). *Theory of prose*, (Benjamin Sher, trans.). Elmwood Park, Illinois: Dalkey Archive Press.

Silverstone, R. (1984). Narrative strategies in television science—a case study. *Media, Culture, and Society*, *6*(4), 377–410.

Singer, P. (2015). *Animal liberation* (40th Anniversary Edition ebook). New York: Open Road Integrated Media.

Stouffer, M. (1988). *Wild America*. New York: Times Books.

Templer, V., Lee, K., & Preston, A. (2017). Rats know when they remember: transfer of metacognitive responding across odor-based delayed match-to-sample tests. *Animal Cognition*, *20*(5), 891–906.

Thompson, K., & Bordwell, D. (2002). *Film history—An introduction* (2nd ed.). Boston: McGraw-Hill.

Worth, S., & Gross, L. (1974). Symbolic strategies. In S. Worth (Ed.), *Studying visual communication* (pp. 134–147). Philadelphia: University of Pennsylvania Press.

13. *From Gay Bars to Hook-Up Apps: Social and Media Change*

David Gudelunas

Gay bars, like brick and mortar retail shopping, print journalism, or Madonna's career, are something that people are obsessed with declaring dead, over with, and not relevant. The reasons for the end of trips to the mall, newsprint on your hands, accessible pop music, and gay watering holes represent a sort of overlapping Venn diagram of internet thought-piece wisdom: we have the world wide web on our phones, the millennials don't want their parent's MTV, and what was once considered the fringe is now the mainstream. Of course, gay bars are not dead. In fact, you can walk into one in most major US cities right now and if you stay long enough you'll likely hear a Madonna song (or at the very least a Madonna-inspired remix).

The possible reasons for the untrue and untimely death of the gay bar (and I use the term 'gay bar' here with colloquial intent realizing that lesbians, heterosexuals and many other identity and demographic groups frequent these spaces) are many and complicated. There is speculation that GPS-enabled sex-seeking apps like Grindr and Scruff have negated the need for gay men to meet less strategically in a semi-public space like a gay bar, that younger GLBTQ individuals are more accepted by and thus more likely to socialize with their heterosexual counterparts, that overzealous heterosexual women (many in drunken bachelorette mode) have somehow soiled the primarily male atmosphere of the gay bar, and that as small, mostly independent businesses, gay bars simply can't economically survive in hyper-gentrified urban neighborhoods that, ironically, they helped create.

And, if gay bars are disappearing what is the big deal? There was much less consternation when travel agencies, 1-hour photo developing storefronts, and music retailers became memories instead of destinations. Gay bars, however, matter both historically and culturally. The modern gay rights movement launched during the Stonewall riots that take their name from the West Village New York City gay bar that police raided as part of routine crackdowns on homosexual activity in the summer of 1969. While many bars and cafes pre-date the Stonewall Inn as catering primarily to sexual minorities, it is in the post-Stonewall era when gay bars become central to individual and community identity formation. Beyond adult bookstores, cruising areas, peepshows or movie theaters, gay bars were the one space in mid-century America where sexual minorities could find and socialize with others like them.

The other space, as Larry Gross's (2001, 2007) important work in this area lays out, was film and television. Especially for those sexual minorities located far from major metro areas where gay bars were clustered, lacking the proper identification or confidence to enter these spaces, or alienated because of racial, class or other barriers, film and television served as an even more important source of finding representations that mirrored their own experiences, desires and identity. Gross argues that media representations were so crucial for GLBTQ audiences because GLBTQ audiences often lacked real-life role models within their own families or immediate community institutions and when homosexuality was discussed it was usually done so with violent disapproval.

Like gay bars, however, conventional internet punditry posits that representations of GLBTQ characters in fictional or reality based programming is far less important today because we are awash with these images and, besides, younger GLBTQ audiences can create their own representations in the space of digital media and they are less starved for any contact with another GLBTQ person, either in real life or through more parasocial forms of contact (Gudelunas, 2012, 2016).

If there is one common denominator about what is changing GLBTQ culture it is new media technologies. Conventional wisdom posits that we don't go to gay bars because we can find other sexual minorities through GPS enabled apps, we don't need GLBTQ newspapers or magazines because we have social media feeds, and we don't crave GLBTQ representations on network television because anyone can be a YouTube star and the proliferation of media platforms from Netflix to iTunes makes the availability of diverse representations easier to obtain. In short, what is changing is how media influence GLBTQ culture.

This chapter explores the influence of media on generational differences. Specifically this chapter looks at how new media technologies serve as a point of differentiation in the coming out and socialization process of younger and older gay men and lesbian women. Through interviews and focus groups with gay and lesbian respondents, this chapter looks at how access to representations of GLBTQ life outside of mainstream media have changed how young GLBTQ audiences are able to learn about a culture that they are generally not born into.

When it comes to generational divides, polls and surveys indicate a large one when it comes to matters of sexual orientation and identity. Younger voters, as an example, are more likely to favor marriage equality, the right of GLBTQ (gay, lesbian, bisexual, transgender, and queer) individuals to serve in the armed forces openly, adoption rights for same sex couples, and a host of other social and political issues (Agiesta, 2011; Egan & Sherrill, 2005; Smith, 2011). And while this generational divide has received much attention from pundits and activists, a generational divide within the GLBTQ community is rarely discussed. At least in popular discourse, the GLBTQ community is typically thought to be fairly monolithic both in terms of political and social attitudes as well as general demographic composition.

Rarely is this "community" described as consisting of multiple communities or a diverse range of sexualities, social positions or other differences. Among the differences not typically discussed within the population are generational ones. When the GLBTQ community is represented at all in popular culture, it is usually depicted as a young man's world and the images of homosexuality that appear (infrequently) in advertising, the news media, and other forms of popular representation are generally dominated by younger men (Drummond, 2010). Despite the progress made in terms of visibility, older GLBTQ individuals are largely absent from this picture (Goltz, 2007; Pugh, 2002). Ironically, when they are included in the picture, it is typically exclusively gay men in reference to being a sexual object ("Daddy" or "Silver Fox") in the eyes of younger gay men, or about the seemingly never ending quest to stay youthful (and relevant) in the GLBTQ community (Kennedy, 2008).

This primary goal of this chapter is to explore generational differences in the GLBTQ community and to specifically question how technology serves as a point of differentiation in the coming out and socialization process of younger and older gay men and lesbian women. The central question here is how does generational cohort and access to digital technology impact both coming out narratives and larger understandings of GLBTQ community?

Generational Cohort Theory

Generational cohort theory, developed by Inglehart in 1977, examines differences and changes across generations. According to this theory, change is associated with historical events, societal attitudes, values and beliefs, particularly during one's formative years (Crabtree & Fisher, 2009; Rogler, 2002). In short, political, economic and social events similarly shape the views and feelings of individuals born during a similar time period. Notably, while social conditions may change, the values instilled by the conditions prevalent during these formative years hold over time (Inglehart, 1977). Generational cohort theory has been used to describe everything from differences in managerial styles, to various waves of feminism, to differences in shopper orientations.

Generational cohort theory is particularly useful in thinking about changing identities of sexual minorities over time where significant progress has been made in terms of visibility and acceptance in the US since the 1969 Stonewall riots. Unquestionably younger and older gay men and women today grew up in very different times, and research demonstrated that the average age of coming out has decreased over time (Grov, Bimbi, & Parsons, 2006). Factors other than social acceptance also mark significant divisions between older and younger gay men and lesbians. As an example, HIV and AIDS defined an older generation of sexual minorities in ways radically different than younger sexual minorities who grew up in a world that has always known about, and largely managed, the disease (Clark, 2010; Duffin, 2009). Media technologies available at the time of adolescence are another factor that divide, and potentially shape the worldview of, different cohorts of the GLBTQ population.

Method

This study employed a qualitative research methodology that included focus groups, and in-depth dyad interviews with both inter- and intra-generational pairs. This qualitative methodology was selected to gain the deepest insights in an exploratory fashion that allowed for a constant refinement of the research question throughout the data gathering process. Research was approved by an Institutional Review Board.

In all, six different focus groups were conducted in Southern California. The smallest group had 9 participants while the largest group had 16 participants. Focus groups were selected as a primary methodological tool of inquiry based on the desire to recreate naturalistic conversations between gay and lesbian participants that approached the collaborative and social process of communication (Kruegar, 1998; Morgan, 1988). Each group lasted for 90 minutes. All respondents were between 21 and 76 years old and self-identified as gay or lesbian in pre-screening questions. A total of 78 individuals participated in focus groups that were divided between one older group, one younger group and one mixed age group. There were three different groups for lesbian women and three different groups for gay men, for a total of six groups. There were no mixed sex groups in order to focus questions in the group around the specific experiences of gay men and lesbians and encourage comfort in more homogenous groups. While bisexuals and transgender individuals were initially part of the call for respondents, recruitment issues prevented their inclusion.

Defining generations is a tenuous task, and this task is made especially complicated in the case of gay men and lesbian women who follow different trajectories when revealing their sexual orientation. For the purposes of this study, 1965 (generally considered to be the last year of the baby boom generation) was used as the dividing line between the older and younger cohorts. Essentially, those respondents born in or before 1965 are considered part of the older cohort (ages 47 and older at the time of the study) while those born after 1965 (younger than 47 at the time of the study) are referred to throughout the findings as the younger cohort. While ultimately this distinction between "older" and "younger" does not provide for granularity, the small number of total respondents prevented further cohort batching. While this dichotomy between "older" and "younger" is arbitrary, it was considered appropriate given the broad focus of the study that was not looking for developmental differences as much as more general cohort differences.

A total of 12 depth interview dyads were also conducted, with six sets of men and women each for a total of 24 participants. For both the gay men and lesbian women, the dyads were divided so that there were two younger pairs, two older pairs and two inter-generational pairs. These dyads were structured as depth interviews between the two respondents facilitated by the researcher in a way that was meant to encourage unfiltered and raw discussions about a potentially taboo topic like age. Each dyad lasted about 50 to 70 minutes and like the focus groups followed a semi-structured question format that allowed for naturalistic conversations. The dyads engaged in conversations about aging, technology and other topics similar to those introduced in the focus groups, though the moderator guide used during the focus groups was not employed for the dyads.

While the qualitative nature of the research methods does not allow for any quantitative measure of reliability, various questions asked during focus groups to judge reliability of individual respondents indicated no significant problems. All respondents filled out a pre-questionnaire for basic data collection that also included some key questions that were asked in during the focus groups or dyads. Two respondents who contradicted their verbal answers with their written answers on the pre-questionnaire were discarded from the analysis.

The overall number of respondents from both the focus groups and dyads was 102. This respondent pool was intentionally diverse in terms of race and socioeconomic status. The qualitative focus group and dyads population contained 61 white, 25 Latino, 5 Asian, 6 African American and 5 other/mixed respondents. While income is not an accurate measure of socioeconomic status since some respondents in the older cohort were retired and members of the younger cohort were sometimes not yet employed, there was a range of educational backgrounds, employment histories and life experiences generally. While the respondents were largely suburban based, many (n = 97) spent at least part of their lives in a major urban environment. The median age for the qualitative sample in the older cohort was 62 and the mean was 61, in the younger cohort the median was 27 and the mean 28.

Results

Media Differences

The two groups of respondents saw the notion of "gay community" in radically different ways. This difference is particularly noticeable in terms of attitudes of respondents toward GLBTQ targeted niche media.

> I don't subscribe to *Out* or the *Advocate* or anything. I know people who do I guess, but I'm just like, what is the difference between gay news or straight news, or gay fashion and straight fashion. I mean it looks good or it doesn't, there is no difference. It happened or it didn't. Why would I read news in the *Advocate* when I can read *Time*? (31 year-old male)

> I think it is important we support the gay press, online and offline. A lot of stories important to me go unreported by the big guys, the gay press covers things that matter to be that are largely ignored elsewhere. (43 year-old male)

The younger cohort, unlike their older counterparts, also indicated that they were more likely to actively produce media instead of solely being consumers of media. As an example, one 30 year-old-woman said: "I actually blog and do web videos about stuff going on in my life, I contribute to lesbian web site as well some reviews of parties and stuff." Similarly, others in the younger cohort reported creating YouTube clips and their own media feeds through social media. One 27 year-old male said, "I don't read many gay blogs or pick up [the gay local newspaper], but on Twitter I follow some folks that are constantly linking to gay stories or causes." In terms of spending time with digital technologies including web sites and social media, the younger cohort was actually more likely than the older cohort to spend time with at least one exclusively GLBTQ-specific mobile application or web sites. While 30 of the

51 younger male respondents and 8 of the 51 female respondents spent time with a GLBTQ-specific mobile app, only 5 of the male responds and 1 of the female respondents who said they used an app were in the older cohort.

These results, however, obscure the sort of media that respondents were referring to. The younger cohort was overwhelmingly using social networking applications like Grindr and Scruff in comparison with the older cohort who reported spending more time on gay news websites, blogs and generally less sexually-driven media. There were some commonalities, including blogs like Towleroad and Queerty, but while both groups reported heavy usage of digital technologies that specifically hailed a GLBTQ audience, the qualitative difference between these technologies is significant. Also, notably, the men were far more engaged in this activity than the women. This is one of the key differences between the male and female respondents in the data.

The older cohort saw gay media as a means of survival while the younger respondents saw gay media more as a means to access desire and information. This points to a larger difference not just in how different cohorts view essentially the same medium, but how they view their sexual identity. As gay sexuality evolves, then, we see a larger shift from sexuality as a matter of identification to more a matter of access to information and desire. Those younger gay respondents using Grindr as a form of gay media, in other words, were less looking to connect to a sense of community and more looking to connect to a physical body.

The two cohorts were also markedly different in terms of the importance placed on scripted or reality-based representations of homosexuality. The older cohort more often mentioned important cultural moments when marginal sexualities made it into the mainstream while the younger cohort was more likely to critique these representations as "stereotypical."

> I think it is important that you see gay characters on TV. I remember when Ellen came out, it was a big deal, it was like 'my life is finally being acknowledged,' and, you know, it has importance because it brought a lesbian into every home in America. (50 year-old female)

> There are a lot of gay characters on TV, I mean look at 'RuPaul's Drag Race,' it is a whole show about gay men. I think a lot of the times these are the extremes, like the most flaming gay stereotypes. I see a lot of gay people on TV, but none are really like me or my friends (23 year-old male)

For the older cohort who remembered a time when GLBTQ representations in mainstream media was a rarity, numbers more so than quality of these representations mattered. While the younger cohort was still very interested in GLBTQ characters in film and television, they were more critical of the fact that sexuality was the most prominent trait of these characters. Both cohorts acknowledged that it is easier today to find representations of GLBTQ life. As one respondent noted: "I'm always being told [by media platforms] you might be interested in any movie, TV show, artist, whatever that happens to be gay. They know I'm gay!"

Digitally Reliant Versus Digitally Able

The place of technology in the lives of the younger and older cohorts served as a significant point of distinction. Both the reliance on gay niche media versus general market media, as discussed above, and the role that new media technologies played in connecting individuals to some larger gay and lesbian community, were interesting points of departure between the two cohorts. The younger cohort was clearly a group that could not envision life without social media and technology played a significant role in the coming out and socialization process for these men and women. The older cohort, while not unfamiliar with these newer technologies, saw social media as additive instead of necessary.

> I remember being in chatrooms and those [online gay communities]. That was my first contact with another gay person. It was online, for sure. (26 year-old gay male)

> I didn't know another lesbian in school, and I came out online to my friends first. In high school I had a real dramatic blog about coming out and all those things you have angst about in high school. It was free therapy I guess. (29 year-old female)

Several of the younger cohort mentioned having explicitly online romantic relationships that were carried out over video chats and other real time messaging devices. Many of the younger gay men and lesbian women noted in discussion that these online relationships occurred before they were out to close friends and family in their offline lives. As one 29 year-old male put it, "I had a gay online life when I wasn't out to my Mom or friends. I sort of tested the water before I came out." In contrast, the older cohort spoke about "testing the water" through other means. One respondent, a 70-year-old male described his earliest experiences interacting with other gay men: "Before I was out, I would go to [a bar] and never take my hat off. Not a disguise, but I rarely talked to anyone, sat alone until I got comfortable. I was just getting my toes wet I guess."

The availability of various communication technologies also played a significant role in access to pornography. While the younger cohort almost universally discussed online pornography as their first (and only) place they accessed sexually explicit material, respondents in the older cohort discussed in detail securing magazines and videos at retail locations. While a few older cohort respondents actually enjoyed buying or renting pornographic material in locations with other customers (and hence potential sexual partners), many others discussed the fear that accompanied potentially being recognized purchasing taboo media. For the younger cohort, the notion of not buying pornography anonymously online was rarely even considered. As one 22 year-old male explained, "I see all those porn shops [in the city], but it is always old men that I guess don't have a computer. I don't mind porn, but those stores seem … shady." The fact that pornography retailers were familiar to, yet rejected by, this respondent was typical of the younger cohort who identified these stores as something for other gay men not like themselves.

This discussion of pornography also highlights another glaring difference between male and female respondents. The availability of digital technology as a structural circumstance allowed younger male respondents to access sexuality in a very different way than younger female respondents. While both men and women in the younger cohort used media technology to first explore their sexuality, men did this largely through pornography as opposed to contact with actual (that is non-actors) sexual others as was the case for the women.

In comparison, while the older cohort was very familiar with social media and other new media technologies, these media tools (including digital pornography) were generally not available for the older cohort during their coming out process. As one 58 year-old male noted: "We came out by actually going out. There was no chance to meet people anonymously online like you can now. If you wanted to be anonymous you wore a hat and sunglasses." This seemingly obvious difference in the availability of digital technologies during the historical moment when the two cohorts were coming of age had ramifications for how older and younger cohorts stayed socially and sexually connected to other sexual minorities. Those respondents who came of age with social media relied on the technology as opposed to simply using it like the older cohort.

One key media effect was the ability to access sex structures and to explore non-normative sexuality for the first time. This difference in access was often discussed, particularly by the older (male) cohort, in relation to HIV/AIDS that positioned bodies as potentially toxic and unsafe whereas those in the younger cohort coming into contact with virtual bodies saw their initial sexual exploration as wholly safe and non-threatening. One older man explained, "I approached gay sex as very taboo, it was something that was definitely outside the normal and so it took me a long time to be comfortable and to not see it as dirty somehow." Comparatively, a member of the younger cohort

220   DAVID GUDELUNAS

explained: "Some of the first pornography I saw was gay, you know, online …
and so it is all I have really known. No big deal really." Another member of
the young cohort explains, "With Snapchat and Tinder and whatever, you
get to know what someone looks like naked long before you ever actually get
naked with them. I've always been curious about black guys, and I'm sort of
exploring that now." Here we see how shifts in media technologies as well as
patterns of consumption have an impact on something as significant as sexual
exploration outside of dominant norms.

The older cohort, depending on specific age wasn't, however, completely
without mediated forms of communication when it came to finding other
sexual minorities. Respondents mentioned using classified ads in gay newspapers and later telephone personals (also facilitated by classified like listings in
gay publications) in order to find romantic and platonic friends alike. One 60
year-old man recalled moving through several different modes of mediated
communication to seek romantic partners:

> I used to use those ads in the back of the [gay newspaper] and I remember actu-
> ally sending letters to a box number at the paper. Actual letters you wrote. Then
> it was voicemail. … same thing, but you heard voices. I met my partner in 1995
> and it was then that everyone was going online I guess to do the same thing, but
> I never made the move … I didn't have to.

Conclusion

One of the most interesting and rarely discussed differences between older and
younger gay men and lesbian women to emerge from the findings centered
on traditional and new media use and how media influences GLBTQ culture
generally. For the older cohort a gay and lesbian press was seen as essential
while the younger cohort were less likely to seek out or use gay specific media
even though they knew about local and national gay media. For the younger
gay men and lesbians who often times created their own self-representations
online through video blogs, websites and social media platforms, the question
of representation by professional media producers was seen as less significant.
These younger gay men and lesbians spent less time with queer-specific media
because, in part, they created their own media and newsfeeds. This ability to
create their own representations had an important effect on how individuals
understood and indeed owned their sexuality.

New media technologies were also essential for this younger cohort connecting with an imagined GLBTQ community before actually revealing their
sexual orientation to others. This allowed many in the younger cohort to
come out and acknowledge their sexual orientation sooner than the older

cohort who generally discussed going to gay bars (as opposed to going online) as the first step in acknowledging their sexual orientation. What effect this earlier "coming out" has over the developmental life span of the individual is best left to other studies, but the findings here do indicate that these different access points to sex structures results in qualitatively different understandings of what sex is. For the younger respondents, (gay) sex was far more normalized and not something so different that it required a distinctive cultural identity to map onto the sexual behavior.

While both cohorts had access to these technologies, the younger cohort was more likely to see them as necessary. For the older cohort GLBTQ niche media was a means of obtaining individual and community survival whereas the younger respondents largely saw gay specific media platforms and channels as access to information (and often times information about gay life). In other words, each cohort approached gay media with very different expectations and these differences help illuminate different and changing notions of sexuality.

While new media technologies have certainly altered GLBTQ life, any pronouncements that they have killed the culture should be viewed with great suspicion. Gay men may be able to locate other gay men with GPS-enabled technology, but this does not mean that the gay bar is dead. Similarly, while it may be easier to locate more and varied representations of GLBTQ life in popular culture, or that sexual minorities can create their own media content more readily, it does not mean that these representations are inconsequential.

References

Agiesta, J. (2011). Poll: Near-split in US over legal gay marriage. *The Associated Press.* Retrieved from The Associated Press website: http://www.google.com/hosted-news/ap/article/ALeqM5gZ8VevKxgXSPRRPtWys2UEzcLgbw?docId=829c-797391f0453a974c44f613cf1afd

Clark, J. M. (2010). HIV/AIDS, aging, and diminishing abilities: Reconfiguring gay masculinity in literature and theology. *Journal of Men's Studies, 18*(2), 137–144.

Crabtree, J. L., & Fisher, T. F. (2009). Generational cohort theory: Have we overlooked an important aspect of the entry-level occupational therapy doctorate debate? *AJOT: American Journal of Occupational Therapy, 63*(5), 656+.

Drummond, M. J. N. (2010). Younger and older gay men's bodies. *Gay & Lesbian Issues & Psychology Review, 6*(1), 31–41.

Duffin, R. (2009). Ageing and HIV—the story unfold. *HIV Australia, 8*(3), 15–17.

Egan, P. J., & Sherrill, K. (2005). Marriage and the shifting priorities of a new generation of lesbians and gays. *Political Science & Politics, 38*(2), 229–232.

Goltz, D. B. (2007). Laughing at absence: Instinct magazine and the hyper-masculine gay future? *Western Journal of Communication, 71*(2), 93–113.

Gross, L. (2001). *Up from invisibility: Lesbians, gay men, and media in America.* New York: Columbia University Press.

Gross, L. (2007). Gideon, who will be twenty-five in the year 2012 *Media/queered: Visibility and its discontents* (pp. 261–278). New York: Peter Lang.

Grov, C., Bimbi, D. S., & Parsons, J. T. (2006). Race, ethnicity, gender, and generational factors associated with the coming-out process among gay, lesbian, and bisexual individuals. *The Journal of Sex Research, 43*(2), 115–121.

Gudelunas, D. (2012). There's an app for that: Thue uses and gratifications of online social networks for gay men. *Sexuality & Culture, 16*(1), 347–365.

Gudelunas, D. (2016). Culture jamming (and tucking): 'RuPaul's Drag Race' and unconventional reality. *Queer Studies in Media & Popular Culture, 1*(2), 231–249.

Inglehart, R. (1977). *The silent revolution: Changing values and political styles amoung western publics.* Princeton: Princeton University Press.

Kennedy, S. (2008). The age of the silver fox. *Advocate* (1012), 32–41.

Kruegar, R. A. (1998). *Focus groups: A practical guide for applied research.* Newbury Park, CA: Sage.

Lyons, A., Pitts, M., Grierson, J., Thorpe, R., & Power, J. (2010). Ageing with HIV: health and psychosocial well-being of older gay men. *AIDS Care, 22*(10), 1236–1244.

Morgan, D. L. (1988). *Focus groups as qualitative research.* Newbury Park, CA: Sage.

Pugh, S. (2002). The forgotten: A Community without a generation—older lesbians and gay men. In D. Richardson & S. Seidman (Eds.), *Handbook of Lesbian and Gay Studies* (pp. 161–181). London: Sage.

Rogler, L. H. (2002). Historical generations and psychology: The case of the great depression. *The American Psychologist, 57*(12), 1013–1023.

Smith, T. W. (2011). Public attitudes toward homosexuality. Retrieved from: http://news.uchicago.edu/sites/all/files/attachments/Public Attitudes Toward Homosexuality.pdf

14. The Hidden Female Face of New York

CARLA SARETT

As a young girl growing up in the 1960's, I loved nothing more than going into the "city" as I then thought of New York. Its landmarks have become fixtures in my personal visual lexicon: fountains and statues of Central Park, the jeweled façade of Radio City Music Hall, the glowing Art Deco interiors. All of it feels magical to me, as it has to many filmmakers and photographers. But, I never imagined that any of that "magic" was created by *women*. To me, cities like New York—that is to say, *great* cities—were designed and built by men—great men, for sure.

In my first mental timeline of Art (which started with the Egyptians and ended at, in those days, maybe Jackson Pollock), there were, oh, three women of note: Georgia O'Keefe, Frieda Kahlo, and Mary Cassatt. My timeline, however flawed, was not an accident; it was cultivated from an early age. My suburban, upwardly mobile parents dutifully took me to The Metropolitan Museum and MoMA. I was given "serious" books like *A Child's History of Art* and, when I was older, John Canaday's *Mainstreams of Modern Art*, and packets from museum gift shops. My elementary school taught Art Education, which forced students to memorize artists, dates, countries, periods. But in all of that, I heard nothing of women in the "fine" (as opposed to the "folk") arts—that is, before Mary Cassatt. Unsurprisingly, I emerged with the impression of a vacuum before Cassatt and then, a spurt of female abstract expressionists, all of whom were beneath Jackson Pollock in importance. (I did see the paintings of "Grandma Moses" in *Life* but lacking a category for folk art, those seemed more curiosity than art to me.)

Before the abstract expressionists ... well, I figured that women's function was to stand, mute, as a model (or even worse from my standpoint, a *muse*) for male artists. (As an aside, I think one reason for the immediate embrace of John Berger is that women like me believed that females were *only* models, *only* objects. Like many women, I bristled with resentment at the notion of women standing naked, freezing, and passive, while male "geniuses" drew, painted, sculpted.)

This contrasted with books where I was raised on a diet of female authors—Noel Streatfeild's "shoe" books (*Ballet Shoes, Theater Shoes,* etc.); *Anne of Green Gables* by L. M. Travers; Helen Hunt Jackson's *Ramona;* Francis Hodgson Burnett's *The Secret Garden,* and of course, Louisa May Alcott's *Little Women.* I knew that writing was open to women, but that requires nothing more than in Virginia Woolf's words, "a room of one's own."

Even as a child, though, I knew that it takes money to buy brushes, paints, canvas, and money for art teachers; and men controlled the money in most families. Young ladies might draw or paint to interest a prospective mate, but not as a career—the academies forbade life modeling to females. As for public art, like sculpture, that required commissions, which I imagined to be an insurmountable barrier. The absence of women made sense.

Except I was wrong. Women were not absent.

Now, a flurry of museum exhibits refer to female artists who are being "rediscovered" or "newly discovered" or, in the case of MoMA's women's abstract art, "unearthed." (A fruitful content analysis might be done of the myriad occasions in which the wearisome adjectives "ignored," "forgotten," "neglected," "overlooked" and "re-discovered" pop up in descriptions of female artists.) The timeline is, ever-so-slowly, evolving to reveal women: portrait painters in Renaissance Italy, genre painters in Rembrandt's Amsterdam, and by the 19th century in America, as painters and sculptors. In fact, in Manhattan, several of my favorite spots were created, in part, by women—the Art Deco muralist, Hildreth Meière, and the sculptors, Emma Stebbins and Bessie Potter Vonoh. Very different artistic sensibilities, from different periods, but the result is the same. Their names are forgotten.

It's the *forgetting* part that intrigues me. Women well-known enough to grab public commissions (no easy matter, regardless of gender), their art in public places, in parks and buildings; and yet forgotten, even *after* the feminist awakening of the 1970s. Scholars and writers were eagerly fighting for the recognition of women, but ignored these glaringly obvious candidates. All anyone had to do was look—public art is, after all, public. It is in plain view. But somehow, its creators became invisible.

America granted women the right to vote in 1920: and Emma Stebbins, Bessie Potter Vonnoh and Hildreth Meiere were born before then. Stebbins died without having cast a vote. Many of today's freedoms, like birth control, were absent. Yet, from their teens, these three women had *big* artistic ambitions, and they were not alone. By 1871, the National Academy of Arts offered a life modeling class for women, presumably fueled by demand. At Philadelphia's Centennial Exposition of 1876, about a third of the artworks were created by women. Among those was Emma Stebbins, who later created Central's Park's *Angel of the Waters.* (Fine, 1973)

Born in 1815 in New York City, Emma Stebbins was the senior member of a group of female artists, known as "New Women." She was encouraged by her wealthy family to pursue art. Stebbins was gifted, but not a prodigy, and by her twenties was diligently working in oils and watercolors. In 1842, she was elected an Associated Member of the National Academy of Design as an "amateur artist." After an early setback (she was not admitted into the Academy), she continued to work as an "amateur" artist; and with her family's money, persisted. In his *Book of the Artists,* in 1867, Henry Tuckerman would write of her:

> If years of study warrant the artistic career, Miss Emma Stebbins of New York is fully justified in adopting it. She long worked with crayon and palette as an amateur—making likenesses of her friends, copying pictures in oil, improving every opportunity to cultivate her taste and discipline her ability. (cited in Milroy, 1993a)

In 1857, Emma's brother, president of the New York Stock Exchange, sponsored Emma to move to Rome, where she could study anatomy (still difficult for women in America.) There, she became involved with the expatriate, feminist community in Rome, known as the "New Women." Her circle included the African-American sculptor, Edmonia Lewis, actress Charlotte Cushman, Louisa Lander, Anne Whitney, Florence Freeman, as well as Harriet Hosmer (her roommate.) These women were independent, unmarried, "jolly female bachelors": some celibate by choice, and others formed lesbian "marriages" (e.g., Harriet Hosmer with Lady Ashbourne, Emma Stebbins with Charlotte Cushman, Anne Whitney with Abby Adele Manning.) Women living together was not *that* scandalous, at least when compared to the evils of living unmarried with a man: the term "Boston Marriage" referred to a union between two upper-class women. Nathaniel Hawthorne called these women a "White Marmorean Flock" in *The Marble Faun,* a phrase pilfered by Henry James in describing these bohemian "lady sculptors." The now immortal phrase, in any event, was quasi-nonsense, since Edmonia Lewis was neither rich nor white. (As a not-quite-irrelevant aside: Louise Lander sculpted a marvelous bust of Nathaniel Hawthorne, and the priggish Hawthorne rewarded her by gossiping that she had posed in the nude, effectively destroying Lander's career.)

Emma Stebbins discovered her artistic identity in this tightly-knit female artists' colony, and her technical skills improved by leaps and bounds. At the relatively advanced age of 42, she embarked upon a professional career. Over the next decade, she produced a dozen marble sculptures and two public works in bronze. During the 1860's, she was awarded three major public commissions, more than any other American woman to date. Her first marble statue, *The Lotus Eater*, along with others, was exhibited in New York in January 1862, and Stebbins was frantic about its reception—but the works won praise from a reviewer in *The New York Times:*

"In the ideal refinement of the treatment, you recognize a woman's thought and a woman's eye, but in the laborious, earnest accuracy striven for throughout, a sense appears of the supreme value of defined and logical expression, which the common and as we *heretically believe*, the correct opinion of sages and scholars, refuses to the daughters of Eve." (cited by Milroy, 1993a—the italics are mine.)

Stebbins, a perfectionist, refused to allow stonemasons to do any carving, in part because her colleague, Harriet Hosmer, was accused of letting others do her work—an accusation that was linked to Hosmer's gender. Stebbins's decision later led to her ill heath from years of inhaling marble dust, but she was determined to be taken seriously—and she was.

Her rise came late, but at a fortuitous time. Her powerful brother now headed the Central Park Board of Commissions, and no doubt wielded his influence to get her a commission. He appears to have been ambitious on his sister's behalf; and hoped, eventually, that the park would be decorated by many of Emma's sculptures. *Angel of the Waters* was the first public commission awarded to a woman in New York. In Rome, Stebbins worked on the statue from 1861 to its completion in 1868 (by which time America's Civil war was over.) The statue was cast in Munich, and dedicated in Central Park five years later (one of the delays was due to the Franco-Prussian War.) Reviews of the statue were mixed. Stebbins nervously wrote to fellow artist and close friend, Anne Whitney,

"I dreaded the comments of the press which in this country respects nothing human or divine and is moved by any but celestial forces. I however sent you only the favorable notices – there have been others, and one which I understood has been copied into a Boston paper … I did not see it myself—not caring to have my mind disturbed by the mean undercurrents of what they are pleased to call criticism here." (cited in Milroy, 1993b)

Angel of the Waters is one of the few surviving American Neoclassical fountains, and the only sculpture commissioned during the Park's original design.

Figure 14.1: Angel of the Waters, Bethesda Fountain, Sculptor—Emma Stebbins. Photo Credit: Ed Yourdon, Wikimedia Commons.[1]

It is part of the terrace of Central Park, which overlooks the lake; and is situated in the middle of the park. At twenty-six feet high and ninety-six feet in diameter, it is one of Manhattan's largest, most beloved, fountains: it seems to define the Park. Stebbins's statue sits atop the fountain. In it, the heroic angel's wings are spread out, triumphantly holding a lily (a symbol of purity) in her hand, and beneath the angel are four allegorical figures, Peace, Health, Purity, Temperance. The fountain celebrated the 1842 opening of the Croton Aqueduct, which brought fresh water from Westchester County into New York City—so New York had much to be joyful about. (Stebbins compared the healing powers of the biblical pool to that of the pure Croton waters.) The statue's feeling of liberation has resonated with subsequent generations; I recall groups of pot-smoking hippies clustering around the *Angel of the Waters* in the 1970s.

Sadly, Emma Stebbins did not go on to greater achievements. In 1869, a year after the dedication, her lover, Charlotte Cushman, developed breast cancer: Emma put her career on hold to nurse her partner, and never produced another major statue. In 1870, the couple returned to the United States, where they set up households in Newport and Boston; and despite family pressures, refused to be separated. (Cushman's rather too colorful past might have influenced Stebbins's family's disapproval: her amorous intrigues apparently inspired James's *The Golden Bowl*.)

But in a fortunate twist, gay history, far more than art history, remembers Emma Stebbins. The NYC LGBT Historic Sites Project spotlights Stebbins's statue on its interactive map and in its important, growing database of historic LGBT sites; and tours of the "secrets of gay history" suggest, quite reasonably, that the central figure in *Angel of the Waters* is modelled on Charlotte Cushman.

Bessie Potter Vonnoh, sculptor of another of Central's Park treasures, represents a second wave of American female sculptors—scrappier, less privileged, less bohemian. Her father's early death left the family poor, and from a young age, she was geared toward money-making (unlike the rich Emma Stebbins and many other "New Women.") In her teens, she studied with a Chicago sculptor, Lorado Taft, at the Art Institute, who recruited her into his all-female cadre of studio assistants, known as the White Rabbits, who helped him on the decorative sculpture program for the Horticultural Building at the 1893 World's Columbian Exposition in Chicago. (Taft coined this phrase for the ability of lightweight women to race up and down the many ladders as nimbly as rabbits.) Taft had a good eye, and several of his White Rabbits went on to sculpt iconic American statues: among these were Julia Bracken's Lincoln in Los Angeles; Enid Yandell's fierce *Daniel Boone* in Cherokee Park, Louisville; and Helen Farnsworth Mears's *Genius of Wisconsin* in Wisconsin's State Capitol.

At the same Exposition, Vonnoh produced an independent commission for the Illinois State Building; and by 1894, established her own studio; and achieved financial success through a group of plaster portraits of fashionable Gibson Girls that she, perhaps self-deprecatingly, labeled "Potterines." (as cited by Tolles, 2012.) In 1898, at only 26 years old, she received the commission for a colossal bust of General Samuel W. Crawford for the Smith Memorial Arch in Philadelphia's Fairmont Park. (Of the eight busts on the Smith Memorial Arch, two are by women—not a bad ratio for 1898.)

The heroic bust proved a detour. Potter Vonnoh was to show her real strengths in decorative, smaller-scale works which are, in the best sense of the word, feminine, and by certain standards, sentimental. One of her early triumphs, *A Young Mother*, now at The Metropolitan Museum of Art, is an example of her gifts for intimacy—and its tenderness brings the works of Mary Cassatt to mind. (She did marry, but, like Cassatt, had no children.)

In 1926, Potter Vonnoh was a logical choice for a group of citizens who had decided to memorialize the classic children's author, Francis Hodgson

Burnett, in the Conservatory Garden of Central Park. By that time, she was an accomplished, prolific artist known for her graceful, life-size fountain pieces. She had received solo exhibitions, including one at The Corcoran Gallery, Washington D. C, and another at The Brooklyn Institute of Arts and Sciences (later, The Brooklyn Museum), and was a full member at The National Academy. Vonnoh appears to have been the only candidate for the Burnett Memorial commission, on which she worked from 1926 to its dedication in 1936.

Like many girls, I was a lover of Francis Hodgson Burnett, and I have a special fondness for this lively, delicate bronze: it has, in Potter Vonnoh's own words, "the joy and swing of everyday life." (as cited by Tolles, 2012.) She had previously sculpted a group of children for Roosevelt Bird Sanctuary in Oyster Bay, Long Island, and that effort informed her concept for the *Burnett Memorial*. She shows a girl standing holding a bowl, and a boy lying beside her, flute in hand—these based on the two major characters (familiar to girls of many generations) from *The Secret Garden*. The charming statue sits, fittingly, on a lily pond—and it captures the feel of a truly secret garden. Today, visitors are asked to be quiet when enjoying this greenspace, and Potter Vonnoh's work still has a magical effect on visitors to the Park, perhaps because so few tourists venture so far uptown these days.

By the time of the *Burnett Memorial*'s completion, Bessie Potter Vonoh was sixty-four; and she produced little after that. I wonder if she retired because of her age, or because of shifting American tastes. Potter Vonnoh, like the other White Rabbits, was a professional, commercial artist—and earning a decent living meant achieving technical perfection in popular genres. She was not out to shatter Beaux-Arts conventions or explore unknown territory.

Today, art critics hop around the historical timeline, looking for evidence of the weird, the iconoclastic, the subversive, and the funky; the photography of Diane Arbus and, more recently, the amateur Vivian Maier, fit the mold perfectly. From this vantage point, even Early American "primitives" (or, for that matter, Grandma Moses) have an edge over a technically refined artist like Bessie Potter Vonoh. She was a virtuoso in America's art academies, not a rebel against them—she had mastered academic technique, climbed a steep, narrow ladder, and was not about to break it. To do so would have been career suicide: thriving in what was still a man's world was tough enough. This absence of formal experimentation might explain the decline in her reputation. (To be fair, most of America's heroic military and equestrian statues are similarly out of critical favor—and the emotional content that informed those public works, as well as those of Potter Vonnoh, collides with today's

Figure 14.2: Burnett Memorial Fountain, Sculptor—Bessie Potter Vonoh. Photo Credit: Another Believer, Wikimedia Commons.[2]

brand of cool irony. Potter Vonnoh's work is beautiful, but it is never cool or alternative.)

Which brings me to the last of the New York trio, the one whose Art Deco works appear across Manhattan. Hildreth Meière was born in New York City in 1892, like Stebbins, to a background of wealth and culture. Her early years follow a similar pattern of intensive training, and the requisite trip to Italy (in her case, Florence rather than Rome.) Meiere was driven from the start. She trained as a mapmaker for the United States Navy during the First World War, which she, cannily, understood would improve her grasp of higher mathematics and rules of perspective, and would allow her to become an apprentice, in her words, to "a mural man." (cited by Brawer & Skolnick, 2014, p. 34.) Meiere may have known that Violet Oakley, in 1907, had earned the first public mural commission awarded to a female.

Although the Beaux Arts Institute in New York barred women, Meiere actively exhibited her designs and won competitions. Her first commission came in 1919—interestingly, from the stage actor Alfred Lunt, for a residential project. In a stroke of luck, in 1923 (Meiere was 31,) she earned her first major commission for the dome of the National Academy of Sciences in Washington, D. C. Its architect, Bertram Goodhue, gambled on the young, ambitious Meiere because he loathed the other designs—and their smooth partnership led to more work for Meiere. After Goodhue's death, she worked with his successor firm on over twenty-three large-scale commissions. From the get-go, she found her style: her work on the Nebraska State Capitol (which has a fabulous Deco design of stylized waves and geometric patterns) earned her a gold medal in Mural Decoration by the Architectural League of New York. Working with an all-male team, Meiere held her own easily, and sought as much control as possible. The voice that emerges from her letters is highly confident, even when miffed (as when her use of Sioux motifs was discarded by the architect.) Meiere later claimed that the State Capital was her "most important secular work." (cited by Brawer & Skolnick, 2014, p. 79)

But her signature Art Deco pieces are in Manhattan, and it is through those that most people know her. These include the mosaics and stained-glass windows for St. Bartholomew's Church, the 75-foot mosaic arch and mosaics surrounding the ark at Temple Emanu-El, the bold metal and enamel sculptures on Radio City Music Hall's exterior, and the mosaic work on the ground floor of Bank of New York (One Wall Street) – an astonishing body of work.

She had just finished working on the chapel of the University of Chicago in 1927, when she was handed the commission for Temple Emanu-El (even today, the largest synagogue in the world.) Its architects had settled on a Byzantine style, and somewhat Moorish façade; and it fell to Meiere to design the mosaics for the eight-story high main arch and the ark behind, with a Judaic feel. She wrote, *"The difficulty in working for Temple Emanu-El came in devising geometric patterns which do not contain a cross. Try and do it!"* (as cited by Brawer & Skolnick, 2014, p. 84) Meiere managed the task with flair; and her intricate designs incorporate Deco-inspired flames, lozenges and Eastern-tinged tulips, as well as (in a happily eclectic spirit) a Sioux-inspired chevron pattern, along with swirling Jewish shofars. The mosaics are varying sparkling shades of gold: Meiere worked as the technical and artistic advisor during their installation, taking special care with their shading and quality. (Meiere loved domes because they captured light so well.)

The work on St. Bartholomew's involved three commissions spanning decades; and to varying degrees, Meiere incorporated Art Deco elements and Byzantine style in all of them. A consummate technician, she studied mosaic techniques that could yield the lush colors she wanted. She plucked ideas from the Genesis Dome at San Marco in Venice, and the fifth century Mausoleum of Galla Placidia in Ravenna; but her geometrics of the Narthex dome are pure Art Deco. Her later work on the church's stained-glass windows involved attacking a new medium (glass): she collaborated with the head of a glass studio, William Haley, to produce a subtle, luminous gray, which she decorated with flamboyant geometrics, stylized clouds and wings.

The pinnacle of her New York work is on the façade of Radio City Music Hall: Meiere's rondels were among the first public works to be completed for Rockefeller Center. The designs are allegorical figures, *Song, Dance,* and *Drama,* each fueled by Meiere's high-power Deco vitality. Mixed metal and enamel had never been used before in large-scale, outdoor art. Meiere's solution was to use the enamel sparingly, with bold colors, and focus on bringing out the specific properties of the different metals. Her use of color is striking: the *Dance* rondel shown below offers a deep cobalt paired with a brilliant yellow hat and cymbals. Her Radio City Music Hall designs won national acclaim as Art Deco masterpieces, and showered her with press.

Meiere's later career was an unbroken stream of hits, including corporate murals and, during the New Deal, murals from the Public Works Administration (for which she had to submit competitive designs, rare in her career.) She was expert at self-promotion: writing about the process of creating murals; exhibiting her sketches in group shows; and her designs were featured in journals like *Architectural Forum.* (Despite this unceasing activity, Meiere somehow found time to marry and have a child.) Her position was so assured, that architect Ralph Walker wrote of her in 1942: "We need more artists in America like Hildreth Meiere!" (Cited by Brawer & Skolnick, 2014, page 167) Most of her murals survive in their original form.

Figure 14.3: Dance, Radio City Music Hall, in Mixed Metal and Enamel Roundel by Hildreth Meière, 1932. Photo Credit: Hildreth Meière Dunn © 2007.

And yet, as with Emma Stebbins and Bessie Potter Vonnoh, New York and America went about forgetting the name of Hildreth Meière. In a short time after her death in 1961, less than a generation, her reputation faded. By the 1980s, when I worked right across the street from Radio City Music Hall, her name had blended into the tapestry of forgotten women.

To me, it is a sad tapestry, almost a cautionary tale.

Is the forgetting of these artists only due to gender? Probably not, or at least not entirely. Nothing is ever *that* simple. History is messy, complicated. Public statues lack the cache, reputation-wise, of painting—and sculpture as a medium is less popular, today, than painting. No question that the sheer scale of murals makes them hard to appreciate from afar, and impossible in reproductions. Moreover, critical tastes are notoriously fickle, and one generation's idol is another's kitsch. I could go on, and there is a grain of truth in all of it.

But a grain of truth is not the truth. The truth is that the works endure, they are beloved, they are part of New York City. The *Angel of the Waters* and the *Burnett Memorial* have been restored, and Radio City Hall's enamel sculptures gleam as never before. And it is unjust that their female creators are left in history's shadows. I feel they deserve our attention. I feel they have *earned* it. Yes, art exists to delight us, to make the world beautiful; but art also tells us *who* we are, and *where* we have been. There is spirit and dignity in the art of Emma Stebbins, Bessie Potter Vonnoh and Hildreth Meiere: women who never stood still, and who in art and life spread their wings. They invite us to fly with them, anywhere we want. It seems the least we can do, by way of thanks, is to remember their names.

Notes

1. Wikimedia Commons link: https://commons.wikimedia.org/wiki/File:Bethesda_Fountain,_Oct_2009,_NYC.jpg; Creative Commons license: https://creativecommons.org/licenses/by-sa/2.0/deed.en
2. Wikimedia Commons link: https://commons.wikimedia.org/wiki/File:Central_Park,_NYC_(June_2014)_-_09.JPG; Creative Commons license: https://creativecommons.org/licenses/by-sa/3.0/deed.en

References

Berger, J. (1973). *Ways of seeing*. Penguin Books.

Brawer, C. C. & Skolnick, K. M. (2014). *The art deco murals of Hildreth Meiere*. New York: Andrea Monfried Editions.

Central Park, Bethesda Fountain, retrieved from http://www.nycgobparks.org/parks/central-park/monuments/114

Fine, E. H. (1978). *Women and Art*. Montclair, NJ: Allanheld, Osmun and Co.

Milroy, E. (1993a). The public career of Emma Stebbins: Work in marble. Division I Faculty Publications of Wesleyan University.

Milroy, E. (1993b). The public career of Emma Stebbins: Work in bronze. Division I Faculty Publications of Wesleyan University.

Musacchio, J. M. (2014). Mapping the "white, marmorean flock": Anne Whitney Abroad, 1867–1868. Nineteenth Century Art Worldwide, 13(2).

Tolles, T. (2010). American neoclassical sculptors abroad. In *Heilbrunn timeline of art history*. New York: The Metropolitan Museum of Art.

Tolles, T. (2012). Bessie Potter Vonnoh (1872–1955). In *Heilbrun timeline of art history*. New York: The Metropolitan Museum of Art.

15. The Cultural and Economic Dimensions of Class in Queerness[1]

Lisa Henderson

Introduction: Sex and Solidarity

In a *Guardian Observer* story of January 2014, British film and stage actor Rupert Everett writes about the police ouster of sex workers from their shared apartments in London's Soho neighborhood (Everett, 2014). The arrests were conducted under the guise of stopping sex trafficking, says Everett, though no traffickers were apprehended. Contrary to the claims of police and morality squads, there is a Soho land grab going on, where police co-operate with property developers and their partners in city hall, greedily warming their hands over a Soho reconfigured for international tourism and sales, as if London weren't expensive enough. It is a "creative class" approach to urban development long promoted by Richard Florida (2002), an approach even Florida (2017) has begun to recant as urban creative classes are revealed to mainly produce dramatic income inequality in cities (Wetherell, 2017). Everett follows his sex worker friends to trial, to witness the proceedings and to write dryly—and knowingly—about the theater taking place there and the revelation of legal done-deals against Londoners with few resources, save their own social networks now ruined by police "protection."

Reading Everett's piece left me wondering about Everett—his posh writing style, his come-and-go fortunes as leading man in popular film since openly identifying as gay in 1989, his friendship and solidarity with maids and prostitutes pooling their housing resources in Soho. Everett is not unique among English cultural figures—part social and cultural elite, part artistic bohemian and old school sexual rebel—indeed he reminds me of Oscar Wilde, whose biography, plays, and film adaptations Everett knows well as performer. Everett is arguably part of the old creative class. Everett's *Guardian* piece, however, re-animates the conversation about sexual culture and class solidarity in queerness—the queerness of being a gay actor who, at one time, traded sex for drugs and money, the queerness of being unmoved (if still displaced) by morality squads working at the service of property development, the queerness of sexual libertinism and the sensible distrust of sexual show trials. Anyone who watched the purification of New York's Times Square and the loss, there, of a mixed culture of rent boys, porn workers, and sexual bohemians will find Everett's account of Soho familiar. Samuel Delaney's writing preserves the Times Square story achingly (Delaney, 2001), as Sarah Schulman's does for New York's East Village (Schulman, 1990).

I start with Everett to trouble expectations, first, about media and sexual scandal. Here is Everett—actor, moderate celebrity, sometimes party-boy in his earlier years, sexual iconoclastic (and punished for it) in the entertainment industry—writing about the shadowy economic conduct of London's development class and its acolytes and payoff-seekers in the police, courts, and city hall. Second, I also want to trouble conventional ideas about class alignment in queerness, in which one professional managerial queer habitus encounters another, and the two live happily ever after. Such a union would likely be sanctioned, at this point, by the state in ways that Soho sex workers only are when their circumstances favor the state. (Nothing ends *laissez-faire* policing like a land grab.) I occupy such a habitus-match, and am not here to deride it or to dismiss its structured predictability (Bourdieu, 1984). On the contrary, I want to think clearly about it. But in addition to signifying a historical type, Everett's support of his sex worker friends is a reminder of the complexity and variability of class formation, solidarity, and loss in contexts of sexual control or exclusion. It is a complexity that Jeffrey Escoffier periodized in U.S. gay history as the closet, liberation, territorial, AIDS, and hypercommodification economies from the 1940s to the 1990s (Escoffier, 1997).

Class, Income, and Wealth

What is class? In the liberal, empirical tradition, "socio-economic status" or "SES" is favored over the Left language of class. SES is a composite variable that takes into account individual and household income, occupation, and formal education. It sometimes also includes wealth, or accumulated capital. The income/wealth distinction is important and easy to see if we consider, e.g., the difference between a first-generation, well-educated, professional-managerial person who earns a whopping $100,000 a year (192% of the average US household income in 2016), whose salary is expected to support an extended family of children, aging parents, and needful nieces and nephews, in contrast to a colleague at the same salary, partnered with another, also salaried, from a professional managerial family, whose financial obligations end at their own front door and who can expect an inheritance. Same salary but different prospective wealth over time, given the effects of an extended economic distribution in the first case and the lower likelihood of inheritance from a dependent older generation. That diminished likelihood of inheritance, moreover, is often the multi-generational outcome of consciously racist policy in the United States, for example where even federal home loans were blocked from African-American borrowers, who could not, then, buy homes and leave property or sale revenue to future generations (Rothstein, 2017).

The Occupy movement re-sensitized people in the U.S. to the current degree of (mal)distribution of wealth, and at this point it is easy to find research in so many corners that reveals the present as bearing the greatest wealth inequality in the United States since the late 1920s. Berkeley economist Emmanuel Saez, e.g., calculates that in 2012 the top 1% of *income* earners in the U.S. (those earning above $394,000) reaped 22.5% of all income. In a recent update, Saez considers the proportion of income *growth* captured by the top 1% between 1993 and 2015.

> The implications of these fluctuations at the very top can also be seen when we examine trends in *real* income growth per family between the top 1 percent and the bottom 99 percent in recent years … From 1993 to 2015, for example, average real incomes per family grew by only 25.7% over this 22 year period. However, if one excludes the top 1 percent, average real incomes of the bottom 99% grew only by 14.3% from 1993 to 2015. Top 1 percent incomes grew by 94.5% from 1993 to 2015. This implies that top 1 percent incomes captured 52% of the overall economic growth of real incomes per family over the period 1993–2015. (Saez, 2016)

That's a big piece of the income pie in 2012 and the income growth pie in 2015, but the slice of the wealth pie accruing to the top 1% is greater still. According to economist Edward Wolff at NYU, in 2010 the top 1% controlled 34.5% of all *wealth* (Pew Research Center, 2014). Another expression, also from Wolff, is that whereas the highest earning fifth of US families earned 59% of all income in 2010, the *richest* fifth held 89% of all wealth. Wealth and income are different but closely correlated; over time, diminished income means even more diminished wealth.

I reiterate these figures for two reasons: (1) they speak to the place of income and wealth in critical definitions of class, though we still don't have reliable, national wealth and income data (to say nothing of SES) by sexual orientation or transgender identification in the United States; and (2) they say a lot about the overall context in which post-Stonewall LGBT generations have come of age, some of whom have also acquired relative visibility and authority in a range of sectors—electoral politics, law, corporate life, the academy, NGOs, government, consumer markets, and cultural production. I have argued elsewhere (Henderson, 2013) that this has meant that thirty years of the amelioration of queer life for some has taken form amid socially and politically crippling economic conditions and a national culture of hyper-accumulation. That's an important way of putting it. It isn't a matter of rich, indifferent gays vs. conscious queers; it's rich, indifferent everyone vs. conscious citizens. If you don't say that, however, you get rich gays vs. poor everyone else and queerness comes to bear a skewed proportion of responsibility for the economic state of things, much as it has historically borne a skewed proportion of moral antipathy. Following Escoffier, call this the neoliberal hyperaccumulation economy.

Although we don't have comprehensive, reliable SES data by sexual orientation or transgender identification in the United States—data that combine occupation, education, and income for a national population over time—we do have regional studies conducted by the Williams Institute at the University of California Los Angeles School of Law and by the National Gay and Lesbian Task Force (NGLTF), among other groups, which demonstrate that gay, lesbian, bisexual, and especially transgender citizens suffer wage and employment discrimination at significant rates relative to their non-LGBT peers, and that those forms of discrimination persist throughout a lifetime, with cyclic and compounding effects. Gay men, the Williams Institute reports, earn 10%–32% less than heterosexual men "who have the same productive characteristics, such as experience and level of education, according to 12 studies" (Williams Institute, 2015). Transgender people, moreover, "are unemployed at twice the rate of the general population, and 15% have reported incomes of less than $10,000 per year, according to the National Transgender Discrimination Survey" (Williams Institute, 2015).

Early discrimination means early wage suppression and diminishes the likelihood of catching up. What is true of non-LGBT society, moreover, is also true in gay populations: *within* sexual orientation discrimination, LGBT people of color suffer disproportionately high employment discrimination and wage suppression relative to their white counterparts. Discrimination overall has been activated through a range of everyday prejudices and state and federal policies, e.g. the deprivations, still felt, from the Defense of Marriage Act (DOMA, whose Article 3 on the definition of marriage as occurring between "one man and one woman" was ruled unconstitutional

only in 2013), which excluded non-married partners from social security survival benefits and spousal health benefits. Wage suppression plus lack of health
care early in life (whether through poverty, discrimination, DOMA exclusion
or myriad other reasons) means less wealth and chronic health problems later,
and thus fewer LGBT people (than non) can expect "golden years" as they
age. Fewer people overall can expect secure retirements, but among those
facing diminished prospects, LGBT people, especially transgender people and
people of color, will fare less well still (National Gay and Lesbian Task Force,
2013). Such economic circumstances are a reminder of one source of the
ardor for marriage equality among political possibilities: it may be less about
romance and relationship recognition (though both are valuable to many)
and more about health care and other cost sharing needs.

This is the thinnest of economic snapshots of the recent period for LGBT
citizens, not a picture that extends in a refined way the broad periodization
Escoffier authored. But, harking back to the recognition/redistribution
debates of the 1990s (e.g. Fraser, 2002), it is a reminder that from wages
to contracts to health care to starring roles (as Everett's career suggests), a
supposedly cultural, identitarian category like sexuality has measureable dis-
tributive consequences.

Class as Culture

But what *else* is class? We know from Bourdieu (1984) that it is a conden-
sation of capitals—economic, social, educational, and cultural. As their
name suggests, capitals are resources acquired, used, and reinvested with
the unself-conscious presumption of return. They are mediated by family
upbringing and formal education, and their non-economic forms (which can
though don't usually fall far from the tree of economic provision) produce
other kinds of value—tastes and dispositions that communicate distinction
and refinement (or not), and networks of similarly-endowed others in whose
company a world takes shape more-or-less hermetically, excluding those without the same or equally-worthy resources to trade. People with elite educa-
tions, for example, will cash in through the prestige value of their schooling
beyond their credentials, and through peer networks where those resources
are circulated and their value deepened. Not all those enrolled in elite schools
come from fancy backgrounds, and those who do sometimes flunk out or
don't get in. But well-heeled people who do, and who do well, go on to consider their rewarding lives the outcome of their hard work, where in fact the
majority of them would have done fine in the world placed by their networks
and regardless of effort. You can get a great job at Morgan Stanley with a

cumulative average of C from Amherst College (or a job as president of the U.S. with a C average from Yale). Amherst College sociologist Jan Dizard, for example, wrote an acute critique of the culture of student effort in his own institution. Effort, he argues, is ritualized and rewarded as though an absence of effort will trouble a student's college outcomes and future. That depends, however, on where the student comes from. Hard-working students from elite backgrounds are trained to recognize their rewards as the outcome of effort, not as the reproduction of status or as the inheritance of economic or cultural capital (Dizard, 1991).

In addition, then, to economic and professional security, educational capital promises footing and faith in the idea of one's self and one's effort as the source of value. Lots of hard-working, working-class people, on the other hand, know from experience that their effort does not predict let alone guarantee reward, though without effort they will surely sink.

Enter sexual difference and desire. As clarifying as Bourdieu's theory of capitals is, there are always mitigating circumstances of personal and historic proportion, and sexual difference and desire have long figured among them. They are not guarantees of class inversion or social mixing, though many historians (e.g. Chauncey, 1994, Kennedy and Davis, 1993, Houlbrook, 2006, and Stein, 2000) have described the perils and pleasures of class mixing in periods of closeted and yet still capacious LGBT world-making. More recently, U.S. historian Chad Heap described the effects of sexual cultures on class practice in the mid-century context of recreational "slumming" in Chicago and New York (Heap, 2009). During the Depression, which was also a period of "pansy" and lesbian "craze" in New York and Chicago, Heap notes (262), for example, that black, heterosexual, working class men identified pansies—effeminate men—as a class of people they could revile, as they lost their own jobs and economic toe-holds and despite their cautions to black women that they support their men lest those men hook up instead—with pansies. The re-configuration of gender, race and class in this example is not progressive in the terms we conventionally imagine departures from class structure or rigidity, least of all for heterosexual black women. But that doesn't set it aside as gender and sexual category trouble, the kind that produces temporary or emerging change. Even regressive transformation introduces new social possibilities that challenge received presumptions about class, race, gender, and sexual difference.

Heap continues:

> Surprisingly, however, a number of black working-class bulldaggers and faggots also exploited the intermediary space created by the pansy and lesbian craze of Harlem and Bronzeville to coax middle-class whites away from the increasingly

hegemonic hetero/homosexual classification. Invoking eroticized notions of racial difference, they created situations in which otherwise heterosexual white women and men could once again indulge in same-sex relations without calling their sexual normalcy into question. (2009, 263)

People, in other words, are always creative if not always liberating. Whether or not we re-categorize social and sexual value in permanent ways, we *re-group* in many directions under the right circumstances. The convergence of sex and culture has long provoked such re-grouping, a trove of kaleidoscopic sociability within and beyond class boundaries. In some contexts, like Everett's or the world Samuel Delaney (2001) narrates in *Times Square Red Times Square Blue*, boundary crossing becomes common cause.

Queer Class Representation

I wrote *Love and Money: Queers, Class, and Cultural Production* (2013) moved to find common cause in queerness across class lines. I was also moved by the transformative economic analysis of JK Gibson-Graham, joint nom-de-plume of co-authors Julie Graham and Katherine Gibson. In *A Post-Capitalist Politics*, Gibson-Graham argue against what they call a *capitalocentric* analysis (2006, xxxiv) in which all economic activity is defined as "capitalist" even before an analyst begins to explore a particular instance, simply because it occurs within or in close proximity to a system dominated by capitalist practice. The language of the economy, they say, bears a paucity of concepts for imagining non-capitalist production. As a consequence, we don't imagine it. Against this grain, Gibson-Graham invite what they call "reading for difference," looking for economic activities, groups, and forms of exchange that cannot properly be called capitalist (which doesn't necessarily make them progressive) and proceeding from there to locate and support durable, alternative forms of economic activity from which a new set of solidarities might be enacted in the present. As feminist political economists, in other words, they sought to *queer* the economy in the name of reparative action, and in that essential gesture were indebted to the work of queer theorist Eve Kosofsky Sedgwick, a debt they took pleasure in acknowledging (2006, 7).

Gibson-Graham's writing inspired me to read for difference at the intersection of queerness and class, to expand how we understand the cultural layer of that intersection (since culture is what I study), and to reimagine the conditions of common cause. Sometimes, of course, one can look and not find, and indeed *Love and Money* observes, first, how commercial cultural production has been the site of the reproduction of class value through what many observers have called the "new queer visibility." "New queer visibility" is a shorthand that refers to the relative burgeoning of queer characters in broadcast and premium cable television in the late 1990s and early 2000s, for example *Ellen, Will and Grace,* and *The L Word* ('burgeoning' is easy when you start with little). It is a symbolic formation best charted by Larry Gross (2001) in *Up From Invisibility: Lesbians, Gay Men, and the Media in America.* In the new queer visibility, the interaction between queerness and class had an economic logic, embedding enough fragmented class recognition—bits and pieces here and there—to appeal to a range of consumers and still flatter those managers and professionals at the crest of advertising trade value, and to sweeten content with a *soupçon* of queer edge, enough to draw newer, hipper, younger audiences in the hyperdiversified landscape of popular forms. Within this logic, queerness delivered cultural expansion, a new commercial horizon broadened beyond old typifications of queer marginality but well shy of heterosexual disarmament. In the case of broadcast and cable television, it was a horizon fitted to the "postnetwork" era (Lotz, 2004), a competitive context in which smaller, more-defined "niche" audiences acquired industrial value, cable outlets competed as targeted brands with each other and with traditional broadcast networks, and distinction relied on a combination of old formats (situation comedy, nighttime soap opera, family melodrama) and new themes and characters, queers among them. In this new environment, an audience of "socially liberal, urban-minded professionals" (Becker, 1998) comes with a high price tag for advertisers and is thus especially desirable for networks, outlets, cable operators, portals, and production companies. Many producers and executives, gay and straight, are themselves a part of that audience, brokering class fantasies, queer trade value, and industrial ratings as they shuttle back and forth between the specialized domain of cultural production and more diffuse forms of meaning-making in everyday life. In Sherry Ortner's terms, the *class project* of queer visibility takes shape through their creative, technical, and managerial labor (Ortner, 2003). Ortner's hitching of "project" to class is apt, reminding us that in economic and cultural terms, class is as much something we do (and do again) as it is something we and others have, or are.

The vernacular and academic critique of the new queer visibility as a class project is that it has promoted a vision of homosexuality populated by rich, white, healthy men detached from sex, lovers and queer political communities. Will Truman of *Will and Grace* comes to mind. There is truth in that critique, but it's partial. In U.S. commercial popular culture the class spectrum is compressed. The ruling class and routine (not criminal) poverty are strikingly absent, and wealth is way out of proportion to the world as we know it. The underrepresentation of lower-middle-class citizens and communities meets an overabundance of superrich celebrities and corporate up-and-comers, and even modest living is more luxurious and better-heeled on television, say, than in strapped neighborhoods and working households. That doesn't mean, however, that amid this compression the engines of class distinction are still. As is true in everyday life, they are steady, neither thunderous, nor silent, but a coarse drone sustained by (1) comportment, (2) family attachment, and (3) legitimate modes of acquisition (not only what we have but how we get it) as the class markers or *habitus* (Bourdieu, 1984, 170) of queer worth. Naming these markers is a different goal than describing class types among queer characters, not least because such markers are variably applied to a range of characters across the familiar categories of blue-collar, middle-class, and rich, shifting characters' relative value in the world of narratives, genres, and moral outcomes.

The class markers of queer worth have organized not only the concentrated narratives of commercial popular culture but the diffuse and contradictory partial narratives of everyday living. Commercial culture's most visible fantasies are not a world apart, but a part of our world, elements of a continuous cultural stream in which ideologies of class and queer worth rooted in managed bodies, family attachments, and legitimately acquired things are as likely to surface off television as on. My conclusion, then, is not that adequate representation in commercial culture will promote adequate representation in social life, or that as critics we ought to expect that popular media will deconstruct popular fantasy. (On the contrary.) Instead, I suggest there is a continuity of affective investment inside the media and out, in a universe where people *really do* enjoy, endure, and equally suffer the terms of existing class projects, including the class project of queer visibility.

That's the bad news, but reading for difference guides us not to stop there. Where else in queer cultural activity can we find class expression, and where, in that expression, are there opportunities for common cause? *Love and Money* goes on to find class expression in narratives of gender queer trauma (*Boys Don't Cry, The Crying Game*), where hard living in bleak circumstances is offered to account for transphobic violence and death. But it uses other narratives and other readers' encounters with narrative for signs of gentle observation and a non-dominative form of class recognition in queerness. Readers of the work of Dorothy Allison, for example, gather across queer lines to articulate, through their readings of Allison's novels, stories, and essays, a classed place in the world, sometimes as queer class "escapees" with lives marked by an upward mobility that has been more or less economically secure but remains shaky in its class ethos, its limited sense of inclusion, its losses or partial-losses of a community of origin, and its guilt and concern for those left behind.

Readers' insights were reminders of the limits of that old claim that Americans don't talk about class, and a testament to the value of doing so consciously and in public. Class, it turns out, is spoken (whether or not through the term *class*) wherever critics imagine class effects to be felt—in conversations about generational change within families, about education, charity, health, migration, police reaction in public, or expectations of taste and demeanor, to name just a few social contexts where talk of class structures the recognition of one's own experience.

Elsewhere in *Love and Money*, I write about cultural producers whose practice of relay running from queer to non-queer sectors and back remind the avant-garde among us not to be too protective against the threat of cross-over. "Queer relay" is an alternative concept for narrating cultural labor. I conceived queer relay to resist the taste hierarchies that come with what I call the "commercial repressive hypothesis", a living idea that says "commerce is bad," sustaining the old opposition between good culture and bad capital and lamenting popular queer taste (for *Queer Eye* or *Ru Paul*) as diminishing sexual and political beauty. Taste hierarchy has long been a sure way to drive class hierarchy into queer solidarity.

As many readers will recognize, my critique of the commercial repressive hypothesis is an adaptation of Michel Foucault's critique of the "sexual repressive hypothesis" (Foucault, 1986), which holds (indefensibly, says Foucault) that the modern history of sexuality has been a history of change from repression to liberation. Instead, Foucault argues, the history of sexuality has been a proliferation of discourses about sex, whether religious, medical, carceral, or educational. The history of sexuality has also been a proliferation of intersections between sex and capital that makes defensive retreat as much an expression of taste as politics.

Finally, *Love and Money* seeks the cultural conditions of "plausible optimism," a category at once inspired by and conceived as a challenge to Lauren Berlant's powerful concept of "cruel optimism" (Berlant, 2011, 2006). In popular culture, as in life itself, we routinely return to attachments we feel we need in order to keep life going, even when those attachments diminish us. Cigarette smoking or bad relationships are easy examples. They are cruel because they attach us to the very possibility of going on with life, despite the likelihood of ruination or loss, because they are what we know. What if we looked for new things to attach to, things that serve us better than the project of familialism, accumulation, and physical propriety as the routes to queer enfranchisement?

In Berlant's theorization, the alternative to cruel optimism is surviving a moment of fracture or impasse without returning to old ways of being. Some characters, Berlant observes, particularly those with enfranchisement and skill, do not lose their footing when the ground beneath them shifts. They navigate broken territory and find their way out, without returning to the familiar but failed conditions that entrap them (2006, 26). Berlant's category of cruel optimism is thus a provocation to discover narratives and histories of plausible optimism, of thriving, even, including among characters and people who do not have class ascendance or social power on their side. I have looked for examples of thriving in narratives and practices of friendship, not in ideal terms but in non-dominative ones, in histories of solidarity (such as that between Soho sex workers and Rupert Everett) where class analysis tells us to least expect it. The life of African-American gay poet, artist and novelist Essex Hemphill was an important place to look, as black queers sought refuge together while many in their communities died of AIDS in the 1980s and 1990s (including Hemphill himself, in 1995) (Duberman, 2014, cited in Henderson, 2015). So was the New York City chapter of ACT-UP, the AIDS Coalition to Unleash Power, whose veteran activists witnessed common cause across the lines of class, race, and gender despite a common critique that blamed the movement's gay white men for persistent self-interest at others' expense (Hubbard, 2012, cited in Henderson, 2015).

Conclusion: Queering Class

The economic and cultural dimensions of class in queerness, in sum, take account of income; wealth; formal education; networks; tastes and dispositions; comportment; familialism; modes of acquisition; life chances enabled, compressed, made precarious, or screwed by medical, legal, and economic policy; class project narratives of hierarchy but also thriving; relay systems in culture-making that counter avant-garde presumptions of liberation through taste and its exclusions; and fantasies of survival through friendship and solidarity in places both unexpected and routine. Such a list is less comprehensive than indicative of the social saturation of class as the economic and cultural co-production of distinction and hierarchy.

Michael Ashton, a young, queer Irish rebel, gay liberation activist, and self-identified Communist living (then dying) in London in the mid-1980s, was the clear-eyed founder of Lesbians and Gays Support the Miners (LGSM), a small, motley organization that raised money for and waged solidarity with striking Welsh miners at the height of Thatcher's redundancy program. The story of LGSM's travels in Wales' Dulais Valley is told in the recent British film *Pride* (dir. Matthew Warchus, 2014), a deliriously encouraging movie based in part on an amateur documentary, titled *All Out! Dancing in Dulais*, about the queers' and miners' joint efforts. The community documentary, thankfully, is embedded in full in *Guardian* writer Kate Kellaway's review of *Pride* (Kellaway, 2014). "One community," says the irresistible Ashton in the documentary, "should give solidarity to another. It is really illogical to say, 'I'm gay and I'm into defending the gay community but I don't care about anything else …'"

Ashton is not Everett, not by roots, *habitus* or, exactly, by political motives. He identifies with the miners not through desire or a shared history of sexual trade, but through the dignity of stigma, aversion, and political demonization in common—all conditions Thatcherism managed to attach to sex *and* work and which the miners and the LGSM re-signified through their solidarity. In current conditions, as averse as those conditions are to sexual liberation and the fair valuation of work, Ashton, *Pride*, and *All Out!* remind us not only of the thick and multicolored braid of class formation and representation, but of the gifts of solidarity that sexual recognition, in its shames and glories, has delivered in the past and can deliver again.

Note

1. Some passages in this paper first appeared in Henderson (2013). Love and thanks to Larry Gross and Scott Tucker.

References

Becker, R. (1998). Prime time television in the gay 90s: Network television, qualities audiences, and gay politics. *The Velvet Light Trap, 42*, 36–47.

Berlant, L. (2006). Cruel optimism. *differences: a Journal of Feminist Cultural Studies, 17*(3), 20–36.

Berlant, L. (2011). *Cruel optimism*. Durham, NC: Duke University Press.

Bourdieu, P. (1984). *Distinction: A social critique of the judgment of taste* (Richard Nice, trans.). Cambridge, MA: Harvard University Press.

Chauncey, G. (1994). *Gay New York: Gender, urban culture, and the making of the gay male world, 1890–1940*. New York: Basic Books.

Delaney, S. (2001). *Times square red, times square blue*. New York: New York University Press.

Dizard, J. E. (1991). Achieving place: Teaching social stratification to tomorrow's elite. *Teaching what we do: Essays by Amherst college faculty*, 145–162.

Duberman, M. (2014). *Hold tight gently: Michael Callen, Essex Hemphill, and the Battlefield of AIDS*. New York and London: New Press.

Escoffier, J. (1997). The political economy of the closet: Notes toward an economic history of gay and lesbian life before Stonewall. In G. Gluckman & B. Reed (Eds.), *Homo economics: Capitalism, community, and lesbian and gay life*. New York: Routledge, 123–134.

Everett, R. (2014, January 19). In defence of prostitutes: There is a land grab going on. *Guardian Observer*. Accessed at https://www.theguardian.com/film/2014/jan/19/rupert-everett-in-defence-of-prostitutes

Florida, R. (2002). *The rise of the creative class: And how it's transforming work, leisure, community, and everyday life*. New York: Basic Books.

Florida, R. (2017). *The new urban crisis: How our cities are increasing inequality, deepening segregation, and failing the middle class, and what we can do about it*. New York: Basic Books.

Foucault, M. (1978). *The history of sexuality, volume 1: An introduction*. (Robert Hurley, trans.). New York: Random House.

Fraser, N. (2002). Rethinking recognition. *New Left Review, 3*, 107–120.

Gibson-Graham, J. K. (2006). *A post-capitalist politics*. Minneapolis: University of Minnesota Press.

Gross, L. (2001). *Up from invisibility: Lesbians, gay men and the media in America*. New York: Columbia University Press.

Heap, C. (2009). *Slumming: Sexual and racial encounters in American nightlife*. Chicago: University of Chicago Press.

Henderson, L. (2013). *Love and money: Queers, class, and cultural production*. New York: New York University Press.

Henderson, L. (2015). Queers and class: Toward a cultural politics of friendship. *Key Words: A Journal of Cultural Materialism, 13*, 17–38.

Houlbrook, M. (2006). *Queer London: Perils and pleasures in the sexual metropolis, 1918–1957*. Chicago: University of Chicago Press.

Hubbard, J. (2012) *United in anger: A history of ACT UP*, DVD.

Kellaway, K. (2014) When miners and gay activists united: The real story of the film *Pride*. *The Guardian* (US Edition), August 31. Accessed at https://www.theguardian.com/film/2014/aug/31/pride-film-gay-activists-miners-strike-interview.

Kennedy, E. L. and Davis, M. *Boots of leather, slippers of gold: The history of a lesbian community*. New York: Penguin.

Lotz, A. (2004). Textual (im)possibilities in the U.S. post-network era: Negotiating production and promotion processes on lifetime's *Any Day Now*. *Critical Studies in Media Communication 21*(1), 22–43.

National Gay and Lesbian Task Force. (2013). *No golden years at the end of the rainbow: How a lifetime of discrimination compounds economic and health disparities for LGBT old adults*. Washington, DC: E. Fitzgerald.

Ortner, S. B. (2003). *New Jersey dreaming: Capital, culture, and the class of '58*. Durham, NC: Duke University Press.

Pew Research Center. (2014). *5 facts about economic inequality*. Washington, DC: D. Silver.

Rothstein, R. (2017). *The color of law: A forgotten history of how our government segregated America*. New York: W. W. Norton & Company.

Saez, E. (2016). Striking it richer: 5 facts about economic inequality in the United States (updated with 2015 preliminary estimates). Accessed at https://eml.berkeley.edu/~saez/saez-UStopincomes-2015.pdf

Schulman, S. (1990). *People in trouble*. New York: Plume.

Stein, M. (2000). *City of sisterly and brotherly loves: Lesbian and gay Philadelphia, 1945–1972*. Chicago: University of Chicago Press.

Warchus, M. (2014) *Pride* DVD

Wetherell, S. (2017, August 19). Richard Florida is sorry. *Jacobin*. Available at https://www.jacobinmag.com/2017/08/new-urban-crisis-review-richard-florida

Williams Institute. (2014). *Race/ethnicity, gender, and socioeconomic wellbeing of individuals in same-sex couples*. Los Angeles, CA: A. Kastanis and B. Wilson.

Williams Institute. (2015). *9.5 million LGBT adults nationwide would be protected under new, comprehensive non-discrimination bill*. (Press release). Accessed at https://williamsinstitute.law.ucla.edu/press/press-releases/9-5m-lgbt-adults-nationwide-would-be-protected-under-new-comprehensive-non-discrimination-bill/

16. The Longest Walk Is the Walk Home: The Theme of Return in Indigenous Cinema

STEVEN LEUTHOLD

In 1968, when Larry Gross first joined the faculty of the Annenberg School, he met the filmmaker and scholar Sol Worth, who had recently engaged in field work with the Navajo. This fortuitous meeting sparked the collaborative development of the fields of visual communication studies and visual anthropology by Worth, Gross, Jay Ruby, Paul Messaris and other important scholars. As a doctoral student at Annenberg in the early 1990s, I was eager to delve into back issues of *Studies in the Anthropology of Visual Communication* (later renamed *Studies in Visual Communication*), a journal that Larry took over editing after Sol's death. When choosing a dissertation topic, this exciting strain of research, which Larry had helped so much to develop, influenced me to consider the expanding world of indigenous media (Leuthold, 1998). In this essay that celebrates Larry's career as a scholar, I return to the emphasis on film and Native culture that had a formative impact in visual communication studies.

One of the observations by Worth and Adair in their seminal *Through Navajo Eyes* (1997) was the prevalence of sequences featuring walking in films made by the Navajo. The scholars stated "… it took us some time to see how deeply the concept of walking was embedded in their way of seeing and of showing the world, and how deliberately they planned and used images of walking" (1997, p. 146). In their analysis, Worth and Adair alternated between a consideration of the relevance of actual walking in Navajo lives and a reflection on the mythic importance of walking within the Navajo worldview. Though I will not focus exclusively on the Navajo, I will follow the second line of inquiry and attempt to frame walking in a particular mythic context, the act of return.

In 1993 the author, Paula Underwood, presented us with an epic: *The Walking People: a Native American Oral History*. A tie to the deep knowledge of the ancestors is one value expressed through the metaphor of walking. Underwood learned the tales of *The Walking People* from her father. She writes, "When I was a child my father sang me endless songs about a People who walked vast distances, struggled against high odds, succeeded, failed, but above all else continued" (Underwood, 1993, p. xi). Such distances, odds, successes and failures are also encountered by modern Native peoples.

A Native poet, Linda Hogan, has expressed how walking relates to a specifically Native way of knowing:

> Tonight I walk. I am watching the sky. I think of the people who came before me and how they knew the placement of stars in the sky, watched the moving sun long and hard enough to witness how a certain angle of light touched a stone only once a year. Without written records, they knew the gods of every night, the small, fine details of the world around them and of immensity above them ...

> Walking, I am listening to a deeper way. Suddenly all my ancestors are behind me. Be still, they say. Watch and listen. You are the result of the love of thousands. from "Walking" (1990)

Walking stands for a sensitive awareness of the environment and for a sense of connection to one's ancestors. For those indigenous people who feel alienated in modern society, it may signify a possibility of *return* to natural and ancestral ties.

Relationships at the Center

Native American cultures have traditionally been defined by a sense of a center. One scholar writes, "A ritually defined center, whether the fire at the center of the Plains tipi or the *sipapu* (earth navel) within the Pueblo *kiva* obviously expresses not just a mathematically fixed point established arbitrarily in space. It is understood as an axis serving as a bridge between heaven and earth, an axis that pierces through a multiplicity of worlds" (Brown, 1982, p. 52). The noted scholar and chronicler of the teachings of Black Elk, Joseph Epes Brown, continues, "One key to the Native American religious perspective, which again speaks to a quality of life sought by contemporary generations in their loss of center and concomitant sense of alienation and fragmentation, may be found in Native American concepts of relationship ..." (1982, p. 53). As expressed in the poetry of walking, relationships of family, band, clan and tribe are intensified through generational terms, and these relation-ships spread outward into the environment. But what happens when the center is lost and one is alienated from these powerful life-sustaining relation-ships? Reflecting the loss of the center, indigenous cinema often tells the story of a quest for return to home, to family and a sense of place.

The longest walk is the walk home. The loss of home and family—or, at the least, a great distance from them—and the attempt to recapture that connection as part of the search for self is common in films about Natives and in indigenous cinema itself. It is tempting to locate the experience of 'the return home' in a larger context such as Mircea Eliade's myth of "the eternal return" (2005). In his formative work on comparative religion, Eliade argued that return to a place or time of mythic origin has been characteristic of most systems of spiritual belief. Eliade explained that the power of a thing, whether plant, animal or object, lies in its origin. The concept of the sacred is closely tied to this understanding of things, places and people as having a point of mythic origin, a point that can be re-enacted through ritual and the retelling of myth.

While Eliade's ideas seem to apply to some traditional indigenous belief systems, it is less clear that they apply to the stories told in indigenous cin-ema. In Native cinema, the story of the return home is often more practical and detailed, especially regarding the challenges encountered in the return and of the conflicts found at 'home' itself. The desire for return is found and clearly expressed, but a sense of alienation that is fundamentally modern in its character tempers the actual possibility of mythic return. There are two sources of the difficulty of return: one is that the hero, or subject, of each story has been changed in some fundamental way by that which he or she has encountered during their time away. A second is that, by the time he or she returns, home is never the same world. Both of these difficulties are treated as themes in indigenous cinema, which shares much with *diasporic* cinema in this regard: "… increasingly the exile's longing for return is tempered by their worries about what they will or will not find once they get back" (Naficy, 2001, p. 232).

The Long Walk of Fred Young

The metaphor of the long walk as a search for the return to center has been present in Native cinema from early in its history. A film that was produced and written by Michael Barnes in 1978, *The Long Walk of Fred Young*, points out the centrality of walking to the Navajo worldview and demonstrates the extreme challenge of walking in two worlds, the Navajo and the white. As rooted in the Navajo worldview, 'Walking in Beauty' is the ultimate expression of living in harmony with Father Sun and Mother Earth. Navajos are taught by their spiritual leaders who rise early in order to greet the sun and to scatter corn pollen as a symbol of life:

> The dawn clothes me. I walk in beauty.
> The light is in my heart. I walk in beauty.
> The dawn is in my awareness. I walk in beauty.
> As I sprinkle the pollen, I walk in beauty.
> As the pollen enters me, I walk in beauty.
> As I walk the world, I walk in beauty.
> (from *The Long Walk of Fred Young*, 1978)

Beauty is not just something to be attained or even created; it is a way of being in the world. Indigenous cinema often focuses on ceremonies and actions that have great spiritual significance; through ceremonies such as the greeting of the dawn, the aesthetic and the spiritual are closely linked. This principle is realized by the film's non-Native filmmakers, as they clearly focus on the Navajo spiritual leader and on the subject of the film, Dr. Young, also known as Dr. Fred Begay (1932–2013).

Dr. Fred Young was a Navajo whose life spanned a nomadic childhood of hunting animals and gathering seeds in the high country, a repressive boarding school education and an advanced education at the University of New Mexico that culminated in a doctorate in nuclear physics. This extraordinarily varied long walk brought into stark contrast differences between traditional Navajo and non-Native worldviews. For Fred, Euro-American culture had become overly dependent on the comforts of life and the structured environments for schooling and work. Fred explained, "Generally, especially with my relatives, there's no concept about schedules. They're pretty much preoccupied with trying to solve the daily problem of getting food and water and to them time has pretty much stood still" (1978). Fred had been close to starvation as a child, so an intimate knowledge of nature was tied to his very survival. It is this sense of wonder at the natural world that ties together his experience as a child with his mature years as a physicist.

Perhaps because this was an early effort at documenting Native life by a non-Native, the filmmaker and Fred found that working with one another presented particular challenges. Dr. Young had never grown completely comfortable with the white world of academe and its social setting: "Even after all these year of living among them, I often find myself surprised by the way they act and I still have a hard time making myself act the way that is right according to them" (1978). For him, then, making a film in collaboration with non-Native filmmakers presented quite a challenge. Fred described the filmmaking experience as "a trying process for myself and my family." But he persisted because he wanted to use the medium to, as he put it, create "some understanding about the American Indian" (1978). To their credit, the film-makers acknowledge this tension and use it as a way to gently explore cultural differences between Natives and non-Natives. A Navajo director of one of the local schools noted that in Navajo culture, there might be a reluctance to talk about oneself. Group cohesion is valued over individual accomplishment. Documenting Dr. Young's walk involved a conflict between two ways, one in which talking about oneself and touting accomplishments was expected, the other in which there was, as the school's director tells us, a "Navajo taboo against putting oneself forward" (1978). In this difference, and in many others, we sense the internal conflict within Fred's path, but behind it all there is an encompassing philosophy:

> I walk in beauty.
> I walk with beauty before me.
> I walk with beauty behind me.
> I walk with beauty all around me.
> In beauty it is finished.
> In beauty it is finished.
> (from *The Long Walk of Fred Young*, 1978)

The concept of 'Walking in Beauty' is the theme of resolution for both Fred and the filmmakers. In an historical sense, Navajos are walkers. They are linguistically related to Athabaskan-speaking peoples from present-day Canada. After their migration south along the Eastern front of the Rockies, they settled in small, isolated family groups. Theirs was not a village pattern as was characteristic of the Pueblos. They were nomadic herders; walking was their way of life, though it is one that has been supplemented by the horse and the pickup truck.

However, much of Navajo mythology and ritual may have been derived from the Pueblos or from the peoples of northern Mexico and is not found in northern Athabaskan groups. For instance, sandpainting was practiced by the Pueblo; the Navajo elaborated and developed the technique. These symbolic paintings result from the belief that illness, injury or other transgressions create disharmony, which must be restored. *Hozho* is the integrated way of being in which beauty, harmony and health predominate. For the Navajo, then, all beings are interdependent, part of a grand scheme directed toward the maintenance or restoration of *hozho*. Thus, the Navajo use of the phrase 'Walk in Beauty,' acknowledges the possibility of disharmony, but invokes *return* to a state of reverence, harmony and health. The early film, *The Long Walk of Fred Young*, incorporates an indigenous concept of beauty by representing key leaders in Navajo spirituality. The film profiles an accomplished man who finds himself most at home in the *hogan*, despite thirty years of having lived in non-Native society.

Red Road: The Barry Hambly Story

A more recent film, *Red Road: The Barry Hambly Story* (2004), restates the metaphor of the long walk by telling the story of a Native man, Barry (Whitecap) Hambly (b. 1967, Lakota), in search of his roots. He is engaged in *waca*, the Lakota term for "connecting to that mysterious place of one's origins" (Lost Heritage Productions, 2004). The veteran writer and director of the documentary, Conrad Beaubien (b. 1947), keeps the focus clearly on the experiences of Mr. Hambly, who is confident, open and comfortable in telling his story on camera.

Barry had been separated from his birth mother, Darlene Whitecap, at the age of five and caught in a tragic home life as a child. The film makes the case that this separation was due to the "Sixties Scoop," a time when many thousands of aboriginal kids were put up for adoption by non-Native families. From the website for the film we learn:

> In British Columbia in 1964, the figure became 1,446 Native children out of a total of 4,228 children, or 34.2%. In his book "Native Children and the Child Welfare System", writer Patrick Johnston coined the term "Sixties Scoop" to refer to the forced migration of aboriginal children.

> The situation was the worst in Manitoba. Between 1971 and 1981, over 3,400 Native children were taken from their homes and removed from their province. More than a thousand of these children were sent to the United States, where there was a demand for children to adopt. American agencies could get $4,000 for every child placed. Native children in the United States had been adopted in a similar way until 1978, when the Indian Child Welfare Act was passed, protecting the children from being taken from their people ... There is still no such law in Canada. (Lost Heritage Productions, 2004)

Though this policy has been labeled as assimilationist or as an example of cultural genocide by some, Barry himself seems to see the cause of his separation from family as his own parents. Speaking of his mother, he recalls how, as a young child of four years old, "I don't remember being with her too often" (2004). She would go off and not come back, leaving Barry and his brothers alone. As he put it, "we were running wild" (2004). It is from this period, when he felt abandoned by his mother, that Barry developed a deep-seated anger toward his parents. (His mother had already fled from an abusive relationship with Barry's father.)

The Children's Aid Society gathered the kids and began placing them in foster homes. Most of these families were fairly caring, with the exception of one home, which, unfortunately, was a Native home. There, Barry was abused through various physical punishments such as being whipped with extension cords. Thus, between his feeling of abandonment from his mother and the later abuse from the Native foster family, Barry carried forth within him negative images of being a Lakota. He was fortunate to finally be placed in a nurturing adoptive home, and, even though his teen years were turbulent, he found work as a bricklayer after high school and established a stable place for himself in Hamilton, Ontario. Now, thirty years after his separation from his Native family of origin, he seeks them out.

The filmmakers follow the story chronologically, bringing us to the moment of reunion with his brothers and mother. His birth family, the Whitecaps, are from the Carry-the-Kettle Reserve on the Saskatchewan prairie. They are descendants of the Sioux who were led to Canada by Sitting Bull in his flight from capture by the U.S. military. Typical of women of her generation, at the age of four Barry's mother Darlene had been placed in a residential school. She says plainly of the experience that "it was awful" and that the children were treated like prisoners; she had run away from the school three times. As a result of this early childhood experience, Darlene had no experience of being mothered and, therefore, no skills on which to base her own mothering. She is an example of another major theme of films about the long walk home: displacement.

When we meet Darlene, she is clearly a woman who has weathered hard times, but she has quit drinking. As she puts it, "I went back to my culture" (2004). Thus, though her initial conversations with Barry feel a bit forced, we feel optimistic about the outcome of this reunion that Barry has so eagerly anticipated. These conversations take place at his aunt's house. However, when he later visits his mother at her place, he is more discouraged. Though she is sober, several of the individuals there are, as Barry describes it, "fall-down crazy drunk" (2004). From his perspective, it is the same "never-ending story" around her, and it reminds him strongly of the reason for the original split-up of the family. Even so, the visit home was positive. He visits his dad in a nursing home shortly before he passes away and during the filming, a long-lost brother is found and a reunion is planned with him. Barry plans on coming back to visit again, but he is clear that he "will still live back East, because I know everybody there" (2004).

What, then, do these two films, separated in time by twenty-six years, tell us about the long walk home? We learn that the gap between Native and non-Native cultures can seem vast. It is hard to feel fully at ease in both cultures. Fred Young, who had grown up in a very traditional setting, never felt fully comfortable in the white culture in which he received an education and excelled in a profession. Barry Hambly had grown up in a nurturing adoptive home and felt much more comfortable within white society, but found the Reserve and, especially, the prevalence of alcohol abuse there to be a troubling place. Thus, the sense of not being comfortable with belonging in both worlds, of being 'between' two worlds, can lead to the abuse of alcohol and other substances.

The Business of Fancydancing

These very themes—being caught between two worlds and the dangers of substance abuse and alcoholism in response to that displacement—are developed in another film that expresses the difficulty of 'going home again'. This example is the *The Business of Fancydancing*, written and directed in 2002 by Sherman Alexie (b. 1966, Spokane/Coeur d'Alene), which is based upon his first book of poetry (1992). Sherman Alexie probably needs little introduction; he is both a poet and a novelist who wrote the screenplay for *Smoke Signals* (1998). That film was directed by Chris Eyre (b. 1968, Cheyenne/Arapaho) and is considered the first feature film to be produced, directed and written by Native Americans. The basis for the screenplay was "This is What it Means to Say Phoenix, Arizona," a short story from *The Lone Ranger and Tonto Fistfight in Heaven* (1993) by Alexie.

The Business of Fancydancing is the first and only feature film that Alexie directed.

The protagonist of the film is an Indian poet, Seymour Polatkin (played by Evan Adams), who has made a name in literary circles. Despite this success, or perhaps because of it, he walks a teetering line between the private world of his poetry, the public non-Native world of literary success and his reservation roots. He is thrust back into an encounter with those roots based upon the death of one his childhood friends, a trickster of a man named Mouse. In addition, Polatkin, who is openly gay, realizes that another of his childhood friends is at the heart of his conflict with 'the res.' He writes about these boyhood friends, now grown men:

> O Mouse, O Aristotle
> The men I loved before I loved men!
> O, salmon boys,
> O, Jesus fish,
> O, divergent rivers,
> Return to me, return to me.
> (from *The Business of Fancydancing*)

The theme of return, then, is as dominant in this feature film as in the documentaries. But, the tension surrounding—or the impossibility of—this return to 'the res' and one's childhood past is the main theme of the film. One of the hallmarks of the story's success, is that Alexie, who is not gay himself, was able to so effectively capture the complex perspective and social position of a "two-spirited" or gay man. But, it is fundamentally a film about the difficulty of the long walk home. In the film, Polatkin responds to a confrontational interviewer who asks, "You've traveled all over the world ... yet 95% of your poems, by my count, are about your reservation. Why is that? He answers, "Every time I sit down and write a new poem, I want it to be not about the reservation, but the reservation won't let me go" (2002).

The film is complex in its structure, with multiple flashbacks and dreamlike dance sequences. These dance sequences, which occur outside of the chronological structure of the narrative, present the possibility of resolution—of gay and straight, Native and non-Native—in the present. It is true that it is in one of these dance scenes that Polatkin meets the white man, Steven, who is to become his lover. A later sequence, though, portrays Aristotle in full dance regalia interweaving amongst people from all backgrounds in a modern tribal dance party that transcends cultural differences. If *The Long Walk of Fred Young* finds resolution in the mantra of 'Walk in Beauty,' *The Business of Fancydancing* finds it in the dance.

The reference to fancy dancing, then, has two meanings. It is a metaphor for Polatkin's embrace of the role of a performer. In his poetry, he performs his culture to the broader non-Native audience and this causes resentment among his brothers back home, who see this performance as an exploitation of them. Polatkin represents them and profits from this representation, but he is no longer *of* them. However, dance is the place where fusion takes place. It is a place of celebration and resolution in a way that interpersonal love is not. Polatkin's loves for his old girlfriend, to whom he had announced that he was gay many years before, to his childhood friends from whom he is now estranged and to his non-Native lover are all limited by circumstances. It is in the spirit of 'Dancing in Beauty' that the limitations of interpersonal relationships are removed.

Alexie does not shy from powerful issues. In particular, he directly confronts alcohol and substance abuse. At one point in the film, Mouse is featured in a short vignette, "how to make a bathroom cleaner sandwich" (2002). In the scene, Mouse sprays bathroom aerosol cleanser onto a piece of white bread, chomps it down and promptly passes into the addict's bliss. Seymour Polatkin is a recovering alcoholic, who admits in the film, "Alcohol is a drum calling me" (2002). Clearly, Alexie's feelings about the costs of alcohol and substance abuse are strong. He had been a drinker during his college years at Washington State University, but chose lifelong sobriety at the young age of 23.

Another issue Alexie presents is the relationship of Native youth to formal education. We have already noted that educational institutions had detrimental effects for earlier generations Natives, who were torn from their homes at tender ages. Still, there remains the case of the modern Native youth, which in the case of the film is Aristotle, who arrives at university with high hopes and much natural intelligence, only to drop out a few semesters later. As Polatkin plaintively asks, "You had everything going for you Aristotle. What happened?" Aristotle replies sharply, "You have more in common with these white people than with the Indians back home ... You're the public relations warrior. You're the super-Indian. But, at home, you're just the little Indian who cries too much." (2002). Taking his leave during this confrontational scene, Aristotle spits on Seymour in the public coffee shop where they are battling. There is a great deal of inner and interpersonal conflict here about what it means to move freely and to succeed in the non-Indian world.

This antipathy for the white world echoes Fred Young's discomfort, who after thirty years had never grown to feel comfortable around his non-Native colleagues. But, *The Business of Fancydancing* reflects more than inner hostility and outward discomfort: it presents us with blatant racism. The expression of this racism can run the range from an ironic, disparaging endearment to physical violence. For instance, early in the film we see Mouse's widow eulogizing about her first meeting with him. He had walked along the banks of the river, playing his trademark violin. Coming upon the pretty young blond white woman, he had asked "What the hell you doin' here Suyapi and when are you leavin'?" She soon learns that Suyapi means "dirty, stinking, ugly white person." While this is clearly a case of racism, the widow recalls "He never really was that nice to me ... but I'm really gonna' miss that mean bastard" (2002).

The so-called solution to deep-seated feelings of injustice and hate is anemic. Polatkin says of himself: "I'm the affirmative action poet. They have to let some brown guy rail about the terrible injustices in the world" (2002). Quoting Paula Gunn Allen in the introduction to *Wiping the Warpaint off the Lens,* Beverly Singer notes, "The oral tradition is a living body. It is in continuous flux, which enables it to accommodate itself to the real circumstances of a people's lives. That is its strength, but it is also its weakness, for when a people finds itself living within a racist, classist and sexist society, the oral tradition will reflect those values and will thus shape the people's consciousness" (2001, p. 3). Racism, of course, involves a sense of others as inferior. Reverse racism asserts 'if you are going to treat me as inferior, then I am going to treat you as inferior and to make you pay for your assumptions'. To his credit, Alexie acknowledges that such feelings continue to exist rather than ignoring or downplaying them.

Is Aristotle a "tragic, beautiful warrior" or a "world champion gas sniffer"? The answer is, of course, that he is both of these and more. Alexie's success with the film is that he takes stereotypes and molds them into complex characters possessing rich, contradictory emotional lives. Aristotle is the one who, when Seymour first arrives back on the reservation for Mouse's wake, offers him the gift of a green apple (a symbolic reminder of their childhood bond). He welcomes Seymour back to 'the res', despite his absence of almost a decade. But, he is also the character who is confrontational, bullying and violent. It is easy to criticize the film for presenting stereotypes, and, perhaps, keeping them alive. On the other hand, there is an element of honesty and realism here that, when viewed in the context of indigenous cinema, reflects a larger, more epic theme: the difficulty of the long walk home.

Indigenous cinema presents profound insight about 'walking'. We do not move solely in order to arrive at a destination. We move because movement is at the heart of life itself; traversing the long road home is an attempt to return to understanding and source. Home is not only a familial concept. It is a universal concept that evokes a fundamental place of grounding and origin, and the act of walking just may take us there.

List of Films Discussed

Alexie, S. (Writer, Director). (2002). *The business of fancydancing* [DVD]. Falls Apart Productions.

Barnes, M. (Director). (1978). *The long walk of Fred Young.* [Video Cassette]. Nova Series, BBC and WGBH. (original PBS broadcast 1/11/79).

Beaubien, C. (Director). (2004). *Red road: The Barry Hambly story.* [DVD]. Hamilton, ON: Lost Heritage Productions.

References

Alexie, S. (1992). *The business of fancydancing.* Brooklyn, NY: Hanging Loose Press.

Alexie, S. (2013). *The lone ranger and Tonto fistfight in heaven.* New York: Grove Press [1993].

Brown, J. E. (1982). *The spiritual legacy of the American Indian.* New York: Crossroad, 1982.

Eliade, M. (2005). *The myth of the eternal return: Cosmos and history* (Vol. 46). NJ: Princeton University Press [1959].

Hogan, L. Walking. *Parabola*, *15*(2), 14.

Leuthold, S. (1998). *Indigenous aesthetics: Native art, media, and identity.* Austin: University of Texas Press.

Lost Heritage Productions, Inc. Ocangu-sa, red road: Finding the way home is not always easy … Lost Heritage Productions. Web. Accessed, 8/10/17, www.novamulti.com/red_road.htm#h.

Naficy, H. (2001). *An accented cinema: exilic and diasporic filmmaking.* New Jersey: Princeton University Press.

Singer, B. R. (2001). *Wiping the war paint off the lens: Native American film and video* (Visible Evidence, Vol. 10). Minneapolis: University of Minnesota Press.

Underwood, P. (1993). *The walking people: A native American oral history.* San Anselmo, CA: A Tribe of Two Press; Sausalito, CA: Institute of Noetic Sciences.

Worth, S., Adair, J., & Chalfen, R. (1997). *Through Navajo eyes: an exploration in film communication and anthropology,* with a new introduction, afterword, and notes by R. Chalfen. Albuquerque: University of New Mexico Press. [1972].

17. Leading and Enabling Research for Social Change

Traci Gillig

"I take it you're doing this because you enjoy it," Larry said with a smile as we discussed my dissertation project. He was 100 percent correct. I truly have enjoyed building a research program and now, diving into the dissertation. Not that the past few years have been challenge-free, but I've felt honored to be able to do the type of work my dissertation involves. Conducting research in close partnership with a pioneering nonprofit organization focused on improving the lives of LGBTQ youth is a rare opportunity. Not only that, but having the chance to do so under the guidance of Larry Gross is even rarer, as there is only one Larry Gross. Here, I reflect on my journey to becoming Larry's advisee, discuss my research and Larry's influence on it, and look ahead to striving to carry on Larry's legacy after I graduate.

To start at the very beginning, I was born and raised in a small suburb of Chicago, IL. My parents were supportive of me in countless ways while I was growing up. They made sure I had a strong education. They helped me pursue the extracurricular activities I enjoyed. They enabled me to see the world at a young age. They taught me to value hard work and kindness. They also let young me run free with a gender nonconforming fashion sense, wearing my hair in a short, "boy" cut paired with sports t-shirts and gym shoes straight out of the boy's section. When I was the only female invited to a male classmate's birthday party, they dropped me off as the group cheered, "Traci's here!" They didn't realize then (nor did I) that my gender nonconformity was tied to queer identity.

That I was perceived as simply a tomboy when I was young—and that my family and friends were shocked when I came out in my twenties—still surprises me. I suspected my parents wouldn't exactly respond with cheers to my disclosure. They were Protestant Christians, and our church's stance was that homosexuality is a sin. I don't have any memories of my parents explicitly expressing disapproval of homosexuality while I was growing up. However, I picked up on comments here and there that implied such an identity was undesirable. This mattered to me. When I experienced some of my first attractions to female peers, I hid my feelings. I thought they were bad and embarrassing. When questions kept bubbling up in my mind, I suppressed them more, at times with damaging coping. It took me finishing college and graduate school, becoming financially independent, going through a rough break up with a boyfriend, immediately moving across the country from Washington D. C. to Los Angeles, and struggling in a new city where I had little local social support to make me finally open up about my orientation. I remember lying on my bed in my apartment thinking, "This has to be rock bottom. So, if things can't get any worse, I might as well do this." Not exactly a courageous emergence from the closet. For far too long, LGBTQ people have had to go through difficult, confusing situations like mine. Helping make the world a friendlier place for LGBTQ people is a key motivator behind my research. However, it wasn't always clear to me whether or how I'd be able to pursue such goals through scholarship. And I wasn't always confident expressing these aims.

In my application essay for USC Annenberg, only one sentence suggested that Larry and I had any overlapping interests. Buried in commentary about designing healthcare interventions, working for federal agencies, and weighing concerns of communication campaign stakeholders, I mentioned an interest in issues pertaining to LGBTQ people. What, in hindsight, looks almost like a passing thought in my essay was the starting point of me ultimately becoming Larry's advisee. However, it took a year and a half of doctoral studies for our advisor-advisee relationship to be solidified.

My conversations with Larry began while I was working on a study exploring the effects of a media storyline involving two gay youth on young viewers. I found myself continually seeking and greatly valuing his advice. I recognized that my knowledge of LGBTQ history, queer theory, and related areas was limited. As I dove into readings Larry recommended, I found myself encountering many questions. During those times, nothing cleared away uncertainty like Larry's candor and insightful feedback. While I appreciated each of our conversations in terms of practical matters, I valued even more the trust that was built. When Larry gives advice, he's typically spot on. At the same time, he allows his students to follow their own paths. While I'm sure he envisions potential trajectories for his advisees, he doesn't impose his opinions. He lets each make their own way. Larry is always there for students for guidance and to challenge them to expand their thinking. His influence emerges through his keen insights. Larry's impact on me has been noticeable in both of my interrelated programs of research: My dissertation research examining the health-related effects of a novel program for LGBTQ youth and my work analyzing the impact of mediated and interactive representations of LGBTQ people.

Under Larry's guidance, my dissertation project explores the effects of a summer leadership camp for LGBTQ youth ages 12 to 18, hosted by the Los Angeles-based non-profit organization Brave Trails. Brave Trails was founded in 2014, establishing the first summer camp in the western U.S. for LGBTQ youth. Few camps focusing on the needs of LGBTQ youth (particularly camps of a non-medical nature) exist in the U.S., and Brave Trails has become one of the largest of such initiatives. Camp Brave Trails kicked off in the summer of 2015 with an inaugural group of 45 campers, and for the summer of 2017, enrollment was capped at 115 youth. Brave Trails aims to develop the communication and related skills of LGBTQ youth, affirm their identity, and build a community focused on social justice. Though the organization's programming was developed under the leadership of a licensed therapist, and many features align with strategies for improving psychological well-being (Cruwys et al., 2014), most activities do not explicitly address mental health. This subtle approach may actually drive the program's demonstrated effectiveness in improving campers' well-being, as indirect methods sometimes work better than "frontal assaults" in changing attitudes and behaviors (Cohen & Sherman, 2014). Additionally, this approach may make the program attractive for a wide range of youth, compared to therapy-oriented programs. In addition to providing a safe, encouraging environment at camp, the organization fosters continued engagement with the camp community after summer. All campers and staff are invited to join a closed Facebook group, where campers share their successes and struggles, staff members provide positive reinforcement, and more. My research with Brave Trails has explored the immediate effects of camp, and the work is expanding to examine the impact of the support provided post-camp through this growing community, as well as seeking a richer understanding of the dynamics that drive positive, lasting change.

For my dissertation, Larry encouraged me to step outside my comfort zone. While I had planned to rely heavily on survey methods, Larry pushed me to extend myself methodologically by attending camp as a participant observer. I was hesitant about asking to insert myself as a researcher into the camp environment. In my mind, it was something of a sacred space where I'd be an outsider. Additionally, I had volunteered with the founders and directors of the organization for a year at a weekly youth support group and had participated in many activities that were ultimately incorporated into camp programming. I thought I knew the "Brave Trails approach," and I trusted the program/community the directors were building. Larry took a broader view of the situation. He helped me think about the additional insights to be gained by experiencing a full session of camp and how those learnings could inform current and future work. So, I went to camp, and as usual, saw that Larry was right. During my time as a utility staff member, I gained a deeper understanding of camp culture, norms, communication dynamics, activities, collective emotions, and more. I was inspired to see firsthand what data from my previous research with the organization had indicated: Positive, observable change was happening for youth. Having firsthand experience that corroborated prior quantitative findings was reassuring and invaluable. It also opened my mind to potential new routes for understanding the effects of the program and sharing those learnings with a broader audience.

Larry has also been influential in another line of my research: exploring the effects of LGBTQ media representations. As I noted previously, my first study in this line—an experiment examining the effects of a media portrayal of two gay youth on young viewers—was the starting point for our relationship. Obviously, Larry's influence regarding scholarly understanding of LGBTQ people in the media is unparalleled. One must look no further than *Up from Invisibility: Lesbians, Gay Men, and the Media in America* to have most of their questions about the history and trajectory of such media representation answered (Gross, 2001). Yet, some of the questions I had for Larry pertained not to historical aspects of representations, but to current issues and analyses at hand. For example, for the experiment I noted previously (which involved a stimulus video derived from the TV show *The Fosters* (Freeform)), it had been suggested to me to change my main analyses so that instead of comparing LGBTQ viewers to non-LGBTQ viewers, the analyses would compare male viewers to female viewers. To me, this seemed problematic on two fronts. First, I viewed the approach as reinforcing a strict gender binary that science has shown to be limiting (Scientific American, 2017). Further, it overlooked what I thought was a more interesting question: How, if at all, did the reactions of LGBTQ viewers—that we'd expect would perceive LGBTQ characters to be part of their "ingroup" – differ from the responses of non-LGBTQ viewers – that may see LGBTQ characters as part of their "outgroup"? I expressed these concerns to Larry. His response? Simply, "Well, if you don't analyze gender, people will ask why not, and *The Fosters* isn't exactly 'breaking the binary.'" Oh. That clarified the situation for me. Based on Larry's feedback, I ran gender-focused post hoc analyses. These new analyses added another element of interest to the paper. Larry's direct, concise assessment was exactly what I needed to take the project another step forward and get it out in the world, where I hoped it would contribute to our understanding of a timely phenomenon affecting both LGBTQ people and TV viewers more broadly.

It sometimes amazes me that I have the opportunity to study what I do, considering the long history of marginalization of LGBTQ people in the U.S. Just two years ago, in 2015, same-sex marriage was illegal in many U.S. states. When the Supreme Court struck down the ability of states to ban same-sex marriage, the milestone was met with backlash. Conservative groups protested, with one Kentucky clerk famously refusing to issue marriage licenses to same-sex couples (Elliott, 2015). Then, the campaign and ultimate election of Donald Trump to the U.S. presidency fueled additional anti-LGBTQ actions. During the campaign year of 2016, hate crimes across the country increased by 20%, with perpetrators emboldened by Trump's rhetoric (Reuters, 2017). Assaults on gay men by attackers proclaiming, "You're in 'Trump's America' now," were reported (CBS DC, 2017; Filosa, 2017). After taking office, the Trump administration rolled back protections for transgender students (Somashekhar, Brown, & Balingit, 2017) and barred transgender adults from entering the military (Terkel, 2017). Yet, these regressive actions stand in contrast to a broader shift in American public opinion. Across the country, Americans' attitudes overall have become steadily more positive toward LGBTQ people and related policies (Fingerhut, 2016).

A recent Pew Research Center survey found one-in-five adults say their views toward LGBTQ people have changed, with most saying they have become more accepting (2016). Support is especially apparent among young people, with an overwhelming majority (73 percent) of Americans ages 18 to 34 supporting marriage equality (Pew Research, 2015). Further, advancements in media and politics have occurred. For example, the number of fictional TV portrayals of lesbian, gay, and bisexual (LGB) individuals has increased to an all-time high of 4.8 percent of regular characters on broadcast television being LGB (GLAAD, 2016). Likewise, media depictions of transgender individuals reached new levels in 2014 in a media moment *Time* called the "transgender tipping point" (Steinmetz, 2014, para. 1). Visibility of transgender people has remained elevated across a variety of platforms since then (Scheller & Love, 2016). This increase in visibility was welcomed by LGBTQ advocates, though as Larry himself has noted, "Visibility, like truth, is rarely pure and never simple" (Gross, 2001, p. 253). Accordingly, LGBTQ viewers have lauded some recent portrayals while critiquing others for reinforcing harmful stereotypes. LGBTQ representation has also grown in political and institutional spaces. In 2016, Oregon voters elected the first openly queer U.S. governor (Domonoske, 2016). The following year, the Boy Scouts of America began accepting transgender males as scouts (Lee, 2017). This progress has occurred thanks to the dedicated activist efforts of earlier decades.

Larry's contributions in founding the field of LGBTQ studies, drawing attention to inequality in media representation, and demanding better of both the academy and media—among a myriad of other accomplishments—have helped propel progress. For any difficulties I have encountered in opening up about my identity and in working as a scholar-activist, I can only imagine how many more challenges Larry faced in his own life and career. I hope to help extend the legacy of rigorous, insightful, dedicated research that Larry himself undertook and that he encourages in his students. I'm beginning my career as a scholar in a much more welcoming climate than Larry experienced, and much of this is a result of his efforts. Larry's paper "The past and the future of gay, lesbian, bisexual, and transgender studies" (Gross, 2005) traces the evolution of such studies from a time when a "semiofficial conspiracy of silencing ... was endorsed" (p. 1) to a current environment that is support-ive to an extent once inconceivable. In 1973, when Larry helped found the Gay Academic Union—marking the first formal organizing of gay scholars—silencing was still common. Now, of course, many programs seek scholars focused on LGBTQ issues, and acceptance of LGBTQ people continues to increase more broadly.

As further strides are made toward equality, the so-called LGBTQ com-munity will further evolve. Larry's exploration of prior transformations of the community, as well as his predictions for its future, have informed my thinking. "Gideon who will be 25 in the year 2012: Growing up gay today" (Gross, 2007) provided an early foundation on which I've grounded my own arguments regarding the potential future experiences of today's young LGBTQ people. Larry discusses how the invisibility of LGBTQ people (in media and elsewhere) characterizing earlier decades has waned, yet many youth are still experiencing isolation and vulnerability. Schools have become a new battleground for equality. Despite remaining challenges, Larry suggests the prospects of today's young LGBTQ people are generally bright, and I agree. Though at times my hope is challenged by current political upheaval, I look forward to witnessing the progress ahead. Years from now, I expect I'll be able to reflect on how far society has come during my own life and since Larry before me fought for equality.

My personal experience as Larry's advisee has been a privilege. At the onset of my doctoral studies, I couldn't have imagined everything working out quite as well as it has in terms of finding a mentor who supports my interests and scholarly trajectory. Having Larry as a model for conducting rigorous research from an activist perspective has been empowering. Likewise, discovering unexpected overlaps in our experiences has affirmed some of my decisions. Overall, looking back on my personal and professional journey, then thinking ahead to future aspirations, I can already see Larry's influence on the arc of my work, and I am deeply grateful that he took me on as an advisee. As Larry has said, "We have traveled far in the past half century" (Gross, 2001, p. 263). I look forward to seeing how Larry's influence continues to reveal itself as his many former advisees, empowered by his guidance, work to close remaining gaps in social and political equality.

References

CBS DC. (2017, February 9). Police: Gay man attacked, hurt by 'Trump America' supporters. Retrieved from: http://washington.cbslocal.com/2017/02/09/police-gay-man-attacked-hurt-by-trump- america-supporters/

Cohen, G. L., & Sherman, D. K. (2014). The psychology of change: Self-affirmation and social psychological intervention. *Annual Review of Psychology*, 65, 333–371.

Cruwys, T., Haslam, S. A., Dingle, G. A., Haslam, C., & Jetten, J. (2014). Depression and social identity: An integrative review. *Personality and Social Psychology Review*, 18(3), 215–238.

Domonoske, C. (2016, November 9). For first time, openly LGBT governor elected: Oregon's Kate Brown. *NPR*. http://www.npr.org/sections/thetwo-way/2016/11/09/501338927/for-first-time-openly-lgbt-governor-elected-oregons-kate-brown

Elliott, P. (2015, November 20). LGBT leaders warn of looming gay rights backlash. *Time*. Retrieved on February 5, 2017 from: http://time.com/4123059/gay-rights-marriage-backlash/

Filosa, G. (2017, February 25). Drunk gay basher tells Key West couple: 'You live in Trump country now,' police say. *Miami Herald*. Retrieved from: http://www.miami-herald.com/news/local/community/ florida-keys/article134965699.html

Fingerhut, H. (2016). Support steady for same-sex marriage and acceptance of homosexuality. *Pew Research*. Retrieved from: http://www.pewresearch.org/fact-tank/2016/05/12/support-steady-for-same-sex-marriage-and-acceptance-of-homosexuality/

GLAAD. (2016). *Where we are on TV report*. Retrieved on January 5, 2017 from: http://www.glaad.org/whereweareontv16

Gross, L. (2001). *Up from invisibility: Lesbians, gay men, and the media in America.* New York: Columbia University Press.

Gross, L. (2005). The past and the future of gay, lesbian, bisexual, and transgender studies. *Journal of Communication, 55*(3), 508.

Gross, L. (2007). Gideon who will be 25 in the year 2012: Growing up gay today. *International Journal of Communication, 1*(1), 18.

Lee, K. (2017, January 5). Here's how the Boy Scouts have evolved on social issues over the years. *Los Angeles Times.* Retrieved on February 5, 2017 from: http://www.latimes.com/nation/la-na-boy-scouts-evolution-2017-story.html

Pew Research Center. (2015). *Support for same-sex marriage at record high, but key segments remain opposed.* Retrieved on February 5, 2017 from: http://www.people-press.org/2015/06/08/same-sex-marriage-detailed-tables/

Pew Research Center. (2016). *Changing views on gay marriage.* Retrieved on February 5, 2017 from: http://www.pewresearch.org/topics/gay-marriage-and-homosexuality/

Reuters. (2017, March 14). U.S. hate crimes up 20 percent in 2016, fueled by election campaign: Report. Retrieved from: http://www.nbcnews.com/news/us-news/u-s-hate-crimes-20-percent-2016- fueled-election-campaign-n733306

Scheller, A., & Love, C. (2016). Transgender people are more visible than ever, but it's still legal to discriminate against them in most states. *Huffington Post.* Retrieved from: http://www.huffingtonpost.com/2015/06/03/transgender-discrimination-laws_n_7502266.html.

Scientific American. (2017). The new science of sex and gender. Retrieved from: https://www.scientificamerican.com/magazine/sa/2017/09-01/?WT.ac=SA_SA_CurrentIssue

Somashekhar, S., Brown, E., & Balingit, M. (2017, February 22). Trump administration rolls back protections for transgender students. *Washington Post.* Retrieved from: https://www.washingtonpost.com/local/education/trump-administration-rolls-back-protections-for-transgender-students/2017/02/22/550a83b4-f913-11e6-bf01-d47f8cf9b643_story.html?utm_term=.216c701ce88f

Steinmetz, K. (2014, May 29). The transgender tipping point. *Time.* Retrieved from http://time.com/135480/transgender-tipping-point/.

Terkel, A. (2017, August 29). Transgender military members at risk of harassment under Trump, says former army secretary. *Huffington Post.* Retrieved from: http://www.huffingtonpost.com/entry/eric-fanning-trump_us_59a47882e4b0446b3b85ba2b

Contributors

Derek Bousé studied under (and was teaching assistant to) Larry Gross at the Annenberg School for Communication, University of Pennsylvania (MA '89; PhD '91). He is the author of *Wildlife Films* (University of Pennsylvania Press, 2000).

Traci Gillig is a doctoral candidate at the University of Southern California's Annenberg School for Communication and Journalism. She studies the psychological mechanisms, social factors, and intervention features influencing the health and well-being of youth, as well as the effects of mediated representations of individuals from diverse, underrepresented groups on attitudes toward people and policies. Traci's recent projects have been published in journals such as *Sex Roles, Human Communication Research*, and the *International Journal of Communication*. Her work has also been featured in major media outlets, including the *Washington Post, Los Angeles Times, New York Times*, and *Newsweek*. Organizations such as the USC Annenberg Norman Lear Center and the USC Dornsife College of Letters, Arts, and Sciences have funded Traci's research, and the National Science Foundation awarded her a 2015 Graduate Research Fellowship Honorable Mention.

David Gudelunas is Dean of the College of Arts and Letters and a Professor of Communication at the University of Tampa. He completed his PhD under the direction of Larry Gross at the University of Pennsylvania in 2004. He is the author of *Confidential to America: Newspaper Advice Columns and Sexual Education* (Transaction, 2008) and co-editor of *RuPaul's Drag Race and the Shifting Visibility of Drag Culture* (Palgrave, 2017).

Lisa Henderson (PhD, University of Pennsylvania) is Professor of Communication in the Department of Communication at the University of Massachusetts, Amherst. She is the author of essays in the *International Journal of Communication, Screen, Signs, GLQ, Journal of Communication and Feminist*

Media Studies, among other titles, and of *Love and Money: Queers, Class and Cultural Production*, a 2014 finalist for a Lambda Literary Award in Lesbian and Gay Studies.

Stewart M. Hoover is Professor of Media Studies and Religious Studies at the University of Colorado at Boulder, where he directs the Center for Media, Religion, and Culture. He is an internationally-recognized expert on media and religion. He is author, co-author or editor of ten books, including *Media, Home, and Family, and Religion in the Media Age*, and *Does God Make the Man: Media, Religion, and the Crisis of Masculinity*, co-authored with Curtis Coats, and the edited volume, *The Media and Religious Authority*.

Eva Illouz was born in Fez, Morocco, raised and educated in France and then later in Israel and the United States. Currently, she is a full professor in the Department of Sociology at the Hebrew University, Jerusalem and Directrice d'Etudes at the EHESS in Paris. Her research interests include sociology of culture, sociology of emotions, sociology of capitalism, and the effect of consumerism and mass media on emotional patterns. Illouz is the author of 11 books about romantic love, Oprah Winfrey, culture, consumer capitalism, best-sellers and self-help culture. Several of her books have won International awards and have been translated into 17 languages.

Dr. Steven Leuthold is a professor at Northern Michigan University, where he teaches a variety of courses in the history of art and design including a course on Native American art and architecture. He is the author of two books, *Indigenous Aesthetics: Native Art, Media and Identity* (University of Texas Press, 1998), which included and expanded upon his dissertation research under Larry Gross at the Annenberg School, and *Cross-Cultural Issues in Art* (Routledge, 2011). His most recent book project is a global history of design from the early nineteenth century to the 1910s; it considers the emergence of modern design in the context of contact and negotiation between expanding and contracting empires.

Dr. Ioana Literat is Assistant Professor in the Communication, Media & Learning Technologies Design Program at Teachers College, Columbia University. Her research examines creative participation in online contexts. Her work has been published in *New Media & Society*, *Communication Theory*, *International Journal of Communication*, and *Information, Communication & Society*, among others.

Paul Messaris is the Lev Kuleshov Professor Emeritus at the Annenberg School for Communication of the University of Pennsylvania. His research deals with visual communication and digital media. He is producing a set of online videos about the persuasive uses of visual media in politics, social advocacy, and commercial advertising.

Bill Mikulak received his MA and PhD from the Annenberg School of Communication at the University of Pennsylvania. His research interests include visual and aesthetic communication as they relate to popular culture and fandom. He is a senior editor at the newswire service, Business Wire.

Michael Morgan is Professor Emeritus in the Department of Communication at the University of Massachusetts, Amherst. He has conducted many national and international studies on cultivation analysis and the impact of television on audience conceptions of violence, sex-roles, aging, health, science, the family, political orientations, and other issues. He was a Fulbright Research Scholar in Argentina and has received the University of Massachusetts Distinguished Teaching Award. He served as Chair of the UMass Department of Communication at Amherst from 1997–2007.

David W. Park is Professor of Communication at Lake Forest College. He studied with Larry Gross at the Annenberg School for Communication at the University of Pennsylvania (MA '96; PhD '01). His scholarship addresses new media and questions related to communication history, with an emphasis on the history of communication study.

Carla Sarett has a PhD in Communications from The University of Pennsylvania, and has taught at The University of California at Santa Barbara and Queens College of The City University of New York. She has worked in television at National Broadcasting Company and Home Box Office, as well as nonprofit international film distribution. She later founded Internet Research Group, a market research firm serving major media and technology clients. In recent years, her short fiction and personal essays have been published in magazines including *Crack the Spine, Page and Spine, The Linnet's Wings, Loch Raven Review, Medulla Review, scissors and spackle,* and *Blue Lyra Review* (nominated for Best American Essay.) She blogs at http://carlasarett.blogspot.com.

Dona Schwartz is a photographic artist who explores everyday life and culture. Her work examines definitions of family and the nature of domesticity, cultural continuity and change, and transitional moments in life. She earned a PhD at the Annenberg School for Communications at the University of Pennsylvania, specializing in visual communication and ethnographic research. She has published two photographic ethnographies, *Waucoma Twilight: Generations of the Farm* (Smithsonian Institution Press, 1992) and *Contesting the Super Bowl* (Routledge, 1997). Her photographic monographs, *In the Kitchen* (2009) and *On the Nest* (2015) were published by Kehrer Verlag, Heidelberg. Schwartz's award-winning photographs have been internationally exhibited and published. Her work is included in the collections of the Library of Congress, the Museum of Fine Arts Houston, the Musée de l'Elysée, the George Eastman House, the Harry Ransom Center, the Portland Art Museum, and the Kinsey Institute. Schwartz is Associate Professor in the Department of Art at the University of Calgary, and she is President and Board Chair of the annual Exposure Photography Festival. Schwartz is represented by Stephen Bulger Gallery, Toronto.

Lois H. Silverman is a museum studies scholar, project director, and consultant who fosters innovation in museum theory, potential, and practice. Author of more than 55 publications, including *The Social Work of Museums* (Routledge, 2010), she is an international thought leader on such concepts as visitor meaning-making, museums as therapeutic agents, metaphysical aspects of museums, and the "next age" of museums. A three-time recipient of Indiana University's Teaching Excellence Award, she currently serves as adjunct faculty of The George Washington University Museum Education Program in Washington, DC, and the Bank Street College Museum Leadership Graduate Program in New York. Lois holds an MA ('84) and PhD ('90) from the Annenberg School for Communication, University of Pennsylvania, and an MSW from Indiana University (2006).

Aram Sinnreich is an Associate Professor at American University's School of Communication, where he currently chairs the Communication Studies division. He is the author of several books on culture, law and technology, including *Mashed Up* (2010), *The Piracy Crusade* (2013), and a book tentatively entitled *A People's Guide to Intellectual Property*, forthcoming from Yale Press.

Cindy Hing-Yuk Wong is Professor of Communication at the City University of New York, College of Staten Island. Professor Wong's areas of research include grassroots media, Hong Kong cinema culture and practices, diasporic media, global Chinese Diaspora and international film festivals. Her book, *Film Festivals: Culture, People and Power on the Global Screen* (Rutgers, 2011) offers the first comprehensive overview of the history, agents, films, and multiple agendas of the global festival world. She is the co-author of *Global Hong Kong* (2005) and the co-editor of the *Encyclopedia of Contemporary American Culture* (2001). Her selected publications include articles and book chapters in *Asian Cinema, American Anthropologist, Asian Cinema, Film Festivals History Theory Method Practice* (2016), *Chinese Film Festivals* (2017). She is now preparing a book manuscript on Global Chinatowns with Gary McDonogh.

Barbie Zelizer is the Raymond Williams Professor of Communication and Director of the Scholars Program in Culture and Communication at the University of Pennsylvania's Annenberg School for Communication. A former journalist, Zelizer is known for her work on journalism, culture, memory and images, particularly in times of crisis. She has published fourteen books and over a hundred articles and essays. Recipient of multiple fellowships, Zelizer is also a media critic, whose work has appeared in *The Nation*, *PBS News Hour*, *CNN* and others. Coeditor of *Journalism: Theory, Practice and Criticism*, she is a recent President of the International Communication Association. Her newest book *What Journalism Could Be* was published by Polity in 2017. In Spring of 2018, Zelizer will launch the Center for Media at Risk, a center devoted to fostering free and critical media practice under political intimidation.

A CRITICAL INTRODUCTION TO MEDIA AND COMMUNICATION THEORY

David W. Park
Series Editor

The study of the media in the field of communication suffers from no shortage of theoretical perspectives from which to analyze media, messages, media systems, and audiences. One of the field's strengths has been its flexibility as it incorporates social scientific and humanist ideas in pursuit of a better understanding of communication and the media. This flexibility and abundance of ideas threaten to muddle the study of communication as it stakes out an interdisciplinary identity.

This series puts on center stage individuals and ideas whose importance to the study of communication can be reconfigured, reinvented, and refocused. Each of the specially commissioned books in the series shares a concern for the history of theory in the field of communication. Books provide sophisticated discussions of the relevance of particular theorists or theories, with an emphasis on re-inventing the field of communication, whether by incorporating ideas often considered to be 'outside' the field or by providing fresh analyses of ideas that have long been considered vital in the field's past. Though theoretical in focus, the books are at all times concerned with the applicability of theory to empirical research and experience and are designed to be accessible, yet critical, for students—undergraduates and postgraduates—and scholars.

For additional information about this series or for the submission of manuscripts, please contact:

David W. Park
park@lakeforest.edu

To order other books in this series, please contact our Customer Service Department:

(800) 770-LANG (within the U.S.)
(212) 647-7706 (outside the U.S.)
(212) 647-7707 FAX

Or browse online by series:
www.peterlang.com